AN ADIRONDACK PASSAGE

AN ADIRONDACK PASSAGE

THE CRUISE OF THE CANOE *SAIRY GAMP*

CHRISTINE JEROME

 Second edition published by the Adirondack Mountain Club. *An Adirondack Passage* was first published in a hardcover edition in 1994 by HarperCollins Publishers.

Design by Alma Hochhauser Orenstein

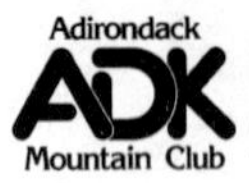

Published by the Adirondack Mountain Club
814 Goggins Road, Lake George, New York 12845-4117
www.adk.org

The Adirondack Mountain Club (ADK) is dedicated to the protection and responsible recreational use of the New York State Forest Preserve, parks, and other wild lands and waters. The Club, founded in 1922, is a member-directed organization committed to public service and stewardship. ADK employs a balanced approach to outdoor recreation, advocacy, environmental education and natural resource conservation.

Library of Congress Cataloging-in-Publication Data
Jerome, Christine, 1943–
An Adirondack passage : the cruise of the canoe Sairy Gamp / Christine Jerome.—2nd ed.
p. cm.
Includes bibliographical references (p.) and index.
ISBN 0-93527294-1
1. Canoes and canoeing—New York (State)—Adirondack Park. 2. Adirondack Park (N.Y.)—Description and travel. I. Title.
GV776.N721 A35 1998
917.47'50443—dc21 98-33343
CIP

Printed in the United States of America
04 03 02 01 00 99 10 9 8 7 6 5 4 3 2

For JOHN,

my point man in life

I hope at no distant day to meet independent canoeists, with canoes weighing twenty pounds or less, at every turn in the wilderness, and with no more duffle than is absolutely necessary.

GEORGE W. SEARS ("NESSMUK")
Forest and Stream
August 9, 1883

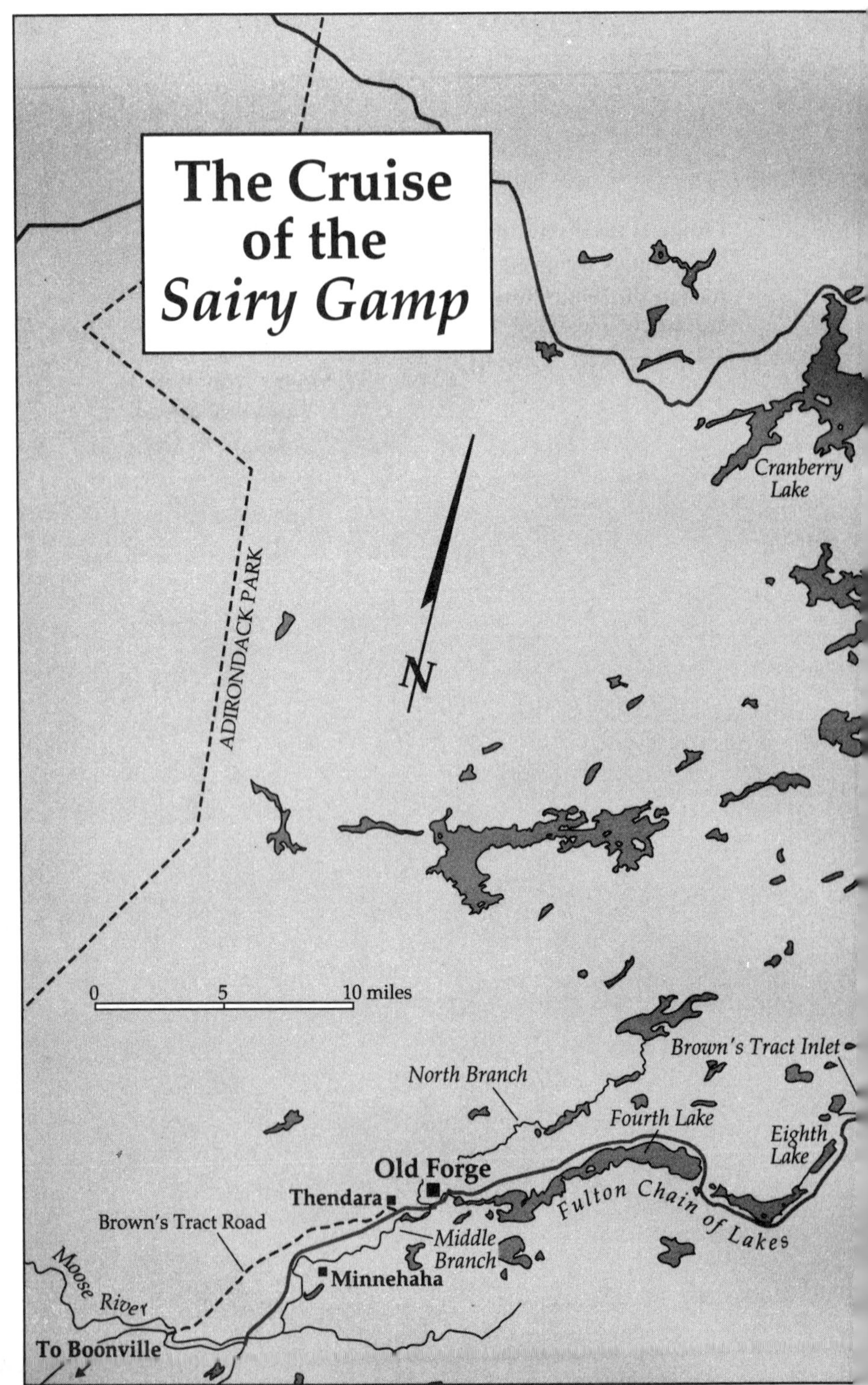
The Cruise of the *Sairy Gamp*
ADIRONDACK PARK
N
Cranberry Lake
0
5
10 miles
Brown's Tract Inlet
North Branch
Fourth Lake
Eighth Lake
Old Forge
Thendara
Fulton Chain of Lakes
Brown's Tract Road
Middle Branch
Moose River
Minnehaha
To Boonville

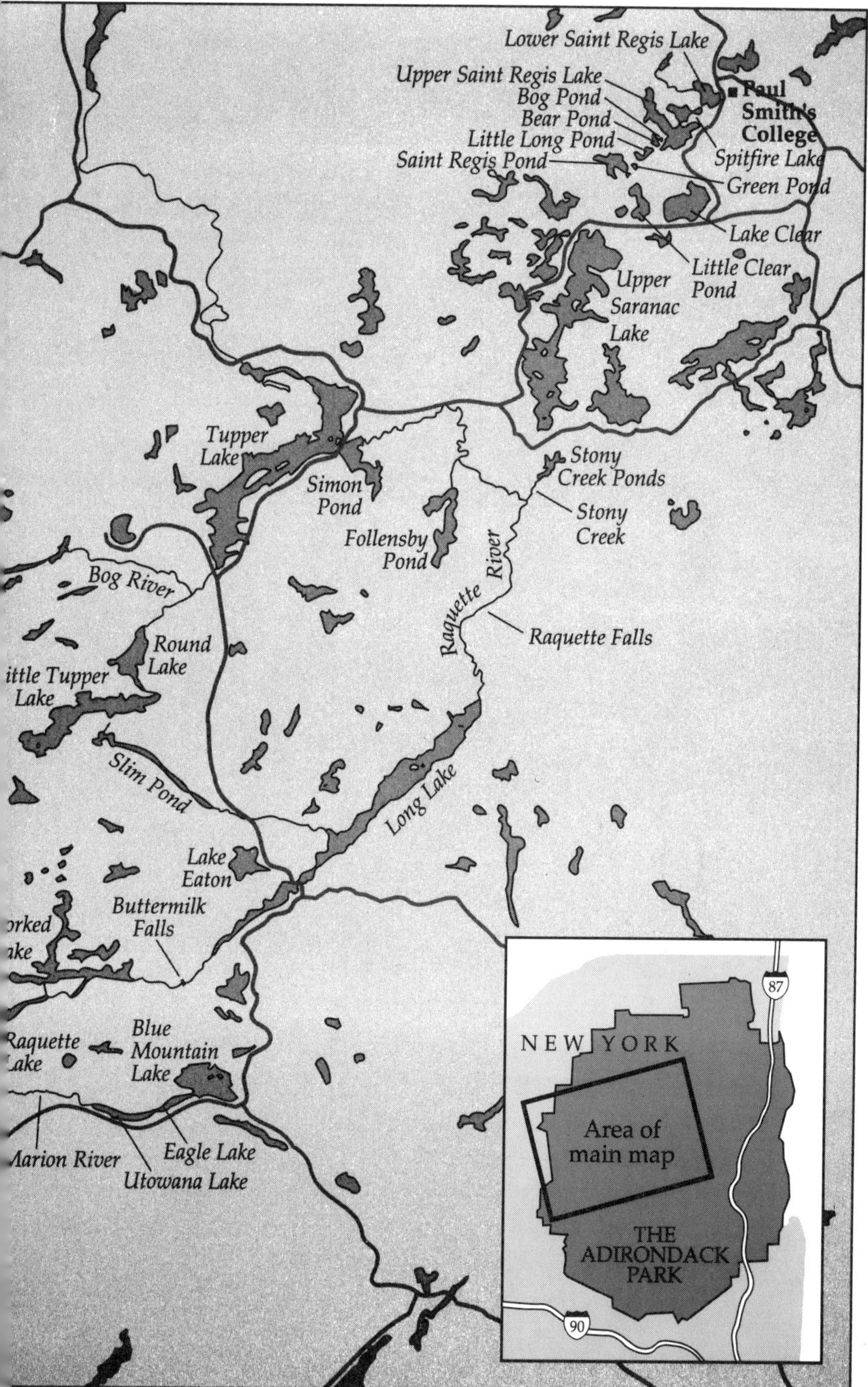

Lower Saint Regis Lake
Upper Saint Regis Lake
Bog Pond
Bear Pond
Little Long Pond
Saint Regis Pond
Paul Smith's College
Spitfire Lake
Green Pond
Lake Clear
Little Clear Pond
Upper Saranac Lake
Tupper Lake
Simon Pond
Stony Creek Ponds
Stony Creek
Follensby Pond
Raquette River
Raquette Falls
Bog River
Round Lake
ittle Tupper Lake
Slim Pond
Long Lake
Lake Eaton
Buttermilk Falls
orked ake
Raquette ake
Blue Mountain Lake
Eagle Lake
Utowana Lake
Marion River
NEW YORK
87
Area of main map
THE ADIRONDACK PARK
90

CONTENTS

ACKNOWLEDGMENTS

THIS WORK (ALTHOUGH IT HAS ALWAYS SEEMED MORE LIKE play) would not have been undertaken had it not been for my *New England Monthly* colleague Julie Michaels, who raved about a canoe trip she had taken in the Adirondacks and insisted that I go. At roughly the same time I happened upon Adam Hochschild's memoir *Half the Way Home,* which fired my imagination and wrung my heart. I went, I saw, and, like so many before me, I was hopelessly hooked.

Librarians were my allies as I ransacked regional history. In particular I want to thank the staff of the Erwin Library and Institute in Boonville; the resourceful Janet Decker and her volunteers at the Saranac Lake Free Library's Adirondack Collection; and Jerold Pepper of the Adirondack Museum, who went out of his way to see that I got what I needed. Ruth Giddings and Rita Dennison of the Town of Webb Historical Association, in Old Forge, were always ready to drop what they were doing each time I popped up unannounced.

The staff of the Adirondack Museum were unfailingly generous with their time and expertise. Jim Meehan helped me find photographs and even took camera in hand to assist me. Alice

Gilborn kindly allowed me to read the revised introduction to *The Adirondack Letters of George Washington Sears* while it was still in manuscript. Hallie Bond's contribution was invaluable: she urged me to consider a Hornbeck canoe, was generous with her own research on small boats, and fulfilled my ultimate fantasy by letting me hold the *Sairy Gamp*.

Chris Shaw steered me right on several issues and gave me my first paddling lesson. Herm Albright led me around Minnehaha and shared memories and photographs. Sears's great-grandson, Dr. James F. Madison, provided genealogical data. I am also indebted for advice, reminiscences, and leads to Bruce Coon, the late Maitland DeSormo, John J. Duquette, Diane Garey, Larry Hott, Ernie LaPrairie, and Gary Randorf. My brother Mike McCall and the redoubtable Jo Currie took us on our first camping trip and showed us how it's done. Their example saved us much grief and opened our eyes to the pleasures of canoeing.

Betsy Folwell, Tom Warrington, and Ann Hornbeck offered friendship, encouragement, and several memorably raucous meals. Nessmuk aficionado Chuck Brumley was unstinting in providing photographs and books from his personal collection. Robert L. Lyon, author of numerous articles on Sears, unselfishly shared his research with me when a lesser spirit might have declined to do so. Most of the memorials you see today in the Wellsboro area are the result of Bob's efforts to gain recognition for Sears. Our lengthy correspondence has been a particular pleasure.

I still marvel at the hospitality extended by Janet and Fritz Decker, whose interest in this project has been one of its greatest rewards. The Deckers opened their home to us, fed us, and encouraged us to come and go as we pleased. On innumerable occasions Janet placed her research skills and her personal library at my disposal. It is one of the many happy accidents of this project that what began as a working relationship has broadened into a warm and special friendship.

Pete Hornbeck gave me good advice on camping equipment, but of course he did a great deal more. He built me a wonderful canoe that never let me down. The *Sairy Damp* carried me safely from one end of the Adirondacks to the other and back again, and she did so with admirable aplomb.

I don't know what we would have done without Karen Gano, who lived in our house, cared for our dogs and cats, and coped with the beaver that appropriated our pond. She made our month-long journey possible and then slipped away, leaving a fabulous dinner to welcome two bedraggled travelers home.

Two artists' colonies sheltered me, fed me, and provided the gift of solitude during the research and writing of this book. To staff and my fellow residents at Blue Mountain Center and the MacDowell Colony I extend my heartfelt thanks for enthusiasm, support, and many happy times. I am especially grateful to Harriet Barlow, Evelyn Thompson, and Kaye Burnett for myriad kindnesses.

Thanks are also due to my friend Richard Todd, who counseled patience when this project seemed to be going nowhere, and to Daniel Okrent, whose kindly advice ("Don't be a schmuck—get an agent") was as always eminently sound. That agent was Don Congdon, who persisted until he found the right home for this book. At HarperCollins, Ed Burlingame and Christa Weil provided a valuable critique, and Hugh Van Dusen cheered me on in the home stretch.

Paul Jamieson, to whom Adirondack paddlers owe so much, has been both mentor and friend from the beginning. His encouragement and advice have meant a great deal, and his willingness to read this manuscript while battling prostate cancer seems to me heroic. Paul is now ninety, and can no longer canoe as much as he used to. I once asked whether this bothered him; yes, of course it did, he replied, and then he smiled.

"But I've pretty much done all of it," he said. "I guess you could say I wrote the book." Indeed he did.

The person to whom I owe the most is John, who helped me believe I could do it, who set aside his own work to paddle with me, and who took over our household so I could go off for protracted bouts of research and writing. He has been there every step of the way; without him this immensely enriching experience would still be no more than a dream.

PREFACE

I HAD NEVER SEEN THE ADIRONDACKS BEFORE SEPTEMBER 1988, when on a friend's recommendation John and I drove over from western Massachusetts to spend a couple of days rubbernecking. As often happens in that upland region, however, the weather closed in and we ended up in a cabin in the village of Blue Mountain Lake, visibility nil, a chill rain battering the windows. Like hundreds of other rainbound tourists, we opted for history over hypothermia and visited the Adirondack Museum, just up the road.

Among the canoes in the boat building, one in particular seemed to beguile the crowds. Her cedar hull had aged to a mahogany glow and her size, at nine feet, was positively lilliputian. *Sairy Gamp,* the card read. Among the details of her provenance was this brief story: In the summer of 1883 a sixty-one-year-old writer named George Washington Sears, pen name Nessmuk, had paddled and portaged her 266 miles, from Boonville to Paul Smith's hotel and back again. I had no idea where these places were, but the distance was appalling. How could anyone have gone so far in such a toy? And who was Sears? When I realized I was creating an eddy of tourists I moved on, but later that day I ducked back for another look.

For weeks afterward the *Sairy Gamp* and George Sears kept elbowing their way into my consciousness. What had he written? How long had his journey lasted, and where, exactly, had it taken him? Could you follow his route today? Finally, in something like exasperation, I went back to the museum for some answers. It was mid-October, and Blue Mountain Lake was again cold and gray. The leaves were mostly down, and waves of Canada geese were passing over, their calls bringing a lump to my throat. The *Sairy* reposed just where I'd left her, and I hadn't imagined it: she really was beautiful. I bought a shopping bag full of Adirondack books, rented a cabin, and shivering beside an anemic space heater, began to tease out the story. I learned that the cruise of the *Sairy Gamp* ran almost the length of the Adirondacks, from the southwest to the north-central part of the region, and returned by a slightly different route. Once under way, the trip took Sears about a month. And yes, you could still do almost all of it; the longest leg, from Old Forge to Upper Saranac Lake, is one of the region's most popular canoeing excursions.

Another discovery awaited me in that frigid knotty pine room: I was, it seemed, inordinately happy to be back in the Adirondacks, although I wasn't sure why. Perhaps it was the mountains. I'd lived for twelve years in northern New Hampshire, and now I realized I missed having wilderness outside my door, missed a way of life dominated by natural forces. I also missed the people, whose code of mutual assistance, capacity for hard work, and impatience with pretension are increasingly attractive the older I get. It occurred to me that in many ways, north country men and women—especially the women—taught me how to be an adult.

Yet it wasn't simply mountains that moved me. This place was special. In his memoir *Upstate,* Edmund Wilson described traveling to the western Adirondacks as a boy and discovering "a foreign country but a country to which I belonged." That was it. From the outset I had felt a powerful tug of belonging. In an act that puzzled me at the time, I had cut short our first visit because I couldn't bear to be treated as a tourist in a place that was so patently home. There was an eerie familiarity to the landscape, but it was months before I understood that the lakes and forests of the Adirondacks reminded me of my childhood, when we escaped our cramped Toronto apartment for brief visits to northern Ontario and Quebec. (I would later discover that my instincts were right: the Adirondacks are an extension of the Canadian Shield, a relic of my native geology adrift in upper New York State.)

At six million acres the Adirondack Park is roughly the size of Vermont, but its character is quite different from that of its neighbor just across Lake Champlain. There is in the Adirondacks an odd, brooding beauty that writers from Dreiser to Doctorow have struggled to capture. It can be a lonely place: only a handful of roads penetrate the densely forested interior, and the hamlets strung along them are small and spaced far apart. Climb one of its mountains and you'll see chains of peaks rolling away in all directions, ridge after ridge growing paler toward the horizon. Deep valleys cup thousands of lakes and rivers. In the Adirondacks the woods run right down to the shore, a constantly reiterated theme of dark trees, granite, and black water. It is spruce and pine and hemlock country, deerfly and punkie and blackfly country, wool and four-wheel-drive country, loon and osprey and raven country. My kind of country.

The more I learned about the cruise of the *Sairy Gamp,* the stronger my urge to retrace it. This would be no wilderness expedition, no two-thousand-mile, woman-against-the-elements feat of derring-do. Most of the larger Adirondack lakes are lined with cottages, and for long stretches a state highway parallels the route. By any standard this would be a modest undertaking, a couple of hundred miles through vacation country. Still, I wavered. I had never attempted anything like an extended canoe trip. My paddling experience consisted of a few tandem runs down an unchallenging local river. Although I was strong and had once been an athlete, years at a desk had left me seriously out of shape. I had done enough day-hikes in the White Mountains to know I liked being in the woods, but I hadn't a clue about how to live there: I had never spent a night outdoors.

On the other hand, when I felt bullish I decided I could find out what I needed to know; this was not, after all, neurosurgery. I was healthy, I was thirteen years younger than Sears had been, and I had had my share of physical adventure. When I was in my teens, a pilot friend often took me along while he practiced stalls and spins. As a journalist in my twenties, I had gone 168 miles an hour in the passenger seat of a race car. I'd also spent a week learning to race a Shelby Ford Mustang, a trick assignment, since I'd never driven a car before. Surely, I thought, I could paddle a canoe a couple of hundred miles. So I decided to follow George Sears. The trip would be great exercise, and besides, it was a way to spend time in a place that would not, it seemed, let me go.

For a year I shuttled back and forth to the Adirondacks, haunting libraries, scouting the route, soliciting advice. Although Sears started out in early July, I decided to wait until late August; this would give me a week of typically crowded waters and then, after Labor Day, an experience more like the one he'd had in 1883. I wanted very much to go solo, but I was persuaded that with my lack of paddling experience this would be a bad idea; if I got into trouble on one of the bigger lakes, no one would know what had become of me. There was another consideration: since I planned to approximate Sears's experience as closely as possible, I would be traveling in a very small boat with almost no space for gear. To my relief, John, who had been intrigued by the project from the beginning, volunteered to come along in a second, larger canoe. A slim, six-foot-two-inch Texan who won my heart with an ability to fix anything and a modest but polished repertoire of clown-diving stunts, he is the best of company. He is also an accomplished writer of nonfiction and a storyteller in the great southern tradition. He has another talent I envy: he can fall asleep so fast it makes him dizzy, and once under is impervious to any kind of mayhem, except my gentle snoring.

The critical piece of equipment was my canoe. I wanted something exceptionally light and sturdy, but I was disappointed by what I saw advertised. Eventually Sears settled on a design by J. Henry Rushton, and in the end, so did I. Hearing that an Adirondack resident named Peter Hornbeck built Kevlar *Sairy Gamp*s, I called him at home in Olmstedville. "I'm not trying to make a replica of the *Sairy Gamp*," he told me. "I build working boats. I use Rushton designs because they're still the best." Many of his canoes, he explained, were used by wildlife biologists because they were easy to carry into the back-country. At ten pounds, his smallest model weighed eight ounces less than the *Sairy* and almost exactly duplicated her dimensions. Best of all, Lost Pond boats, as he called them, could be bolted to a pack frame, which freed the hands for other gear and eliminated the drudgery of "doubling the carries"—making separate trips to haul canoes and equipment over each portage. Hornbeck also made double-bladed paddles because nothing on the market had the resiliency he liked.

I hadn't dreamed I could come this close to the *Sairy Gamp*. Hornbeck himself was a bonus. An elementary school teacher, he had a gentle, self-deprecating sense of humor and a passion for hiking and canoeing. Besides, how could I resist someone who'd named his cat Velcro? We ordered a nine-foot boat for me and a ten-and-a-half-footer for John, and in February 1990 I drove over to pick them up. Hornbeck turned out to be taller than I'd imagined, over six feet, with a puckish face framed by curly white hair. After showing me around his small operation, he introduced me to my boat.

I don't know what Sears thought when he saw the *Sairy Gamp* for the first time, but when I saw my nine-footer I laughed out loud. She was tiny. *Tiny.* Her manila-colored hull was translucent in the sunlight, and when I lifted her, the Kevlar under my fingers flexed. Could material this thin really be strong? Absolutely, Hornbeck assured me; more of his boats were damaged by blowing off cartops than by hitting rocks, and in those cases it was usually the mahogany gunwales that needed fixing.

He showed me how to attach the canoe to my pack frame and how to stoop underneath, slide into the straps, and shrug the whole affair onto my back. It was peculiar to see the bow looming over my head, but the harness was comfortable, the weight nicely balanced. He insisted on checking John's rig himself, adjusting several of the buckles and then striding off down his snowy driveway, a tan banana on legs. When he came back, he was beaming and shaking his head. "You know, for the Adirondacks," he said to no one in particular, "this is really the cat's ass."

Seven weeks later the ice went out of our pond and we could finally haul our boats out for their baptism. Mine was trickier to get into than John's, but once under way, both canoes felt so maneuverable they might have been part of our bodies. They were fast too, flying the length of the pond with a couple of strokes. We paddled around in delirious circles while our Lab and our golden retriever watched in utter disbelief from the shallows.

That summer we assembled our equipment and made two shakedown cruises with experienced canoeists. By the last week of August, John had mailed off his book manuscript and I'd finished the stories I was editing for *New England Monthly*. The cars were loaded, the house sitter was ready to move in, and at last there was nothing more to do.

When Sears told his friends he was taking a nine-foot canoe through the wilderness, they were so skeptical about his chances they took out five thousand dollars of insurance on him. He himself had no qualms. "I am as sure to make that cruise as you are to turn in when you start for your berth," he wrote in *Forest and Stream* magazine. "It wouldn't take a strong rope to hang me, but a bear trap on one leg and a grindstone on the other wouldn't drown me in ten fathoms." In a matter of weeks he was boarding a train for his rendezvous with the *Sairy Gamp*.

AN ADIRONDACK PASSAGE

BOONVILLE TO OLD FORGE

THEODORE ROOSEVELT was twenty-four the summer his doctor sent him to Richfield Springs, just south of the Adirondacks, to recover from an attack of asthma. The year was 1883, and the junior state assemblyman improved rapidly, in health if not in temper. By the first week of July, when he wrote his sister Corinne, he was well enough to complain of being "bored out of my life by having nothing whatever to do, and being placed in that quintessence of abomination, a large summer hotel at a watering place for underbred and overdressed girls, fat old female scandal mongers, and a select collection of assorted cripples and consumptives." While Roosevelt was nursing his ire, a consumptive outdoorsman and writer named George Washington Sears was swinging down from a train in Boonville, forty-five miles to the northwest. A gnomish man, sixty-one years old, with a high forehead, thinning white hair, a full beard, and penetrating brown eyes, Sears was embarking on a project that would certainly have raised Roosevelt's spirits: a cruise through the heart of the Adirondacks in a radically small canoe, stopping along the way to mail dispatches back to *Forest and Stream* magazine.

With practiced ease Sears shrugged on his knapsack and slung his rifle over his shoulder before sauntering off toward the freight depot, where his new boat awaited. The *Sairy Gamp* had been shipped direct from her builder, and she was indeed phenomenal, ten and a half pounds compared to the standard Adirondack guideboat's eighty or more. Sears must have smiled when he saw her for the first time, saw the graceful flare at bow and stern, the beamy waist, the shallow depth amidships. Beneath coats of oil and shellac, her lapstrake siding, three-sixteenths of an inch thick, seemed recklessly delicate, but her maker had known what he was doing. He had compensated for her thin skin by stiffening her hull with thirty-nine ribs, and thwarts fore and aft. The lightest boat J. Henry Rushton had ever produced, she was so small that Sears could lift her with one hand.

She appeared too frail for the task ahead, yet by the end of August she had carried her skipper from one end of the wilderness to the other and had secured his place, and her own, in canoeing history. The cruise of the *Sairy Gamp* was a triumph for owner and builder alike, a demonstration that twelve strips of cedar, properly designed, could float a man—at least a little man—safely and in style. The cruise of 1883 was significant for another reason, although Sears only suspected it at the time. After a lifetime of adventuring, he was embarking on the last physically demanding tour he would ever make.

The man who squatted on the platform inspecting his canoe was not, to judge by his clothing, a man of means. He wore a knitted gray cap, a frayed blue shirt, and pants of a thin woolen weave. Only his lightweight boots, of fine French calf, bespoke quality, but this was to be expected: a shoemaker by trade, he had made them himself. The cobbler's bench provided him with a tenuous living, but Sears was temperamentally unsuited to indoor work. From his earliest days, he had exhibited "a liking for adventure, intense love of nature in her wildest dress, and a strange fondness for being in deep forests by myself." These affinities he ascribed to his friendship with a Nipmuck Indian who "was wont to steal me away from home before I was five years old, and carry me around . . . day after day, until I imbibed much of his woodcraft, all his love for forest life, and alas, much of his good-natured shiftlessness." In tribute, Sears later adopted his mentor's name, Nessmuk (meaning "wood drake"), as his byline.

By 1883 Sears was a leading contributor to *Forest and Stream,* the most respected sporting weekly of his day. Based in New York City, the magazine gave him a national audience for his articles on woodcraft and a bully pulpit for addressing environmental evils. Sears had traveled widely and he had lived outdoors much of his life. He could therefore speak with authority about the changes he was seeing, the depletion of fish and game by overhunting, the pollution of rivers by industry, and the degradation of watersheds as the nation's old-growth forests were logged. His was not the only voice raised in alarm, but it was an influential one.

He was also one of the most famous canoeists in the country, although his reputation derived more from his promotion of lightweight boats than from the distances he covered. Extended trips, he admitted, "always began to peter out in the first 100 miles or less, if I happened to strike a model camping spot." All his life he had sought "the blessed calm of lonely places, where the bright-eyed, wary wood folk come almost to your feet as you sit quietly smoking; where the arch rascal man does not intrude; where one may camp for months without seeing a human face or hearing the buzz of civilized racket." His was, he happily confessed, a "lone, light, hunter style of outing" that "cuts off all possibilities for women and children." A world-class loafer, he liked to line his boat with ferns, lie down, and let the wind push him where it would as the rocking motion lulled him to sleep.

As Nessmuk, George Sears taught America how to camp. "We do not go to the green woods and crystal waters to rough it, we go to smooth it," he explained in his classic *Woodcraft.* He told readers what equipment to take, what to wear, the best way to make a campfire, how to cook a porcupine, and most important, what they didn't need. He was the first to advise middle-class "outers," as he called them, that they could dispense with professional guides and go it alone—as long as they traveled light, the way he did: "Each and every [camper] has gone to his chosen ground with too much impedimenta, too much duffle; and nearly all have used boats at least twice as heavy as they need to have been. The temptation to buy this or that bit of indispensable camp-kit has been too strong, and we have gone to the blessed woods, handicapped with a load fit for a pack-mule. This is not how to do it. Go light; the lighter the better."

He himself had no choice but to travel light. A poor man, he could not afford to pay a guide three dollars a day to look after him and carry his gear. And while he had all the skills he needed to go solo, he was limited by his physique. Five foot three and at most 112 pounds, he was, fellow sportsman Fred Mather recalled, "nearly as big as a pound of soap after a hard day's washing." Nor was he the man he had been. By the time he collected the *Sairy Gamp* in Boonville, Sears's physical powers were sadly diminished. His 1881 Adirondack tour had been cut short by illness, and in 1882 he canceled his cruise altogether. He suffered from asthma and tuberculosis, and a mysterious pain in his side had troubled him more than forty years. To his diary he confided another worry: an entry circa 1883 listed two syphilis remedies. His canoe may have looked like a toy, but it was all he could manage on the many portages—called carries in the Adirondacks—that lay along his route.

Finding a light but sturdy boat had not been easy, because at the time few American boatbuilders knew much about canoe design. Following its crucial role in North American exploration and trade, this native craft had been all but forgotten by whites, until a Scot named John MacGregor modified an Inuit kayak and came up with a decked sailing canoe he called the *Rob Roy.* Propelled by a double-bladed paddle and often equipped with an onboard tent, this miniature yacht quickly became popular in the United States after the Civil War.

Sears did not consider boats with masts and rudders real canoes. He had been paddling open (nondecked) models all his life, starting with a Micmac birch when he was eighteen. He had even tried making his own, but they were far too heavy, and those he saw advertised seemed little improvement. In 1879 he wrote to several builders and only one, J. Henry Rushton, of Canton, New York, thought he could make what Sears wanted: a canoe that weighed less than twenty pounds. A genius with wood, Rushton succeeded handsomely on this and subsequent orders. Between 1880 and 1885 he built five canoes for Nessmuk, three of them for Adirondack expeditions. They still seem ethereal today: the ten-foot *Nessmuk No. 1*, or *Wood Drake* (1880), weighed less than eighteen pounds, the ten-and-a-half-foot *Susan Nipper* (1881) about sixteen and a half.

Like her predecessors, the nine-foot *Sairy Gamp* was made of white cedar with copper fastenings. Her keel and gunwales were cedar too, her stem and stern posts were spruce, and the split dowels used for her ribs were red elm. She was twenty-six inches wide and only six inches deep, "too small, too frail," Rushton believed, "for any but a light weight enthusiast, who is willing to incur some risk and sacrifice some points of comfort that he may be able to say he has 'done the wilderness' in the smallest, lightest craft that ever floated a man." Her maker had reservations about the sturdiness of each of his canoes, but he was particularly concerned about the *Sairy.* "Now you must *stop* with *this* one, don't try any smaller one," he told Sears. "If you get sick of this as a *Canoe* use it for a soup dish."

The *Sairy Gamp* was named for the nurse-midwife (spelled Sairey) in *Martin Chuzzlewit,* and like her tippling namesake, Sears hoped she would take no water. Dickens's Mrs. Gamp was a blowzy apparition in snuff-stained clothes with an aura all her own, "a peculiar fragrance . . . as if a passing fairy had hiccoughed, and had previously been to a wine-vault." In choosing this name, Sears was reaching back to his childhood. He once recalled, "A snuffy old nurse who was present at my birth was fond of telling me in after years a legend like this: 'Ga-a-rge, you on'y weighed fo' pounds when you wuz born, 'n' we put yer inter a quart mug 'n' turned a sasser over ye.'"

Rushton built the *Sairy* in fall 1882 and stored her until Sears sent word that he was ready. Early the following July she was boxed, loaded onto a freight car, and sent south to the depot in Boonville. (The board-and-batten building still stands, beside a weedy spur line at the edge of town.) The cruise of the *Sairy Gamp* did not begin at landlocked Boonville, however; twenty-five miles of bad road lay between the depot and her launch point on the Fulton Chain of Lakes. Although wagons plied the route, Sears feared their jolting might puncture his boat's delicate flanks, so he hired a guide named Si Holliday to carry her on his shoulders to the halfway point, at Moose River Settlement; from there he would take her himself. The two men set off, and within a mile the broad vistas of the Black River Valley had yielded to forest. The track dipped and rose, now corduroy, now slithery sand, two ruts leading off to the northeast through a tunnel of birch and hemlock.

The country Sears was heading into is a vast circular uplift rising out of the valleys formed by the Saint Lawrence River to the north, Lake Champlain and the Hudson River to the east, the Mohawk River to the south, and the Lake Ontario basin to the west. The northeastern quadrant of this dome is studded with four- and five-thousand-foot mountains, but to the west, gentler gradients prevail. There, the last glacier scooped out thousands of lakebeds and scraped new paths for the rivers. The dome is a weather-catcher, battered by storms that sweep off the Great Lakes and down from Canada. Winters are severe, and they linger: lakes are often icebound into May.

Until the nineteenth century the Adirondacks were little known to whites. Indians fished and hunted there but built their permanent encampments elsewhere. The region was claimed by both the Algonquins, who lived to the north, and by the Iroquois of the Mohawk Valley ("Adirondack" is thought to be Iroquois for "bark-eater," an epithet for their enemies, who were driven to this food in fierce winters). The French and English skirmished on the dome's periphery, and when peace brought settlers, they clustered there. Later, hundreds of thousands of New Englanders abandoned their rocky farms for the Midwest, but when they reached the dome they streamed south and west and kept going.

Only when the better land had been appropriated was the Adirondack interior breached. Speculators bought vast tracts and began luring settlers into the wilderness. Iron ore was discovered, the virgin timber attracted loggers, and soon primitive roads were inching up from the valleys. Even so, great swaths of territory remained unexplored; until the 1830s no reliable map of the region existed. As Lincoln Barnett has written, "The headwaters of the Columbia River in the Far West were discovered more than a half century before the highest headwaters of the Hudson. Stanley had found Livingstone in darkest Africa before most New Yorkers knew much about the wilderness at their back door."

Surveyors' reports and newspaper accounts by enthusiastic sportsmen brought a trickle of visitors in the 1840s and 1850s, but the Civil War soon drew attention elsewhere. Then, in the spring of 1869, everything changed. *Adventures in the Wilderness; Or, Camp-Life in the Adirondacks,* by William H. H. Murray, caused a tourist stampede that overwhelmed every facility in the north woods. In the following decade hotels were built, stagecoach lines were expanded, a railroad penetrated to North Creek from fashionable Saratoga, and a fleet of steamers was loosed on the lakes.

By the time George Sears visited what was called the Northern Wilderness, much of it was wilderness no more. Along popular routes, hotels were so crowded in July and August that the overflow had to be billeted in private homes. Women in high-necked muslin dresses promenaded on piazzas or trooped down to the water, where guides steadied cane-seated boats reserved for days of sightseeing and botanizing. Men went off with their own guides to hunt or fish. Getting around was now easy, with horse-drawn wagons stationed at the carries to haul boats and gear. In the evening the click of billiard balls could be heard in the parlors, while down by the water, at the guides' lean-to, the traditional bonfire set shadows dancing in the woods.

One could avoid the hordes by heading into the backcountry, and this is what Sears intended to do the first time he toured the Adirondacks, in 1880. "I am going through alone," he promised *Forest and Stream*'s readers. "The faithful guide and the festive landlord of the woodland hotel will not work me to any extent." In the end, however, he paddled the main routes and succumbed with some regularity to the blandishments of resort life. His dwindling strength was clearly a factor, but he was also a sociable creature—on his own terms, of course. "I like the sort of woods life," he once wrote, ". . . that has a spice of convenient civilization mixed up with it, where, for instance, I can visit with intelligent men from different sections of the country, and get in [my canoe] and paddle in an hour to a secluded spot where I may camp for a month without seeing a human face."

He made friends everywhere he went, particularly among the guides, of whom he had been suspicious at the outset. Their kindness won him over. Encountering the exhausted old man on the trail, these good-natured fellows routinely shouldered his knapsack or found some other way to lighten his load. "Uncle Nessmuk," as they called him, might have been quirky, but he was bright and witty, and like the guides he never lied about his exploits "more than the occasion seems to demand." They appreciated his easygoing nature and his mastery of woodcraft, and they introduced him to the hoteliers and camp owners for whom they worked. And so by July 1883, when he headed into the woods with the *Sairy Gamp,* Sears could count on running into friends all along his route, from the Fulton Lakes to Paul Smith's.

Half a day's walk brought Sears and Holliday to Moose River Settlement, where Sears took a room at the clapboard hotel and spent several days "trying to brace up weak muscle, which sadly needed it" by testing his canoe in the river. The *Sairy Gamp* proved stronger and more stable than he'd expected. "Her maker had warned me that he would not warrant her for an hour," he told his *Forest and Stream* readers. "'She may go to pieces like an eggshell,' he said. . . . 'He builded better than he knew.'" Fully loaded, she had five inches of freeboard, and thanks to the thwarts Rushton had added, she did not appreciably deform when Sears climbed in. As it would throughout his trip, Sears's project drew considerable interest. The following week the local correspondent for the *Boonville Herald* had much to write about:

> MOOSE RIVER, July 18.—John O'Grady has finished peeling his bark job of 2,000 cords. . . .
> —Charles Hawker, who was so badly kicked by a horse the other day, is improving fast.
> —E. W. Kennedy has taken the job of removing and finishing the stock from the old tannery yard.
> —Miss Maggie Holmes, our school "marm," spent last Sunday with friends in and about Forestport. . . .
> —Hersey & Company's new sawmill is now in running order, it having been destroyed by the late fire. . . .
> —Mr. G. K. Sears [*sic*], of Wellsboro, Pa., has been spending a few days in town. He is using the lightest boat ever seen in these parts. It is 9 feet long, 24 inches wide and weighs 10½ pounds. The entire weight of the man, boat, etc., is 111½ pounds. The boat is built of white cedar. He will spend the summer on the Fulton Chain of lakes.

Originally no more than a fording place, by the 1880s Moose River Settlement had become a boom town with two tanneries. One, the largest in the region, burned just before Sears arrived, but the other continued to operate right next to his hotel. Sears worked leather for his livelihood, but he detested the industry that produced it. "The tannery village . . . springs up at a month's notice on every considerable stream where bark is available," he observed, "and the long, low tannery, with its labyrinth of vats and villainous refuse, commences its vocation of poisoning and depleting the purest trout streams in the land." Back home, Sears had joined a lawsuit over the destruction of a local river, but his side was no match for the corporations. "They said they would wear us out; beat us by appeals and delay; and they did," he reported. "Half a million can make a couple of hundred look sick."

Still, Sears was able to take the long view. As soon as local hemlock supplies were exhausted, he predicted, the tanneries would be abandoned, their buildings left to rot away. "The floods of a single season will sweep the streams clear of spent tan bark and poisonous chemicals," he wrote. "The denuded forests will be replaced with dense cover and the dried up streams will be restocked, and a wiser generation will conserve the game and fish instead of destroying." He was right. By the time of his visit, Adirondack tanneries were increasingly unprofitable, and one by one they closed.

Its industry moribund, Moose River Settlement withered away. For a few years a curious little railroad called the Peg Leg (it ran on wooden rails) carried tourists from the ford to a spot eight miles upstream, where they could catch a steamer to the lakes. But in 1892 a modern railway pushed through to the east, and the tourists stopped coming. The Peg Leg, the buckboard service, and finally the hotel disappeared. Today there is no town center, only a few cottages straggling along the undulating blacktop and a faint track leading down to the ford. Saplings and brambles along the riverbank hide the remnants of foundation walls and row upon row of tanning vats.

At length Sears gathered up his duffle for the remaining thirteen and a half miles to the lakes. His outfit weighed about fifteen pounds and consisted of his Billinghurst rifle, his double-bitted hatchet and hunting knife (both his own design), fishing tackle, compass, tin cookware, blanket bag, ditty bag, tent, and extra clothing (one shirt, one pair of socks). Most of these items were consigned to a knapsack, which he preferred to the wooden pack baskets favored by guides. Once across the river, he lashed his paddle to the *Sairy*'s thwarts, balanced the boat on his head, and struck off north along the Brown's Tract Road. It was not quite 5:00 A.M. and barely light.

The Brown's Tract Road was a relic of one of the region's most spectacular failures. In the early 1800s the merchant John

Brown of Providence (Brown University is one legacy) acquired 210,000 acres, which he had surveyed into eight townships: Industry, Perseverance, Unanimity, Frugality, Enterprise, Sobriety, Economy, and Regularity. The idea was to sell lots to farmers; to lure them, he had a dam thrown across the outlet of First Lake to power a sawmill and a gristmill. In spite of these efforts, only a handful of families came to clear and work the land.

Brown died, and a son-in-law, Charles Frederick Herreshoff, tried to make good on the family's investment. He had the Brown's Tract Road built from Moose River Settlement to the dam, and not far from its northern end he erected a frame house known as Herreshoff Manor. He lived there alone, however; his wife and daughters were too refined to inhabit a howling wilderness. A cultivated man, he did everything he could, but he failed to grasp one essential fact: the climate and soils of the region are unsuited to agriculture. Nothing went right in the struggling colony. Crops failed or were blighted by drought, the merino sheep driven all the way from Rhode Island sickened, and in 1816 a volcanic eruption halfway around the world caused "the year of no summer," when killing frosts occurred every month.*

One by one his disheartened colonists departed and Herreshoff's depression deepened—until iron ore was discovered. With renewed energy he built a forge beside the dam, but the vein proved spotty and the Brown family bankers cut off his credit. Then, a week before Christmas 1819, the mine flooded. The 1860 *Gazetteer of the State of New York* tells the story: "[Herreshoff] made preparations for going to Providence, and

* Brown's Tract settlers endured every kind of privation, but the hard-luck award surely goes to Captain James Gould. On a lovely spring day in 1814 he rode off in his best clothes, his neighbors' good wishes ringing in his ears, to claim the widow who had agreed to marry him. He returned alone and disconsolate; the widow had jilted him for a wealthier neighbor. Three years later, Gould was kicked in the testicles by an ox and died.

gave particular orders for his men to go out the next morning after he left and fill up a large hole that had been dug for ore. They went out to perform their labor; but one of them went down to see if any tools had been left, and at the bottom he found [Herreshoff] who had secreted himself there, intending to be buried. The next day he accomplished his object by a pistol shot." The settlement was abandoned and the old forge became a landmark for passing hunters.

But Herreshoff's road endured. In 1855 the Honorable Amelia M. Murray, maid of honor to Queen Victoria and all-around good sport, floundered over it on foot. "Planks had been laid down and corduroy bridges made," she observed, "but, as no settlement followed, left to entire neglect, the rotten timbers only made bad worse; and I imagine that it would be impossible to find anywhere a track so difficult to get over as that through which we patiently laboured . . . "

Ten years later, buckboard service was instituted, with wagons leaving Boonville at 8:00 A.M. and arriving at the Forge House, at First Lake, at 4:00 P.M. "An unwarranted degree of optimism entered into the publication of this schedule," historian Joseph Grady has written. The wagons were crude, the passengers liable to minor injury as they jounced from mudhole to mudhole. Small wonder that Sears elected to travel on foot.

It was soon clear, however, that unwarranted optimism had entered into Sears's own schedule. "I . . . made the first three miles bravely," he wrote. "Began to weaken a little. Got some breakfast and went on. At the 'six-mile tree' felt beaten. Buckboard came along with party. Party got out to lift and admire canoe. Driver said if I would leave my knapsack at the tree he would fetch it in on his return. Left it gladly.

"Went on and got caught in drenching thunder storm. Crept under canoe until it passed over. Road a muddy ditch. At the 'eight-mile tree' caught another and harder storm. Kept sulkily on, too mad and demoralized to dodge under canoe. Arrived at 'ten-mile tree' pretty much tired and stopped (4 p.m.) to get some tea and lunch. Felt it to be the hardest carry I had ever made . . .

"Just then along came Ned Ball, a muscular young guide, and though he had four hounds in charge, he volunteered to hoist the canoe on his head and carry it in. 'It don't weigh more'n a stovepipe hat,' he said.

"The last three and one-half miles of road were much better, and at 8 p.m. I arrived at the Forge House, wet, bruised, and looking like an ill-used tramp. Some dry woolens, much too large, with a bright fire in front of the hotel, a night's rest, and a good breakfast brought me around and 'paradise, reached through purgatory,' was attained."

After serving for eighty years as the southwestern gateway to the region, the Brown's Tract Road abruptly fell out of use in 1892, when the Adirondack and St. Lawrence Railroad pushed through. The southern half of the road subsequently fell into private hands, and elsewhere it was rerouted, but one section survives as a state-maintained hiking path. Near the spot where the eight-mile tree stood, the Brown's Tract Trail winds through a pretty forest of beech and maple. You will still find plenty of the mudholes travelers used to revile, but now, instead of wagon ruts, each one bears a palimpsest of deer tracks, dog pugs, and waffled lug soles.

Paradise, aka the Forge House, occupied a gentle slope just south of John Brown's dam. In those days the hotel was a two-story board-and-batten structure with a fenced garden out back and a deep verandah furnished with split-bottomed chairs overlooking the pond. When it opened in the early 1870s the Forge House was the only real hotel in the area, yet its first years were lean ones. Tourists clung to the routes recommended in the guidebooks, which entered the region from the northeast, via Lake Champlain; the Boonville gateway was the gentlest ascent onto the dome, with none of the awesome peaks that stimulated nineteenth-century rhapsodies. While more northerly lakes were being transformed by development, the Fulton Chain remained something of a backwater.

Across from the hotel a channel led to the first of eight lakes strung along the central arm of the Moose River. These were known as the Middle Branch Lakes until 1811, when the steamboat designer Robert Fulton was commissioned to determine whether they could become a link between the Hudson and the Great Lakes. Although Fulton soon deemed the idea impracticable, his influence persisted: thereafter the lakes were known as the Fulton Chain. Eventually the state acquired John Brown's dam and in 1879 raised it by several feet. Water was backed up more than eleven miles, all the way to Fifth Lake, and the narrow, rocky rapids between the lakes were turned into stillwaters.

"Have paddled the *Sairy Gamp* on the four first lakes until my arms are lame," Sears reported on July 20. "Sitting in her this afternoon I took in six fine trout. She yields to the rush of a thirteen-inch speckle like a split bamboo. For a 10½-pound canoe she is a marvel of steadiness. I ride her in pretty rough water without a wiggle. I shall try no lighter one, however. She makes a good side-show wherever she appears, but a larger canoe would be more comfortable; say eighteen pounds."

He was sorry, he wrote, that he could not be in Manhattan to help celebrate *Forest and Stream*'s tenth anniversary. "Since the days of *Porter's Spirit of the Times*," he declared, "I have not written for any paper or magazine with which I seemed to be so fairly *en rapport*. . . . " In 1860 he had been a front-page correspondent for *Porter's*, another sporting weekly based in New York City, but after the journal changed hands, Sears disappeared from its pages. Thereafter he published occasional poems in literary magazines—*The Atlantic Monthly, Lippincott's, Putnam's, The Aldine*—but eventually even these efforts ceased. "I dropped the pen in '71," Sears explained. "[Writing] was pleasure, but, like Mr. Micawber's 'coals,' 'not remunerative.' I found that there were several thousand aspirants for literary honors and emoluments who were constantly boring publishers without ever getting a show on any respectable journal—or deserving it—and I stepped aside. For nine years I . . . attended to business, and that is not very remunerative, either."

Sears had good reason to be grateful to *Forest and Stream.* It resurrected his literary career. In 1879 a reader wrote in to ask what had become of Nessmuk, and Sears responded with his plans for an Adirondack cruise. The editor was interested, and Sears's account of his 1880 tour was so successful that he went back in 1881 and 1883. Over the next decade he published roughly ninety pieces in *Forest and Stream* and wrote others for various angling publications. (Although he was a bait fisherman, he was even asked to contribute a chapter to Charles Orvis's anthology *Fishing With the Fly.*) It was *Forest and Stream*'s parent company that published both of Sears's books: *Woodcraft* (1884) and *Forest Runes* (1887). The latter, a collection of poetry, quickly vanished, but *Woodcraft* went through fourteen printings. Had there been no *Forest and Stream,* there may very well have been no *Sairy Gamp.*

Using the Forge House as his base, Sears visited friends on the first four lakes. A week passed, and still he had not set off on his much-touted cruise. "I had several excuses for such utter laziness," he wrote. "I said the weather was too stormy, too 'catching' for a start through the woods in a boat where a man can carry no change of clothes save an extra blue shirt and a pair of socks. Moreover, I had met with an accident on the Brown's Tract Road that made my port deadlight look as though I had been in a 'fight mit table legs' at 'Hans Breitmann's Barty';* looking like a tramp with a black eye, I disliked to introduce the *Sairy* among strangers."

But at least one stranger immediately became a friend. Retired navy captain L. A. Beardslee happened to be passing through. He too was a *Forest and Stream* contributor whose byline, Piseco, was well known to Sears. Ten years afterward, Beardslee recalled walking up the hill to register at the Forge House: "On the stoop lay the very prettiest little boat I ever saw. I will not describe her, for who of you all would fail to recognize at sight the canoe *Sairy Gamp*. While I was inspecting her a little grizzly old fellow came up and kindly answered my questions about her. . . . In the evening he came to my room, and although for a few moments he occupied the chair I offered him he very soon, as we engaged ourselves in the pleasing amusement of comparing and overhauling gear, slid off to the floor and spent the rest of the evening sitting Jap-fashion on his heels." Beardslee thought he'd pared his equipment to the minimum but changed his mind when he saw what Sears was taking. The two fished, and one night camped out, an experience Beardslee never forgot. "The wood nymphs touched him with their charms," he wrote, "and the store of prose and poetry with which he entertained me made of it a bit of dreamland." Self-educated, Sears could quote from a wide range of literature. "I carry a sufficient supply of Shakespeare, Pope, Byron and Burns under the little gray hunting cap, which I can draw on at need," he once remarked. He could have added Dickens to this list, and Emerson and Whitman.

* Paul Jamieson, who edited the original introduction to *The Adirondack Letters of George Washington Sears,* explains, "The reference is to a now nearly forgotten humorous poet of Philadelphia, Charles Godfrey Leland. He published a series entitled *Hans Breitmann's Ballads,* 1856 ('Hans Breitmann gife a barty' is a recurring line), in a kind of Pennsylvania Dutch dialect. The theme is the reverse of Henry James's and Mark Twain's American innocence abroad; it's the old world culture of a German gentleman disintegrating under the influence of American society."

By July 26 Sears's black eye had faded and he was ready to go. "There came a bright, clear afternoon," he wrote, "with good promise of one clear day, and the next morning the *Sairy* was making good time up the inlet of Fourth Lake." The cruise of the *Sairy Gamp* was at last under way.

2

OLD FORGE TO INLET

ON A SUNDAY AFTERNOON LATE IN AUGUST 1990, John and I drove to the Adirondacks, left one car in a parking lot at Long Lake, and continued forty-five miles south to Old Forge, where our trip would begin. Our motel occupied the same hillside, although not the exact site, where the Forge House had stood, overlooking the pond where the *Sairy Gamp* began her cruise 107 years earlier. Near our patio a sprinkler was *tick-tick-tick*ing across the motel's putting green while in the distance a brass band cheerfully mangled an assortment of marches. As the shadows crept across the lawn I imagined drawing up a chair for Sears, handing him a shot of his favorite "cereal juice," and watching him try to grapple with what has happened to the area around John Brown's dam. A powerboat roared up to the dock below; on the opposite shore, bobbing gently in the backwash, two replica steamboats awaited tomorrow's sightseers. Muscle cars blatted through the streets, and across the road a line of kids inched to the top of a giant water slide, their screams carrying above the sounds of traffic. Two rooms away a television anchorman droned on about the latest global mayhem. How could you explain a late-twentieth-century resort town to a nineteenth-century sensibility?

We turned in early, yet in spite of a long day, sleep eluded me. I worried, rationalized, worried some more—about supplies and equipment, about unscouted put-ins, about our cars being vandalized. What had I forgotten? How would our boats perform? How would we perform? I stared into the darkness and saw myself capsizing, my canoe being snatched away by the wind. At last I drifted off. When I opened my eyes the ceiling was pale.

I had always imagined that we would set out on a bright, crisp morning, the kind of day, Sears would have said, "to mark with a white pebble." But when we drew the curtains, we found the world immured in fog so dense that the pond at the foot of the hill might not have existed. One of those late-summer fogs, we assured each other; bound to burn off in an hour.

A lone tourist was patrolling the waterfront as we loaded our boats at the children's beach, lashing packs behind the rear thwarts and sleeping pads in the bows. John carried our tent and food; I had room only for the waterproof bag that held camera and binoculars. The stroller, a middle-aged fellow in a windbreaker, plaid pants, and white sneakers, watched intently and finally addressed us.

"Where you going?"

"Paul Smiths," I said, tossing my life jacket onto my seat.

"Where's that?"

"Oh, about ninety miles north of here."

He shook his head. "Long way. I'd like to do a long trip some day, but my wife don't care for it. How much those canoes weigh?" Ah yes, the question most frequently asked of Sears, and, as it turned out, of us.

Time to get going. We dragged our boats into the shallows

and climbed gingerly aboard. During his week here Sears practiced getting into and out of the *Sairy*, which struck me as odd until I got my own canoe and discovered that this Rushton design is tippy as hell until your bottom is firmly planted on the seat (whereupon it becomes semi-tippy). My early attempts at embarkation were highly entertaining, even to me. Eventually I learned to squat down beside the boat, grasp the gunwales behind me, swing my right leg over the side, and fall backward onto the seat as I brought my other leg aboard. This slo-mo pratfall was not exactly elegant, but it worked. Like Sears, I found it easier to climb aboard at a shallow beach; stepping in from above, at a breakwater or dock, was nearly impossible.

It was 7:40 when we shoved off. Above the muted rumble of traffic came the sound of a mourning dove and a pair of jays jeering. Nothing else was afloat. I was filled with a shy kind of happiness mixed with anticipation. Every canoe trip, no matter how modest, is an adventure, because every one is different, depending on the time you launch, the season, the weather, your mood, your expectations. Best of all are the long trips, when a single thrust of the paddle fends off the land for a happily indefinite period. In a moment the obligations of everyday existence are behind you. There are no faxes in the woods, no cellular phones, no sound bites, no car alarms. No one is trying to sell you anything. With life pared to its essentials—paddling, portaging, arranging food and shelter—you find manifest delight in small things. Canoeing is like meditation, forcing you to remain firmly in the moment.

We headed out to mid-pond, our double-bladed paddles stroking a rhythmic *plip-plop, plip-plop, plip-plop*. In Sears's time you could still find traces of John Brown's grist mill and the tumbledown forge his son-in-law built, but their foundations have since been obliterated. Miraculously, a millstone and two rusty trip-hammers survived and are displayed on a sidewalk in the center of town. And although a concrete dam succeeded

Brown's crude log barrier, it occupies the same spot, where the Middle Branch of the Moose escapes fourteen miles of impoundment to become a river once more.

Peering up at the hillside where the Forge House used to be, I imagined a bruised and exhausted Sears stumbling up to the door after his trek from Moose River Settlement. The hotel was decidedly homespun then, but it didn't stay that way long. Eleven years after Sears's visit the railroad laid a spur from its main line, to the west, to the waterfront. As the trains brought more people, the hotel accreted stories, ells, dormers, and verandahs. By the July afternoon in 1924 when someone noticed smoke curling out of a gable, the Forge House had become a five-story behemoth. In a few hours it was glowing rubble. The hilltop has remained empty; a squat motel now sits at its foot. The railbed lies buried beneath an asphalt street.

We turned our backs and headed for the mile-and-a-half channel that leads to First Lake, a small contingent of mallards escorting us. The forty-five miles from Old Forge to Long Lake would take us four or five days and represented our longest stretch on the water (our limited carrying capacity meant we had to stop often to reprovision and leapfrog cars). This first leg would harden us off physically and, in a way, psychologically: the scenery we'd encounter was typical of the alternating wild and developed country we'd find along our route.*

As we made our way down the channel I was swept with the sensuous pleasure of paddling, the soft plash of each stroke, the rocking of my boat, the sweet tang of fresh water. Because my

* The largest park in the lower forty-eight states, the Adirondack Park contains a stunning ninety percent of the wilderness remaining east of the Mississippi. A state park, it is also noteworthy for its peculiar pattern of ownership. In 1892, New York legislators drew a blue line on the map to define the region they wanted to preserve (to this day the park's boundary is called the Blue Line). By that time, however, the state had lost title to much of that land, and it has never been recovered. Today, about forty-three percent is publicly owned Forest Preserve designated forever wild and fifty-seven percent remains in private hands, with public and private parcels alternating in a giant crazy quilt.

polyfoam seat was placed right on the bottom of the boat, I was not only on the water, I was in it, my outstretched legs actually below surface level. The low vantage point made me feel I was skimming along at inordinate speed—getting over the water, Sears put it, "like a scared loon." The sensation of speed was sheer illusion, but it was an illusion Sears shared, and it was right here that he had his comeuppance. In 1880, paddling his first Rushton canoe, he challenged a guide named Fred Hess to a race. They started from the Forge House landing, Sears with his double blade and Hess rowing a much larger guideboat. By the time they reached the finish, less than two-thirds of a mile away, Sears was lagging. He ascribed his loss to age and lack of conditioning, but his defeat so rankled him that he directed Rushton to build him a faster canoe. Rushton demurred, explaining that a double blade is by nature slow, and instead built him the ten-and-a-half-foot *Susan Nipper.**

Although I had never kayaked I found the double-bladed paddle easy to get on to and a sensible solution for a boat this size. A canoe wants to veer away from the side you're paddling on; the smaller the canoe, the sharper the veer. With a single blade you have to switch sides every few strokes or constantly twist the shaft (the venerable J-stroke is one way to do this) to compensate for this tendency. With a double blade stroking on both sides, you're automatically correcting all the time. The only problem I had in the beginning, and it soon became second nature, was learning to keep a quiet lower body while my arms did the work. Leaning too hard into the stroke tipped the canoe radically and threatened a capsize. This preternatural responsiveness, in which a wiggle of the hips translated into a substantial wobble of the canoe, would come in handy later,

* The following summer, on Seventh Lake, the *Nipper* also lost to a guideboat. Sears's boyish love of racing despite his failing strength is one of his more disarming traits. He was still at it in 1885, at a regatta in Florida, where he pitted the eight-and-a-half-foot *Rushton* against a field of yawls. "I held way with them, too," he reported, "until the wind freshened, when they soon left me astern."

when rough water called for maximum maneuverability.

The channel, uninhabited in Sears's time, is now lined with homes, docks, boathouses, cottages, and waterside patios. A light rain began, tracing Escher patterns on the water, delicate rings growing, merging, and dissolving. With visibility limited by the fog, the landscape seemed oddly intimate. In the orange glow of a table lamp a man sat by a kitchen window with coffee and his morning paper. The sight gave me a swift pang; it would be a long time before I sat in my kitchen again. Paddling side by side, John and I chatted desultorily as we slid past yards decorated with whirligigs, plaster elves, ducks, flamingos, deer, and one three-foot-tall reclining black figure holding a fishing pole, its line trailing in the water. The Museum of American Lawn Art.

At the entrance to First Lake a dozen herring gulls were perched on the rocks at Indian Point, a peninsula that stood well out of the water until the dam was rebuilt. This spot became notorious in September 1833, when a marksman and trapper named Nat Foster secreted himself in the woods and picked off a Saint Regis Indian named Drid as the latter paddled up the channel. Foster, who had installed his family in the abandoned Herreshoff Manor, had been feuding with Drid for a year, but on this day the two had quarreled bitterly near the dam. Foster stomped off ostensibly in the direction of the Manor but doubled back through the woods to ambush his enemy. The dead man was roundly disliked and Foster was eventually acquitted, but, fearing reprisal, he left the area. (Oddly enough, for a time he lived in Tioga County, Pennsylvania, where Sears settled.)

Drid, whose English name was Peter Waters, was buried beside the dam, his grave marked by a boulder inside a low railing. In the early 1940s the town decided to move his remains because a building was planned for the site. Photographs of the dig show four men in shirtsleeves, suspenders, and fedoras leaning on shovels and squinting at the camera. They never found their man. Some said he had long ago been exhumed and buried nearby in an Indian ceremony; others claimed his family had taken his remains to a reservation up north. I like to think he still rests beside the dam, his spirit heaving up the asphalt in a corner of the Chamber of Commerce parking lot.

As we passed Indian Point the gulls flapped into the air, their gray-and-white bodies swallowed by the fog. Although First Lake is small, we could make out no shoreline. The entrance to Second Lake lay somewhere ahead and to our right, between a long point and an island. We struck out blindly and were startled when a drifting boat materialized nearby, two ghostly fishermen huddled over their poles. The rain had stopped.

The point was right where it was supposed to be, and we quickly passed through the strait into Second Lake, which is even smaller than First. In Sears's time there was, on the north shore, a sandy bluff covered with poplars. "Passing this," he reported, "you come in sight of the Eagle's Nest, the most-noted landmark on the Fulton Chain. The oldest guides could not tell me how long the nest had been there. For several years the birds deserted it, owing to the fusillade kept up by the cockneys of the Muggins tribe, who usually considered it the correct thing to empty guns and revolvers at the eagle's nest, occasionally hitting a young eaglet. The thing is better ordered now. With one exception, no one has fired at them this summer. . . ."

The sandy bluff is still there, but the eagles departed many years ago, victims of harassment, loss of habitat, pollution, and the effects of DDT. Of New York State's once-healthy population of bald eagles, only one nesting pair remained in 1976, and they could produce no viable eggs. Now the state Department of Environmental Conservation has undertaken a vigorous effort to restore the species, releasing eaglets in remote areas of the Catskills, the Saint Lawrence River valley, and the Adirondacks. As of 1990 the DEC's work had paid off in ten nesting pairs, three of them in the northern section of the park.

By the time we reached Third Lake the fog was beginning to lift but Rondaxe Mountain (formerly Bald Mountain) was still veiled. We could make out a row of cottages on the north shore where in Sears's day there had been only one building, a place owned by Charlie Grant, who one April day overestimated his strength and froze to death on the Brown's Tract Road. On both previous trips Sears had stayed at this camp, and it may have been here that he contracted tuberculosis. In 1881 he found the place jammed, but he could not get away. For days a cold rain slanted out of the northeast. "In less than forty-eight hours after landing," he reported, "I had joined the little band of coughers, coughing oftener and louder than any of them. As I had made the trip to the woods for health mainly, this was most provoking. I thought it was only a surface cough, so to speak, but it was constant, hard and irritating." The cough would remain with him for the rest of his life.

In 1883 Sears found new camps everywhere, evidence of a building boom that continued for years. At the turn of the century a politician named Martin Van Buren Ives remarked, "The shores of these lakes are ornamented by innumerable private camps or cottages, which serve to give the locality a sort of camp-meeting appearance." By the First World War the region was hopelessly civilized: "The Fulton Chain," journalist T. Morris Longstreth observed, "is a navigable string of lakes dedicated to the summerer. He lines their banks. His victrolas fill in the natural vacancies of an evening in the woods. His womenfolk enjoy themselves shrilly. . . . Stores are not so far apart that you will suffer if you've left the ax at home. Steamers are at hand to pick you up if blistered. The carries are supplied with carriers if your pride goeth before a haul."

In the short channel that leads from Third to Fourth Lake, a cramped trailer park extends for much of the distance along the left bank. Those who live here, in units separated by inches, must be as gregarious as the mallards that dodge among the patio boats and outboards tethered by the shore. This has always been a friendly place. At the turn of the century three community rowboats used to be kept at the far end of the channel for people headed to the other side of Fourth Lake. If you took the last boat you were expected to tow one of the others back for the next traveler.

When the channel broadened into Fourth Lake, we followed the south shore to a state picnic area where we could stop for breakfast. No sooner had we claimed a table than a ranger appeared to collect three dollars. He nodded when I asked if he'd heard a weather forecast; there was a chance of a thunderstorm, so if we headed out we should stick close to shore. We could camp just across the way, on Alger Island, but it would cost us extra. This news we digested along with coffee and cold cereal.

"What do you think?" I asked John.

"Well, we've already come what?—four miles?"

"Four and a half. But the next campsites are nine miles from here. If things get hairy . . . "

"Yeah, but it's only quarter after nine. I can't see stopping this early. We'd have to kill the rest of the day. Let's keep going. We'll stay right by shore."

"I guess we could get a motel room at Inlet if we had to. That's only five miles or so. Okay, let's go for it."

I had shipped a bootful of water when we landed at the log breakwater, and reembarking there in knee-deep swells provided a refresher course in such principles as displacement, volume, and gravity—physical laws I would test, with precisely the same result, throughout the trip. I had chosen boots that were cut too low, which meant that at any depth greater than six inches, water poured over the tops to engulf my feet and ankles. This was unpleasant but not a disaster: my mother did not raise me to be a sissy. No, the difficulty occurred at the crux of my slow-motion fall into my canoe, as my left leg cleared the gunwale and the accumulated liquid cascaded down the back of my calf and thigh to pool—I cannot say this delicately—in my crotch. The sensation, which would intensify as autumn advanced, often caused me to utter strange sounds and to curse Leon Leonwood Bean, whose fault it was not. Wet underpants smack of childhood, but at least in childhood there was a moment (oh, too fleeting!) of suffusing warmth.

Off we went down the largest and most populated lake in the chain. The fog had dissolved into lowering clouds that hid everything above a few hundred feet, and the water was gunmetal gray and restless. Fourth Lake—"the Stormy Fourth" to Sears—has long had a reputation for treachery; in 1881 Sears barely outran disaster here. "I have been in a white squall in the tropics, in a *pampero* off the Argentine coast, and have seen the terrific electric storms of the West," he recalled. "But I never saw so heavy a sea kicked up on an inland lake at such short notice. In two minutes the water was dashing up the sloping landing to the door of the boat-house; sharp, steep, white-crested waves were chasing each other like racehorses; the gale tore their spumy tops off and sent them whirling to leeward in a white mist of blinding spray; tall trees a century old were seized by the hair of the head and dashed to earth, while the zig-zagging of lightning and the heavy bellowing of thunder were just the adjuncts to make the scene perfect. . . . In twenty minutes the storm had howled and whirled itself away to the northeast, the sun came out warm and mellow, the air was a delight, and the lake subsided to a placid, sleepy roll as quickly as it had risen."

A gusty west wind had come up while we ate, and I felt increasingly apprehensive. We crossed over to Alger Island and paddled along its protected south shore, then cut back to the mainland as a moderate rain began. Once we left the island's lee the water became rougher, tossing our boats around and spraying over the gunwales. Hugging the shore wasn't nearly as reassuring as I'd hoped: where the land ran straight, waves bounced off the breakwaters and collided with incoming rollers to create extra turbulence; where headlands thrust out, all hell broke loose and the chop became deep and disorganized. (I later asked my oldest brother, a former naval officer, about this phenomenon: "What's the nautical term for that condition around a headland where the seas are, you know, confused?" He put on his most owlish face and said, "Well, for a couple of hundred years we've called it confused seas.") Beyond each headland we found a patch of calm water that allowed us to regroup. We were learning a lot in a hurry about the physics of wind and water.

It soon occurred to me that instead of using my life vest to pad my backrest, I ought to be wearing it. In twisting around to retrieve it, however, I leaned too far and shipped several quarts of water, which proceeded to slosh back and forth around my outstretched legs. It was not possible to be wetter, but the extra weight was deadening the canoe's handling, so we headed for a private beach where I could unload and swab out. I half expected someone to bolt out of the boxy brown house nearby and run us off, but apparently only idiots were abroad in such weather. It took no more than a minute to toss my gear on the sand, raise the canoe over my head to drain it, and then reload.

Within half an hour the rain had stopped and the sun was making brief appearances through racing clouds. Now I could lower my hood and look around. The north shore was nearly a mile away, our destination somewhere on the hazy green horizon. We passed a house with a luncheon party in progress, nicely dressed people lounging on steps with drinks in hand, clinks and tinkles and laughter floating over the water. Farther along a monarch butterfly hovered over a coppery hydrangea, perhaps as amazed as I at the sight of these great blowzy flowers at the edge of the forest. As the sun strengthened we shucked off jackets and let the warmth soak into our skin. Suddenly the world seemed altogether fresh and fine.

INLET TO RAQUETTE LAKE

At the community of Inlet, a breakwater studded with mooring cleats lines the short channel to Fifth Lake. The dock was too high and sheer-sided to accommodate our canoes, but right next to it was a gently sloping, deserted swimming beach. We glided over the rope enclosing the children's area and disembarked under the bored gaze of a lifeguard and her male companion, who immediately went back to their books. Beyond the sand a lawn ran back to some tennis courts where the Arrowhead Hotel once stood.

The Arrowhead enjoyed a moment of fame in the summer of 1906 when a young man named Chester Gillette was arrested there after drowning his pregnant girlfriend, Grace Brown, in a lonely bay on Big Moose Lake. Gillette had made his way south, on foot and by steamer, to the Arrowhead, where he posed as a tourist until detectives tracked him down. The trial was a national media event featuring Brown's pathetic letters to her increasingly indifferent lover. Gillette was executed at

Auburn Prison in 1908, but the story lived on in Dreiser's *An American Tragedy* and the movie *A Place in the Sun*.

We hauled our food bag to the base of a massive white pine, flopped down, and devoured our lunch. As I stood to brush the crumbs from my lap I noticed on the opposite side of the tree a sign forbidding picnicking, pets, and alcoholic beverages, $50 fine. Looking around, I realized there were signs everywhere: No Parking, No Walking Through Tennis Courts, No Dogs, Picnicking at Tables Only. The beach had its own list of no-nos concerning horseplay, float etiquette, diving, running, glass containers, and whistles. Oh, right, whistles. *Défense de tweet-tweet.*

While we were loading our boats, a man in a short-sleeved white shirt strode up and began berating us for using the beach instead of the breakwater. I explained our problem and apologized, but he was not to be appeased. If the state found out about this there'd be trouble; we were to leave at once. We did, with pleasure.

After the chop on Fourth Lake, the protected passage to Fifth was easy going, a shady glide past a marina and the backsides of homes and businesses lining the road. Smallest of the chain lakes, Fifth was a "good frogging ground," Sears wrote, "but only a pug-hole of nine acres." In 1880 he had camped here and enjoyed "a night just such as a woodsman loves. There was not a soul within miles of me, and the shriek of the steam whistle was afar off, beyond the keenest earshot. The owls were plentier than usual, and in exceptionally good voice, while a loon . . . kept up his strange wild cries at intervals through the night." The sounds you hear today are more likely to be trucks downshifting on the state highway along the north shore. The day had become hot and humid. At the take-out, hidden in a marsh on the far side of the lake, the wet grass under our feet was intensely fragrant.

We prepared for our first carry, using screws and wing nuts

to attach canoes to the top of our pack frames and lashing sleeping pads to the bottom. Our hands were left free for paddles and the rest of the gear, the tent bag for me, the food bag for John. The trail was only seven-tenths of a mile, but the first half was uphill and I was so out of shape I had to stop for a rest. We stood on the shoulder of the highway, traffic rushing past at speeds that seemed extraordinary to our water-lulled senses.

The Sixth Lake launch area is the size of a miniature-golf hole and is flanked by a road, cottages, and No Trespassing signs. Beside the landing sits a prim little dam where a sixty-foot waterfall once tumbled down to Fifth Lake. When Sears first passed through, in 1880, the dam was under construction. By the next summer it was finished, and the waters of Sixth and Seventh lakes had been raised eight feet. "The water at and above the dam," he wrote, "was clogged with rotting vegetation, slimy tree-tops, and decayed, half-sunken logs. The shoreline of trees stood dead and dying, while the smell of decaying vegetable matter was sickening. Last season Sixth Lake, though small (fifty-three acres), was a wild, gamy place, and the best of the chain for floating. Its glory has departed. None care to stop there longer than is necessary."* Although Sixth is now anything but wild and gamy, we could see no trace of this devastation. Homes, boathouses, and docks dot its shores and throw back the drone of seaplanes taxiing to and from the charter business near the dam.

In the time it had taken us to walk from Fifth to Sixth the

* A century before Edward Abbey advocated sabotage in defense of nature, Sears was reasoning along similar lines. "Does it ever occur to the average guide," he thundered, "that he has a better moral right to explode a can of dynamite under one of these dams than a selfish monopolist has to poison the air that men, women and helpless children are forced to breathe and drink? . . . To say nothing of the destruction of fish, the converting of a beautiful sheet of water into a scene of desolation that will last long after the porcine instigator has rotted in his grave, and his ill-gotten gains are scattered by his pampered worthless offspring."

clouds had regrouped. The hardest rain of the day greeted us as we paddled out, billowing curtains sweeping across the lake, pocking the surface. The drumming on my nylon hood was deafening, and I could see nothing through my streaked glasses. I began to feel aggrieved. Probably everything in my pack was soaked by now. Probably all the campsites were taken. Probably all the firewood was wet and we'd go to bed chilled and hungry.

In the midst of this poor-me maundering I recalled how I had airily dismissed the notion of waiting out bad weather, telling friends, "Hey, if you don't like to get wet, you've got no business on the water." Much of the appeal of the Adirondacks, I had insisted, lay in the brooding ambience of dark forests, black water, lowering skies. Well, yes—but that was then; now I was tired and wet. Now I was forty-seven going on twelve. *Why couldn't it have been nice, the way I imagined it?* whined the brat inside me. John, paddling steadily beside me, seemed gently amused that I was taking the rain personally but had the grace not to laugh out loud.

The rain slackened as we slipped through a narrows and under a low bridge to find what Sears termed "the Noble Seventh" filling the horizon. As if to mock me the sun broke through. Wisps of vapor curled off the water; the world sparkled. Off to our left there was once a lean-to where Sears camped in 1881 and hooked up with two guides, one of them "Slim Jim" Phifield.

Phifield was somewhat eccentric, according to historian Joseph Grady: "his mannerisms, philosophies, solemn observances of outworn social amenities, and even his clothes were characteristic of a man fifty years behind the times." A bachelor, he'd built himself a place on the south shore of Fourth Lake, and when guiding was slow, he took in paying customers. A few years after his meeting with Sears, a couple arrived for an extended stay. The husband was ill when he got there, and in spite of the mountain air and his wife's ministrations, he died within a month. Phifield awkwardly offered condolences and arranged for the widow's transportation to the Boonville train station. When she asked him to accompany her, he assented; she was a good person, so kind that he had revised his opinion of the fair sex. Says Grady,

> On the way to Moose River Settlement the two sat side by side in the buckboard as it followed the heavier vehicle which bore the rough box. Slim Jim's arms were constantly alert to shield his gentle companion from the shocks of travel engendered by the rutty surface of the road. In turn, she reciprocated, nestling trustfully. Their conversation, impersonal at first, graduated to subdued intensity. Slim Jim's platitudes in vernacular and her conventional responses gave way to an animated exchange of confidences. The strong arms slowly tightened their hold, and the two voices dropped to intimate whisperings as words almost inaudible passed between them, earnest, low-spoken utterances which the straining ears of the buckboard driver failed to catch. When they reached Moose River the pair were engaged, or so the driver reported when he returned to the Forge House the next day. At all events, Slim Jim followed the deceased not only to Boonville but to his home: he stayed for the funeral, made himself useful afterward, and some time later married the widow.

Within ten minutes of the sun's appearance, John had taken off his shirt; within twenty we had found the archetypal Adirondack campsite atop a granite bluff on the north shore. Our first night out would be spent in style: we had a lean-to tucked into a grove of old white pines with a carpet of sweet brown needles underfoot, a fireplace with grate, a picnic table, a clean privy, and a fine view of the western end of the lake. When we'd lugged everything up to the shelter we got into dry clothes and draped our sopping pants and socks on sunny bushes by water's edge.

A previous camper had observed woods etiquette by leaving

us dry firewood. Other amenities included newspapers for tinder and a swatter for the numerous houseflies. Near the edge of the clearing a bronze tablet bolted to a boulder read:

THIS LEAN-TO
IS DEDICATED TO THE MEMORY OF
ROGER DUCK & TOM FINKLE
BY THEIR FAMILIES AND FRIENDS
SCHENECTADY, NY

I would later learn that the two men had spent many happy hours here; when they died in a car accident, their families underwrote construction of a new lean-to. I can't think of a finer memorial.

After dinner we lounged on the bluff overlooking the lake and congratulated ourselves on having made more than fourteen miles our first day. Just below us, two teenage boys beached their canoe at Arnolds Rock and spent an hour drinking and braying at the setting sun before paddling away. The flies at the lean-to were so persistent we decided to sleep in our tent. Racing the fading light, we set up our nylon dome, hoisted our food bag into a tree, brushed our teeth, and made a last trip to the privy. Our sleeping bags, spread out on self-inflating pads, felt utterly luxurious to muscles already stiffening from the day's work.

A scraping sound came from the rock offshore, followed by familiar voices. The boys had left, it seemed, only to fetch another six-pack. More adolescent bellowing, hooting, and haranguing, as the two defined themselves, to each other and themselves, by what they liked, what they hated, by their music, their movies. I remembered how poignant the last week of August is at their age, what a watershed between the sweet days of summer—sandy towels, stifling knotty pine bedrooms, music across nighttime water—and the gathering momentum of the future. In a week or two they'd start a job or go off to college, and their lives would change forever.

At last we heard the screech of aluminum on granite, and the voices faded. I got up once in the night to discover that fog had settled in. From Arnolds Rock a navigation light blinked relentlessly at the dark lake.

The fog was still there when we woke, graying out the sky and the far shore. On stiff legs I tottered around making pancakes while John fed the fire and began packing up. For Sears, avatar of traveling light, breaking camp was a matter of rolling out of his balsam-bough bed, brewing a pot of green tea—"the sort that takes you by the throat and moistens the roots of the hair"—and tossing his knapsack into his canoe.

For us the process was vastly more complicated and thus slower. After breakfast we dressed in "wet clothes"—quick-drying paddling pants and jackets—and stowed our camp clothes in plastic bags in our packs. (Donning dry clothes and shoes in the evening provides an instant attitude adjustment.) Next we dismantled the tent, removing rain fly, shock-corded poles, pegs, and ground cloth, and rolling them all into a tight bundle that would slip into its nylon bag. Sleeping bags and pads also had to be tightly rolled to fit into their stuff-sacks. Dishes went into another bag, along with cookware, utensils, and the small Swedish stove we used to supplement the fire. Finally, everything had to be hauled down to the water for loading. We became accomplished packers, yet it was difficult to cook, eat, and get on the water in less than an hour and a half; often it required two.

From Arnolds Rock we made our way along the state-owned north shore, its unbroken forest a visual relief after miles of development. The fog was lifting as we paddled around a point and into the inlet bay. Here we had a choice: we could land at the head of the lake and make a mile-long carry or, if the water was deep enough, we could push down the north arm and cut our walk in half. Since paddling is a lot easier than carrying, we opted for the shortcut.

Lily pads pottled against our hulls as we headed into a slack-water channel. Just below the surface stood a forest of stumps, relics of the flooding that once disfigured the lake. The exposed trunks had long ago toppled, but their bases, some of them massive, had been preserved for a century by the cold water. In 1881 Sears had a miserable time of it at this spot. The master napper had overslept after lunch and was late getting away. "The afternoon was cloudy," he wrote, "and my watch . . . had got wet, and, though keeping up a feeble semblance of life, had become utterly reckless as to any proper division of hours and minutes. The hands pointed to half-past two. The hands lied."

The dam on Sixth Lake had raised the water so high that the channel was no longer recognizable in the maze of dying trees. After taking one wrong turn, Sears managed to get his canoe wedged fore and aft in "a fearful mess of dead logs, submerged tree-tops and sunken brush." As dusk fell a thunderstorm approached from the west. He worked his way free, but by then it was pitch dark and the marshy shores offered no place to land. He spent most of the night on the water as the storm raged around him. "On the heel of the wind came the rain," he wrote, "and how it *did* pour; while the lightning was almost incessant, and the thunder was highly creditable for a country with so few advantages." All in all it was, he admitted, "a trifle scary."

When the sky cleared he made his way back to his lunch spot, hung up his wet clothes, and lay down. He was not a happy camper: "It is not to be supposed that a man far on the wrong side of fifty years can take an all-night soaking in a wicked storm, seated in a . . . canoe, where to rise, or even turn around, may mean drowning—[or that he] can turn out, after needed sleep, with a general disposition to throw hand-springs, or perform feats of muscular agility. I awoke at about 10 a.m. . . . lame and sore, . . . made some strong coffee, and tried my best to make a cheery thing of it.

"It wouldn't do. The miserable dead-line of timber was about the only cheerful outlook; it was a long distance either way to human habitation or to human sympathy, and—I was just mad. I limped down to the sodden beach, sat down on a soaked log, and 'nursed my wrath to keep it warm.'"

It was reassuring to know that a canoeist of Sears's experience could get into such trouble. Even more comforting was the realization that within him dwelt a child as petulant as the one I'd discovered in myself.

At the head of the stump-strewn bay a small bridge marked the carry to Eighth Lake. When we pulled up we saw a strapping dark-haired fellow in his late thirties shouldering the last of his gear. We had seen him the night before as he paddled past our spot with a little girl in the bow. "I *wondered* how you got all your stuff in those boats," he said. He inspected our outfit, asked where we were headed, and suggested a prettier campsite than the one we'd planned on. Maybe we could travel together, he suggested, but just now he had to get back to his daughter, who was waiting at the far end of the carry.

The trail was a pleasant green tunnel for the first quarter mile. At a crossroads we turned left onto an asphalt road and strolled through a state campground crowded with RVs and trailers. At the beach our new friend was just pushing off, his little girl and a black puppy in the bow of his blue canoe. "You'll probably catch up with us at the next carry," he shouted over his shoulder. "I've got to keep moving."

Eighth Lake is narrow and only a mile and a half long, with a pretty island about midway. Its shores are all state-owned, and once we'd cleared the beach the tranquillity of the forest reasserted itself. The wind was picking up but it was at our backs, gently nudging us along. At the far end we found the mile-long trail to Brown's Tract Inlet. It was pretty in the woods, sunlight dappling the dirt path. We soon passed the blue canoe propped against a tree, and shortly thereafter our friend appeared on his way to retrieve it. A little farther along his little girl waited patiently with her puppy beside a heap of camping gear. She was five, she told us, and her name was Chelsea. Her dog was Wiggles. No, she wasn't afraid; her daddy would be back soon.

The state highway appeared on our right and paralleled the trail almost to its end. There, a floating dock led through a marsh to the winding channel that would take us to Raquette Lake. The put-in was an awkward squeeze, a narrow strip between the rushes and a dock that sank under our weight and left us working calf-deep in water. We were hungry, but there was no way to manage lunch here. The fellow with the blue canoe arrived and set it down on the opposite side of the dock. Farther back on the trail Chelsea began screaming and kept it up in spite of his shouted reassurances. He jogged off and returned with her in his arms, the puppy floundering gamely along behind, its paws slipping through the slats of the dock with every other step.

By the time her father stowed her in the canoe Chelsea had regained her composure. The rest of his gear was back on the trail where we'd passed it, and he readily accepted our offer to stay with his daughter. Chelsea's mother might be joining them, he explained. He was in a hurry to get to Raquette Lake where he could telephone to find out whether she was coming. Off he went. What would he have done if we hadn't been there—would he have left a five-year-old and a puppy afloat in the middle of nowhere? For Chelsea's sake I hoped her mother was on the way.

The wet puppy climbed onto a pack, turned around three times, curled up, and fell asleep. Chelsea sat on the front seat and explained that she'd been crying because she hated mud and she'd got it all over her sneakers. I took them off, sluiced them out, and set them in the bottom of the canoe to dry, then sponged her grimy feet and toweled them off. When I offered her a handful of gorp she extracted the red M&M's and chattered happily, swinging her perfect little legs. The day had turned brilliant. The trip she was making was about ninety miles, a long haul for a five-year-old. In thirty years, what would she remember of this experience—muddy shoes, the bow slicing through the waves, waiting alone in the woods?

Sears's memories of childhood were painful enough that he invented a rosier version for public consumption. He was born December 2, 1821, in South Oxford (now Webster), in south-central Massachusetts. Six brothers and three sisters followed, but from the beginning George was different, a small but intractable child who had his share of sessions with his father behind the barn, "at which a yearling apple tree sprout was always a leading factor." As long as the boy stayed in school his family reluctantly allowed him to roam the woods with "them dirty Injuns," as one of his aunts described the residents of the nearby Nipmuck reservation. But the classroom was a poor substitute for "the great book of nature," and much of the time he was truant.

His family owned a few books about Indians that caught George's fancy, and in trying to decipher what the pictures meant, he was stimulated to learn to read. The stories left him, he recalled, "with an intense romantic passion for forest life and scenery—for hunting, trapping, and fishing, that pervaded my whole being by day, and my dreams by night—a passion that has never left me for an hour . . . and that burns as steadily, if not as fiercely, now, as when at eight years of age I ran away 'to join the Indians for good,' as I thought and said."

But at eight years of age he did not join the Indians. It was decided, probably by his father, that it was time for George to begin earning his keep, and so he followed several of his relatives to the local cotton mill owned by Samuel Slater, who had imported both the factory system and the Sunday school movement from England. "Although I had a taste for reading, second only to my passion for outdoor sports," Sears wrote, "I *could not* bear restraint or confinement." Yet confined he was, in a stifling, clangorous factory, day after day, his only freedom coming during occasional mill shutdowns. He was ashamed and bitter about his childhood servitude; small wonder that Charles Dickens became one of his heroes and that for the rest of his life he despised industrialists and organized religion.

At age twelve he became an oarsman on a commercial fishing boat based at East Dennis, on Cape Cod, where his forebears had settled. During the winters he apprenticed at his father's shoemaking bench. Eventually the family moved to Brockport, in western New York, but the Erie Canal held none of the fascination of the sea. At the age of nineteen he signed on with the whaler *Rajah*, out of New Bedford, for a three-year voyage to the South Pacific. It was 1841, the same year Herman Melville shipped out of the same port on the *Acushnet*, bound for the same whaling grounds. (Melville jumped ship at Nukuhiva, in the Marquesas, two weeks before the *Rajah* put in there for supplies. The two might have met, had Melville not been sequestered with the Typees in an upland valley.) One trip as a green hand proved enough; when the *Rajah* returned, Sears rejoined his family and in 1848 followed them to Wellsboro, in northern Pennsylvania, where he lived for the rest of his life.

The country around Wellsboro, at the edge of the Allegheny plateau, was an outdoorsman's paradise of rambunctious streams and rolling hills alive with fish and game. The restless young man hunted and camped until he knew the western headwaters of the Susquehanna as thoroughly as his own backyard. Gradually he was drawn farther afield, and by his late twenties he was in the habit of disappearing for months at a time on solitary wilderness expeditions that tested his stamina and resourcefulness. Twice he came close to dying in the backcountry, yet he persevered. He spent a winter trapping with a Saint Regis Indian friend near Lake Simcoe, in Ontario; for several seasons he lived by his rifle, shooting game to feed railroad construction crews. He went to Minnesota to trap and by 1857 had made seven trips to Michigan, which was then largely unsettled. On one expedition he walked the sixty roadless miles across the lower peninsula, from Saginaw Bay to the Muskegon River, in ten days. In 1867 and again in 1870 he traveled to Brazil, where he poked around the Trombetas, an Amazon tributary.

In later life he blamed Nessmuk and his tribe for the obsession with nature that took him so far afield. They had carried him through Douglas Woods on their shoulders, swum him across Junkamaug Lake, and let him ride in the canoe when they went out to fish. He had been Chelsea's age, or thereabouts, and I caught myself hoping this little girl would imprint on woods and waters in the same way.

When her father returned, he lost no time getting under way. We dallied, rearranging gear and fiddling with wing nuts, until the blue canoe had disappeared around a bend. We wanted Brown's Tract Inlet to ourselves: it was the kind of intimate landscape we both responded to, a narrow stream snaking lazily through a marsh. The turns were lined with rafts of white water lilies and the spires of pickerelweed; beneath us a forest of aquatic plants—golden-green grasses, feathery boughs, whorled streamers—swayed in the slow current. The sun stood at the meridian and time stopped. There was no sound except the plop of my paddle tips. Sears had not been as enchanted as I with this place. The inlet was, he wrote, "modeled after the letter S, with an occasional oxbow thrown in for variety, and a dull, sluggish stream, deep and dark, . . . with not a place in its course of four miles where I would like to venture a landing."

I fell back to savor my surroundings. In the distance I could see the tips of John's paddle rising rhythmically above the grass. At one bend a curl of white duck down rested on a lilypad, an Adirondack haiku. Here no historical squinting was necessary to travel back a century: Brown's Tract Inlet is such unpromising terrain that in a hundred years no one has figured out a way to exploit it. "Thank Heaven," Sears once remarked, "there are a few green spots on this green earth that it does not pay to 'improve,' but they are remote." This one felt very remote indeed.

Three times we negotiated beaver dams. I learned how to pull alongside, lever myself onto the springy but solid top, slither the canoe across, probe for a foothold on the other side, and lower myself back in. The last dam was tucked beneath a concrete bridge, and when I resumed my seat my boat had for some reason become wildly unstable. It turned out that my life vest, used as back padding, had fallen forward and was underneath me. Although this raised my center of gravity less than three inches, it was enough to radically alter the boat's equilibrium. I was in a bind: I couldn't clamber back onto the dam because the slightest movement threatened to capsize me, nor was there anyplace to land in the marsh. I paddled on gingerly, body rigid, paddle tips barely grazing the water. At least it wasn't far to civilization; I could see a steeple off to the left. In minutes the river widened into a broad bay and the marsh grasses gave way to the button-topped rushes called hatpins. The blue canoe was drawn up on a small beach near the Raquette Lake town dock. The puppy had slipped its tether and scrambled out but stayed near the boat, yipping hysterically.

Raquette was the handsomest lake we had seen so far, its surface dotted with islands of every size, its shoreline so serrated by bays and headlands that an early traveler named Joel T. Headley likened its shape to a scallop's. "This waving outline," he wrote, "completely deceives one, in sailing over it, as to the extent and direction of the main body of water. As you round one point, the lake seems to take a turn, for it goes miles away, piercing the very heart of the distant forest. But, by the time a second point is weathered, a broad and beautiful surface is seen spreading in another direction." Five miles long by about three wide, its shoreline measures some fifty miles. It's easy for a newcomer to get lost on Raquette; Sears did, in 1880. "Its quaint bays, points, headlands and islands [were] so mixed and mingled to the eye," he wrote, "that although my directions had been lucid I was puzzled just which way to steer."

No one is sure how the lake came to be called Raquette (pronounced *Rack*-et). The legend that most appeals to me concerns a group of Loyalists fleeing to Canada during the Revolution and leaving a heap of snowshoes (in French, *raquettes*) by the shore when the spring thaw rendered them useless. The first permanent settlers, men named, wonderfully enough, Beach and Wood, arrived in 1837. They subsisted by hunting and trapping, supplemented with crops they grew in the short summers. William Wood was a man in the Adirondack tradition. It was around 1850, as Headley told the story, when "by exposure in the woods and snow through a cold winter's night, his feet and limbs were so badly frozen, that it became necessary to amputate both below the knee joints. Since that time he has used his knees as a substitute for feet; and strange as it may seem, he follows his line of traps for miles through the wilderness, or with rifle in hand, hops through the woods in pursuit of deer. He may be seen plying his oars, and driving his little bark over the lake and along the streams; and when he comes to a portage, the upturned boat will surmount his head, and take its course to the adjacent waters."

By the end of the nineteenth century there was no more fashionable summer watering place than the area around Raquette Lake, where William West Durant built the luxurious enclaves that came to be known as Great Camps. These camps (a "camp" in the Adirondacks can mean anything from a lean-to to a mansion) were unique to the region, sprawling complexes of lodges, guest cabins, dining halls, and recreation rooms fashioned from native materials and finished with distinctive rustic accents. From the outside the buildings were sophisticated marriages of American log cabins with Swiss chalets; interiors were finished with handsome woodwork and stonemasonry, and many boasted decorative touches such as twig furniture. Since it took a small army to staff a Great Camp, miniature villages of employee housing and service buildings were located a discreet distance from the camp's nucleus.

Adirondack history is replete with spectacular business failures, but none is more compelling than that of W. W. Durant. His father, Thomas Clark Durant, raised the money for and supervised the building of the Union Pacific, the country's first transcontinental railroad. Too busy for family life, he exiled his wife, son, and daughter to thirteen rootless years in Europe. Once he was held hostage in his railroad car by workers demanding their back pay. In the famous photograph taken at Promontory Point, Utah, where the last spike was driven, Durant *père* towers, hat in hand, at front row center. A cool and apparently ruthless operator, he amassed large tracts of land in the central Adirondacks and built a railroad, from Saratoga Springs to North Creek, that opened the region to tourism. There seems to have been little affection among the members of the family. Not surprisingly, in view of their long separation, father and son had little in common.

The son was tall and slender, with dark hair and eyes and a handlebar moustache. When his father died he took over the family business and proceeded to spend vast sums in preparation for the land boom that was sure to make him a multimillionaire. He created an extensive transportation network and built his Great Camps to attract the wealthiest families in the country—Camp Pine Knot was sold to the industrialist Collis P. Huntington, Camp Uncas to the financier J. P. Morgan, and Camp Sagamore to the sportsman Alfred G. Vanderbilt. Durant *fils* was a bold entrepreneur with refined tastes, but near the end of his life he admitted to historian Harold K. Hochschild that he had been "handicapped . . . by having been brought up in wealth without being taught the value of money." Exacting in his standards, he once had a massive piece of stonework torn down when he discovered that one rock had been laid with its cut face visible. At the height of his power he commissioned an opulent steam yacht, the 191-foot *Utowana,* for transatlantic travel. In her elegant saloons he entertained British society.

By the mid-1890s Durant's world was beginning to unravel. First his marriage to Janet Stott disintegrated; next, his sister, after trying for years to discover what had become of her share of the inheritance, successfully sued him for his handling of the family fortune. Then, in the summer of 1900, his friend Collis Huntington, who was his largest creditor, suddenly died. Huntington had promised additional help but had not had time to put his offer in writing, and his executors declined to honor his word.

Piece by piece, Durant lost his empire—thousands of acres of real estate, the transportation company with its railroad and six lake steamers, his yacht, the country club on nearby Eagle Lake. When he appealed for help, most of his wealthy cronies became hard of hearing. At one point the man who had directed hundreds of workmen was reduced to managing small Adirondack hotels. "He was hired by a former employee," wrote Durant family biographer Craig Gilborn, "and . . . some of the people who had worked for him went out of their way to see him and thereby assuage old grudges at his expense." A brief stint in the optical business and an attempt at mushroom cultivation failed. In time he remarried, and his wife took in boarders. Now and then friends threw small jobs, such as Adirondack title searches, his way.

There is a photograph of Durant taken in 1931, three years before his death, on a visit to one of the camps he built. Handsomer than he'd been in his youth and elegantly turned out, he was, in Gilborn's words, "resolutely but not stiffly posed as if to invite the camera or viewer to find the slightest sign of weakness or regret. He was a man who, after all, had entertained the future King of England and other members of European royalty on his own yacht. Most of the people who worked for William admired and respected him. [One] admitted that Durant was hard to get along with, particularly during the difficult period at the end of the century, but 'I always regarded [him] as a wonderful man . . . a great man to teach a person; I learned more from this man than any man living. He was a driver, but he had a great heart.'"

It was Durant who founded the hamlet of Raquette Lake with a telegraph office and a post office on the eastern shore, then a store, a school, two churches, and a cemetery on land he donated. The community eventually migrated across the lake to its present location, and it was there, in the summer of 1900, that it really began to prosper—just as its founder's fortunes were ebbing. The boom was stimulated by the arrival of a railway that connected the town to the New York Central line to the west. The Raquette Lake Railroad was only eighteen miles long, but its incorporators were some of the most influential men of the time, including Durant, Huntington (president of the Southern Pacific), J. P. Morgan, former Secretary of the Navy William C. Whitney, and Chauncey Depew (president of the New York Central). Private railroad cars deposited the wealthy and their retinues at the town dock, where Durant's steamers waited to ferry them to their woodland homes. The community flourished until one night in the winter of 1927, when a fire gutted its center. Two years later a highway arrived, dooming both the railroad and the steamers.

Today the place has a curiously attenuated feeling. Nowhere

in the Adirondacks is it easier to see the past than in its tracery of empty lots, gaping foundations, and the weedy right-of-way that leads to the water. With a little imagination you can reconstruct it all, the dock and the steamers, the railroad station, the hotel, the general store, the tracks that once stitched the hamlet together. Along the waterfront stroll Gilded Age ghosts, long-gone financiers and their patrician wives, their well-dressed children, their valets, governesses, maids, chefs, the ranks of trunks and barrels arrayed by the siding. Around them stream the local men and women who in summer serve them and in winter regale one another with tales of their employers' foibles, their heedless waste. In the midst of this silent clamor, deep in conversation with his superintendent, stands a tall, spare figure impeccably attired, the man who set it all in motion and then watched helplessly as it slipped away.

RAQUETTE LAKE TO FORKED LAKE

On the day in late July 1883 when George Sears paddled wearily out of Brown's Tract Inlet, the hamlet of Raquette Lake did not yet exist. W. W. Durant had not yet succeeded to the family business, had not yet married Janet Stott, had not yet told her, in the course of an argument with his sister, "You are my wife, your rooms are around the corner; go and stay there." And so when Sears reached the lake he turned not left but right, and paddled two miles along the south shore to "Honest Joe" Whitney's camp at Rush Point.

Wherever Sears went he collected admirers, and Whitney was no exception. "There is a sort of freemasonry among woodsmen that only woodsmen know," Sears told his *Forest and Stream* readers. "Joe and I had heard something of each other—not much; it took us about five minutes to get acquainted. In two hours we were thick as thieves." The two talked late into the night, and Sears slept deeply, having traveled more than fifteen miles from Fourth Lake. He arose early enough "to take in a glorious sunrise on scenery that I shall not disgrace by attempting to describe. It was all the more welcome in that sunrises during the summer of 1883 have been mostly inferential."

Seduced by good weather and companionship, he decided to postpone his departure: "What though?" he wrote somewhat defensively. "May there not come one glorious day in the weary year when we may cast aside every grief and every separate care and invite the soul to a day of rest? And in the future, when the days of trouble come, as they will come, I shall remember that grand day of rest, and the abundance of trout and bass wherewith I was comforted."

Over lunch by the Raquette Lake waterfront, we decided to head for the spot Chelsea's father had recommended, at Clarks Point. Having located it on my map, we set off at about two o'clock, heading north with renewed energy. A strengthening west wind began to worry the boats as we paddled out into a broad bay, the transition from smooth water so gradual that at first neither of us noticed what was happening: a gust, a lull, a stronger gust, another gust, a lull, a slamming gust, then a strong, steady wind that gathered force as it swept down a long reach. From our vantage point right at water level, the ranks of whitecaps were hidden until we were among them. Soon we were being pitched around so violently that a clammy dread settled over me. There had been no wind while we lazed through Brown's Tract Inlet and along the protected southwest shore, but I should have been more alert: I'd had ample warning that the larger lakes could be tricky, particularly Raquette. Sears once had to make a dash for shore here, observing that "Raquette Lake can get too rough for a ten foot canoe very easily." In his erudite contemporary guidebook *Adirondack*

Canoe Waters: North Flow, Paul Jamieson is succinct on this matter. "Open parts of the lake," he says, "should be avoided on windy days."

With rollers smashing my port side and slopping over the gunwale, I was having trouble staying afloat. Paddling in John's lee was a small help, but only temporary, since I had to quarter into the wind to avoid being broadsided. The only way to maintain my direction was to zigzag along, angling first my bow, then the stern, into the waves. Yawing and pitching, we discussed what to do if one of us dumped. My lashed-in pack and foam seat were the boat's flotation; my life jacket was mine. The rough water would sap energy fast; I'd have to relax and scull, float and kick, and try to keep my head out of the waves. With no place to camp behind us but several possibilities ahead, there was nothing to do but keep pulling for the green shore before us. It seemed a very long way off.

There are no atheists in tiny, wave-tossed canoes, only pragmatists. You stick with what works and abandon what doesn't. The rollers seemed to have a periodicity, three or five big ones in a row, followed by a lull. I learned it was better to give the canoe its head and let it ride out the biggest waves, resting my arms and unclenching my fingers, which had whitened around my paddle shaft. Although quartering into and away from the wind worked best, this tactic had its downside. With the wind at my back, waves tended to slop over the stern; I could tell when I'd shipped a big one when the pool of water I was sitting in got colder.

Rushton's designs have many virtues, but under certain conditions the smaller hulls do take on water. "Every well built canoe, yacht or ship, has some individuality, some peculiar trait of its own," Sears remarked. "The peculiar trait of the *Rushton* is to take in spray heavily when going to windward, say four points off. This is owing to her sharp, short curved lines. . . . [When] I tried her with the wind about four points abaft the stem . . . she plashed the spray in, a few spoonsful at a time, until I was obliged to creep under [a friend's] lee and sponge out."

With quarts of water washing back and forth around my outstretched legs, it occurred to me that my canoe was not so much a soup dish, as J. Henry Rushton had dubbed the *Sairy*, as a hip bath. She was, however, a hip bath without a name. "I would as soon have a wife or daughter without a name as an unnamed canoe," Sears had written, yet in six months I had been unable to come up with anything that stuck. In the end I decided not to impose a name; the right one would eventually occur. Thus it happened that in the middle of Raquette Lake, my boat christened herself: henceforth she would be the *Sairy Damp*. As the gap to the shore closed and it became clear that we would make it, I felt a rush of gratitude and affection for her. Wet she may have been, but she had carried me through. Huzzah for the *Sairy Damp!*

We stopped at a private dock to bail out, then made our way past a succession of deserted cottages to the tip of the point, where we explored a still, shallow bay but found no campsite. Rounding another headland we found ourselves in a bay deeper and wider than the one we'd just fought our way across. I then did what I should have done forty minutes before: pulled to shore and fumbled my map out of my pack. If I'd kept it in front of me, we'd have been lounging around a lean-to by now. We had overshot our goal and rounded Indian Point, where Messrs. Wood and Beach settled so long ago. There were no lean-tos in this bay, but three tent sites were clustered toward its head.

First, though, we had to get there. The wind was now in our faces and the chop by the shore was formidable. Conversation lagged as we concentrated on pulling. As we passed a cottage a gray-haired woman on a deck yelled something to me. I cupped my ear and she tried again: "What kind of boat is that?" I called out, "Lost Pond!" When she shouted something else the wind snatched it away and I could only grin, shrug, and press on.

It was becoming clear that we were too exhausted to reach the end of the bay. We were approaching a group of rocky islands called the Hen and Chickens when we spotted a thinning in the forest to our left. No campsite was marked on my map, but fatigue made us desperate. We threaded our way into a cove strewn with boulders and clambered stiffly up the bank. It was a good site, with a flat spot for the tent and a fire ring with logs drawn up on three sides. There was something odd about it: the ground wasn't trampled, nor had the woods been scoured of firewood. Perhaps it was someone's private refuge. An old-fashioned milk can stuffed with garbage leaned against a tree.

Wearily we fetched water, changed into dry clothes, and strung a line for our sopping pants and socks. That done, we dug out plastic bottles and treated ourselves to a celebratory drink as we puttered around. I'd just started heating a packet of onion soup when I noticed roiling black clouds above the western horizon where minutes before there'd been clear sky. "Amid this mountainous region," W. H. H. Murray wrote, "tempests give brief warning of their approach. Walled in as these lakes are by mountains, behind which the cloud gathers unseen, the coming of a storm is like the spring of a tiger." Now I understood that the wind we'd been fighting was not some malevolent force bent on breaking us but the leading edge of a front.

As the dark curtain advanced the light faded and we had to move fast. We gobbled a dreadful freeze-dried entrée, cleaned up, hoisted the food bag, leaned our packs against a tree, and scuttled into the tent. A passing hiker might have thought he'd stumbled on an orgy, but the groans of pleasure drifting out of our dome were chaste, the sounds of aching bodies sinking into down. We were wasted.

The storm hit with spatters of rain and a racing wind that tore through the treetops. Lightning illuminated the tent, thunder rolled and crashed. The sound level was astonishing. What seems like a middling thunderstorm from the comfort of your living room is a wildly different experience when you're out in it, at night, in the middle of nowhere. In our snug nylon cocoon we lay side by side and worried, I about the wind toppling a tree on us, John about our boats blowing away. At the height of the fury he crawled out to tie them down, his headlamp like a strobe flashing around the clearing.

For a couple of hours the storm raged overhead. John drifted off—how could anyone sleep in such a racket?—and I lay on my back reviewing our first two days. We'd seen a little of everything: fog, drenching rain, wind—surely the whole trip couldn't be like this . . . could it? Well, yes. Sears had extraordinarily bad luck with weather: in his first twenty-one days out of Old Forge it rained nineteen, and the temperature hovered around fifty. At Upper Saint Regis Lake, not far to the north, a resident called the summer of 1883 the coldest in the twelve years he'd spent there.

Judging by our experience so far, our worst enemy would be the wind. Especially on the larger lakes we were going to have to get on the water early, while conditions were relatively calm. No wonder Sears started by five o'clock. Packing it in by midafternoon would eliminate a lot of desperate paddling and give us our pick of campsites. I'd learned my lesson: tomorrow we'd get safely across the wide open spaces of Raquette before stopping for breakfast. And oh yes, I'd keep the map beside me.

The storm moved slowly off to the east. As the wind fell I drowsed in my sleeping bag. I could still feel the rocking of my canoe.

We shoved off at 7:30 under partly cloudy skies. Had I not been so paranoid about getting across the lake I'd have poked around the next bay to the north, where in 1857 William J. Stillman spent the summer painting. In *The Autobiography of a Journalist,* Stillman described his stay on Raquette Lake:

> Here the morbid passion of solitude grew on me. The serene silence was seldom broken save by the cry of an eagle or an osprey, high overhead, the chirping of the chickadee flitting about the camp to find a crumb, or by [the] complaining note of the Canada jay, most friendly of all the wild birds, seeking for the scraps of venison we used to throw out for him. No other birds came to us, and one of the most striking features in the wilderness was the paucity of bird life and voice. As I sat painting, I would see the gray eagle come down with his long cycloidal swoop, skimming along the surface of the water, and catch, as he passed, the trout that sunned itself on the surface; or the osprey, seizing it with his direct plunge into the lake, from which, after a struggle that lasted sometimes a minute, the only sign of his presence being the agitated water, he would emerge with the fish in his claws and sail aloft, hurrying to escape to the forest with his prey lest the eagle, always watching from the upper air, should rob him of his hard-earned booty. Once I saw the eagle make the mighty plunge from far above, the frightened osprey dropping the fish to escape the shock, and the eagle catching it in mid-air as it fell.

An artist, diplomat, and journalist, Stillman loved the Adirondacks, and unlike many who wrote about the region, he knew its winter bleakness as well as its summer glory. He was a graceful writer whose charm and intelligence gained him the respect of some of the major figures of his era. The year after his sojourn on Raquette he led a group of friends to Follensby Pond, to a spot that became enshrined in Adirondack history as the Philosophers' Camp. The party of ten included James Russell Lowell, Louis Agassiz, Ralph Waldo Emerson, Judge Ebenezer Rockwood Hoar, and Oliver Wendell Holmes's brother John. Longfellow was invited but declined when he learned that Emerson was taking a gun. At any event, the eminent campers had a wonderful time, hunting and fishing, zoologizing and botanizing, paddling and swimming, competing as marksmen. Stillman painted a group portrait and left a charming prose sketch of the holiday; Emerson celebrated it with a poem.

Our plan had been to retrace our route along Indian Point, cross over to Needle Island for any wind shadow it might provide, then make a dash for the far shore. But in the morning the wind was a zephyr, and we realized we could take a direct course across the middle of the lake. With leisure enough to look around, we saw how lovely the north end of Raquette was. At its head rose Pilgrim Mountain (called Niggerhead in less enlightened days). On all sides rolling hills cupped bays deep enough to be lakes in their own right, each with its own character. Here and there a swath of green lawn, always a shock to the eye in the middle of the forest, sloped up from the shore.

We were well into the center of the lake when a shaft of golden light streamed through the clouds and swept over the water nearby, a child's Bible illustration, at once corny and sublime. Twenty minutes later we were across the open water and paddling along the south shore of Outlet Bay. The water was getting choppy when we stopped for breakfast, and by the time we pushed off it was worse. I took a wave as I climbed aboard and had to empty my boat before trying again. I was getting good at draining the *Sairy Damp;* she was so light it was a pleasure to swing her over my head.

The freshening wind at our backs fairly drove us along, our task simply to keep clear of the turbulence by the shore. The wind lifted the water off my paddle blades and sprayed it into the boat, soaking my thighs and trickling down the inside of the hull. Within half an hour I again had to stop to relieve my canoe of her load. We weren't relishing the dash to the opposite shore for the carry to Forked Lake, but at least the bay narrowed at the end. Narrows are good news and bad news, good because the crossing is shorter, bad because bottlenecks intensify winds and waves. This time we were lucky, hightailing it across during a lull.

We could not find the landing, or even anyone to ask about it, so we took out at a small glade with a rutted lane leading in the right direction. The clearing was awash in wildflowers—closed gentians, spotted touch-me-nots, goldenrods, asters, pearly everlasting—that seemed especially beautiful after the dark uniformity of the woods. As we screwed canoes to pack frames the sun broke out and warmed our backs. We trudged up to the gravel road to discover that we had taken out too early and had to walk a quarter of a mile east to find the spot where the carry trail crossed the road.

Once there was an inn known as Cary's at the Raquette Lake end of the trail. A writer named H. Perry Smith passed through circa 1870 and declared the hotel "a model one—the worst model ever conceived. . . . Outside it looks like a great overgrown barn. . . . The back end of the house stands up eight feet from the ground on one or two crazy abutments and is higher than the front, giving it the appearance of a mule that has just kicked a man up in the air, and had been propped up in that position. It is wood-colored, and its numerous windows are shaded entire inside by white curtains, making them look like white caps in a great sea of brown clap-boards. . . . There is quite an extensive clearing around Cary's house. Trees can't grow much in sight of it." They can now; the clearing has been swallowed by the woods. A few years later, after Cary's closed, part of the building was trundled to the far end of the trail, where it resumed life as the Forked Lake House.

In 1883, after his idyll at Joe Whitney's camp, Sears made his way to this hotel. He took his time, paddling slowly up Raquette Lake's eastern shore and stopping to visit old friends along the way. He spent a couple of hours inspecting a new private camp that had been built, he declared, in "perfect sylvan taste."

The place made him wistful. "I never feel the lack of wealth so sadly as when visiting these private camps," he wrote. The cost for a family, he was told, was roughly three thousand dollars for the summer. "Yes, it is cheap—for a millionaire," Sears noted. "But it would break some of us to run such a camp for a single week."

Sears was born poor, and he remained so all his life. Some of his schemes foundered for want of money or contacts, others as a result of a soft heart. He had, for example, developed a hybrid strawberry he called the Crispin, in honor of the patron saint of shoemakers, and in 1875 he planted three thousand hills. Unable to afford enough netting to protect the fruit from robins, cedar waxwings, and other fruit-eaters, he planned instead to shoot the birds, but a few days of gunning were all he could manage. The peeping of the parentless, starving young tormented him, and he abandoned the project.

On both of his trips to Brazil he tried to interest officials in a process he'd devised to improve rubber production, but he failed to penetrate the government bureaucracy. "I had waited three mortal months for nothing," he recalled late in his life; "I had gone daily to the palace, only to be put off with '*pacienza*' and '*logo mais*'. . . " This debacle, in which he persuaded a number of his Wellsboro friends to invest, was a paradigm of other ventures—in boat design, orange cultivation, the marketing of pocket knives—that consumed whatever small resources he'd managed to accumulate and invariably ended in disillusion. (A poem about his Brazilian fiasco is even called "Desilusao.")

But on the day Sears made his way up Raquette Lake, his spirits were high. People were enchanted with the cockleshell he was paddling, and besides, the weather was glorious. "For once it did not rain," he wrote, "and I was dry—no small item for a man who runs too light for even a change of clothes." He made the carry as dusk fell and reached the Forked Lake House in time for supper. Almost immediately "the demon of storms resumed his sway" and he was stranded at the hotel.

Today there are several small outbuildings and a covered dock at the far end of the carry, along with a multitude of signs prohibiting hunting, fishing, trapping, camping, trespassing, and parking. Welcome to Whitney Park, a private preserve that has remained in the same family since 1897, when it was acquired by Secretary of the Navy William C. Whitney. The Whitney name has been intertwined with American fortunes since the eighteenth century, when Eli Whitney invented the cotton gin and the system of interchangeable parts. Mount Whitney in California is named for another family member. In our own time, a Whitney was publisher of the New York *Herald Tribune,* another owned the New York Mets, and yet another bankrolled *The New Republic.*

William C. Whitney, who bought an Adirondack fiefdom, was a political kingmaker who made a fortune in New York City street railways, although his triumph was tainted by accusations of watered stock and shady financial manipulations. His son Harry Payne Whitney was a sportsman who married Cornelius Vanderbilt's daughter Gertrude, who founded the Whitney Museum of American Art. At the age of thirty-one, their son, Cornelius Vanderbilt ("Sonny") Whitney, inherited twenty million dollars. Like his father and grandfather he bred and raced horses and managed substantial mining interests, but he also went his own way. He was a flight instructor in the First World War and won the Distinguished Service Medal in the Second. He was a founder of Pan American Airways, and served as first assistant secretary of the Air Force and under secretary of commerce. Sued in his youth by a Ziegfeld Follies showgirl for breach of promise, he married four times. He invested in Marineland, in Florida, and in a number of David O. Selznick's movies, among them *Gone With the Wind* and *A Star Is Born.* He and his wife

Marylou revitalized and for years reigned over the social scene of Saratoga, New York. Sonny died in December 1992.

Whitney Park, managed for its timber, now encompasses some fifty-one thousand acres, about half the size it was in its heyday. But the property remains the jewel of the western Adirondacks, an untrammeled preserve of clear rivers and thirty-eight lakes and ponds. Conservationists covet it as the heart of a proposed four-hundred-thousand-acre Bob Marshall Great Wilderness, the largest wild sanctuary east of the Mississippi, room enough to reintroduce long-lost species such as the eastern timber wolf and the cougar. Unfortunately, New York's fiscal crisis deepened while the state was negotiating to protect the land from development, and in 1990 voters rejected a bond measure that would have financed acquisition of this and other choice parcels.

The good news is that the family has retained the Nature Conservancy and the Adirondack Land Trust to come up with a natural-resources inventory of the property and a long-range plan for managing it. (The Conservancy has more than once saved valuable parcels for the public by buying and holding them until the slow-moving state can do its paperwork and come up with the purchase price.) And in 1992 the Whitneys sold the Trust a purchase option on four hundred acres along the Raquette River and the shore of Forked Lake, the very corridor we were passing through.

Forked (pronounced *Fork*-ed) Lake has been prying superlatives from travelers for 150 years. In the mid-1840s Joel T. Headley vowed that he "never was more struck by a scene in my life: its utter wildness, spread out there where the axe of civilization has never struck a blow—the evening—the sunset—the deep purple of the mountains—the silence and solitude of the shores, and the cry of birds in the distance, combined to render it one of enchantment to me."

Fifteen years later Headley returned and spent a night at the only building on the lake. He dreamed he was back in the mountains around Chamonix. "The delicious prolonged notes of a French horn were filling all the air, and coming back in surpassingly sweet echoes from the breast of the bold mountain across the lake. . . . It was a plaintive air, that swept in sweet, softened gushes over the water, and I lay and wondered if really invisible fingers were playing it. . . . I went out, and there sat my host of the evening before, barefoot, with nothing but his shirt and pantaloons on, leaning back against the log hut and pouring forth those ravishing strains from a veritable French horn." The woman who cooked for Headley's party turned out not to be the host's wife. The latter lived in Boston, and once a year journeyed to the outskirts of the forest to visit her husband. "The great tragedies of human existence," Headley concluded, "are not acted outwardly on the public stage, nor are its strangest romances to be found in the imagination of the novelist. . . ."

Forked Lake is shaped roughly like an inverted T, with a long arm stretching off to the north and a seven-mile east-west reach. We were working our way along this reach when we were overtaken by a squall. One minute we were lazing along with the sun glinting off our paddles; the next time we looked behind us the sky was black and the surface was wrinkling before a rising wind. The hard rain lasted perhaps five minutes—just long enough for us to struggle into wet-weather gear and life vests.

The rugged shores were lined with white cedar, the strong, flexible wood used to make the *Sairy Gamp*. The lowest branches of each tree had been sheared off at the same level, as if a squad of gardeners armed with pruning shears had descended on the forest. You see this phenomenon on many an Adirondack lake, and no one has explained it better than an astute observer of nature named Noah John Rondeau. "This six-foot trim is due 100% to Deer Brousing," he wrote to a friend. "An old Buck comes along to breakfast and he trims a cedar; but only as far as he can reach. Then he goes to another cedar and without knife and fork, napkin or prayer—he trims it likewise. And during the winter without spirit-level or measuring tape the deer establish a line. Further you'll observe such a border until you find a spruce. You'll find the spruce like a woman of the gay nineties—wearing its skirts to the ground just because Deer don't eat spruce."

We passed a mountain ash leaning over the water, its Chinese-red berries aglow against the dark forest. Farther along an agitated kingfisher hovered over John's boat and rattled out its call. The lake's only lean-to was unoccupied, and we claimed it with relief, wolfing our lunch in its shelter while a light rain fell.

The Adirondack lean-to evolved from the three-sided bark shanties erected by hunters and pioneers in the eighteenth and nineteenth centuries. The modern version, built of peeled logs, is far more comfortable than its predecessors, with an overhanging roof and often a plank floor edged with a sitting log, or deacon's seat. The lean-to is open on the front to gather heat from the fire, and each has its own personality, depending on its location, construction details (shake or asphalt shingle roof, built-in shelves, and so on), and most of all its graffiti. Names and dates of visits carved into every accessible surface give a rough indication of the structure's age, but there are always other inscriptions, mostly sweet, funny, or exasperated (the weather is lousy, the fish aren't biting). At Forked Lake we admired B. Kingsley's elaborate signature and a bas-relief handprint by someone named Keith, a meticulous piece of work that seemed as fine as anything hidden in the black recesses of Lascaux.

Even in Sears's time the lean-tos carried graffiti. Of the one at Seventh Lake he remarked, "It has been there for many years, and many are the names and dates carved on the square logs of which the sides are built." In *Woodcraft* he wrote that "the best bark camps I have ever seen are in the Adirondacks," an opinion I share. Built and maintained by the state's Department of Environmental Conservation, most of them are tucked back in the woods for minimum visual impact, and many have amenities such as privies, picnic tables, fireplaces, and grills that are godsends at the end of a hard day of paddling. Sadly, some people litter and abuse these oases—particularly the lean-tos located near roads or within reach of powerboats—but most of the ones we used were surprisingly tidy.

Having found a nice spot, we decided to give ourselves the afternoon off. Our first three days on the water, we agreed, had left us fairly depleted. We threw down our sleeping pads and snoozed, lulled by the patter of rain on the roof. From time to time a canoe passed by and disappointed voices drifted up as their occupants realized the lean-to was taken. At about five the rain stopped. We could see the state campground at the east end of the lake but we were far enough away that it might not have existed. A few tents and tarps were visible on the opposite shore, and we could occasionally make out a figure moving among them, but our sense of privacy was complete. There were no buildings in sight, no motorboats on the water.

After supper a luminous pink glow spread into the clearing and drew us down to the water. The sky had cleared; Pilgrim Mountain, bulking up in the west, was backlit by the sinking sun. The lake had stilled, and it was impossible to tell where the mountain ended and its reflection began. There were, as Morris Longstreth put it, two skies. Thirty yards from shore three loons swam and dove. We settled down on a boulder and watched the sky deepen to purple, to light blue, to royal blue. Unable to turn away, we sat there until the stars appeared and the mountain dissolved into night. The silence was immense.

FORKED LAKE TO LONG LAKE

IN THE MORNING THE WORLD WAS MUFFLED IN GRAY GAUZE, the only sound the drip of condensation falling from the trees. The supersaturated air—God's own moisturizer—beaded on my clothes and hair and made my face feel thirty years younger. By the time we pushed off the fog was dispersing and long tendrils of mist were writhing off the water. The view to the west was a Japanese print in which the bold strokes of Pilgrim Mountain softened into the glassy sweep of the lake. I kept turning my canoe around to look at this tremulously beautiful scene.

The day's route lay along the Raquette River, which rises in Blue Mountain Lake and describes a giant reversed **S** as it makes its unhurried way north across the Adirondack plateau. Some 172 miles from its beginning, after metamorphosing from river to lake and back again many times, it slips down off the dome to join the Saint Lawrence near Massena. The Raquette is the state's second longest river, after the Hudson, and it has a history commensurate with the distance it travels. For centuries before whites came it was a thoroughfare, and it is still one of the most heavily used waterways in the Adirondacks, what Paul Jamieson has described as "a companionable stream."

Below the dam where the Raquette leaves Forked Lake, a series of rapids stretch a mile and a half before the river subsides to a gentler gradient. Since the late-summer water level was low and our whitewater skills were minimal we opted for the mile-and-a-third carry, but Sears ran these rapids, albeit in an empty canoe. The fellow who hauled boats over the portage took his knapsack "out of good nature."

At the state campground a couple of men watched us assemble our rigs and diffidently asked what were becoming the standard questions about the boats (weight, length, maker, cost). We were heading out when my eye was caught by a yellow sign detailing black bear etiquette. One item was sobering: don't sleep, campers were advised, in the clothes you cooked in.

A short way down the gravel road two deer bounded across in front of us and melted into the woods. Their ungainly beauty is always a shock to me—the delicate face, the huge wing nut ears, the head too small for the body, the glowing white flag of the tail. White-tail populations fluctuate in response to the severity of winters; these two, a doe and fawn, looked to be in excellent shape. The species has made a good recovery since the nineteenth century, when overhunting for sport and for hotel kitchens thinned their numbers considerably. At present there are about seventy-five thousand in the park. Small herds shuttle between traditional summer and winter ranges, moving in winter to river valleys and lowlands where food and shelter are plentiful and in summer to higher ground as much as fifteen miles away. Groups are organized as matriarchies, with female offspring staying to share their mother's range while young males wander off to join another herd. In winter they're often visible near the shores of Adirondack lakes, nibbling browse and venturing onto the thin ice near open water to drink. Major white-tail predators are coyotes, bobcats, and us.

A group of teenage girls straggled by, in ones and twos, returning to the campground for their packs. They were Girl Scouts from Skaneateles, their leader told us. For the next day and a half we'd be bumping into each other along the route, and before long our shyness would turn to smiles and then to kidding in the casual intimacy of the trail.

At the landing the river was so shallow we had to wade our canoes downstream before we could climb aboard for a mile and a half of flatwater. The Raquette is at its prettiest here, as it passes through a corridor of dark green softwoods, its banks stippled with the bright red spires of cardinal flowers. (Since it has a dam to regulate its flow, this part of the river has little of the tattered wildness we would encounter below Long Lake, where spring flooding undermines the banks and litters the shores with dead trees.) The river bed was studded with boulders, the largest of which, lurking just below the surface, bore streaks of silver, blue, green, and red from passing boats. Paint scrapes are hallmarks of canoe country, especially at campsites, where loaded boats grind onto the shallows.

Twice we encountered flocks of common mergansers, diving ducks that swim with their faces in the water, peering for fish. The females, gray and rust colored, remind me of the Katzenjammer Kids of the old comic strips, their swept-back crests giving them an oddly startled look. Unlike the dabbling ducks that feed on shoreline vegetation, these birds are adapted for underwater pursuit, lunging forward to surface far upstream with silver prizes clasped in their saw-toothed bills. If the light is right you can sometimes see them streaking through the depths, wings and feet working the water like air, bodies as stylized as a petroglyph. In my own version of evolution, I like to imagine that mergansers learned to dive because they were unwilling to look as ludicrous as dabblers, who feed with their heads completely submerged and fannies directed defenselessly at the sky.

The din of Buttermilk Falls was at first so subtle that it might have been a breeze stirring the pines, but with each bend the noise grew until the muttering had become a roar. There is nothing like the sound of fastwater somewhere ahead to quicken your pulse. Even the sound of a stream shouldering its way over a beaver dam is exhilarating when you can't see how far the water's falling. A sign on the right bank warned us to pull in for the short carry.

Buttermilk Falls gained lasting notoriety under the name Phantom Falls when W. H. H. "Adirondack" Murray wrote a story about it in *Adventures in the Wilderness.* Although his tale was clearly apocryphal ("I . . . advise you to believe no more of it than you see fit"), Murray was roundly condemned for implying that he had run the falls. The episode merely added to the controversy that swirled around him after 1869, when his book sent a stampede of city folk into the woods. Murray described a vast wilderness in northern New York (some readers didn't get far enough inland to find it). He said blackflies were gone by July (in the cold summer of 1869 they lasted into August). He claimed the north woods were a healthy place to summer, that the guides were honest, that game was plentiful. For these and sundry other enthusiasms he was vilified by those who knew nothing of the outdoors.

The Reverend Murray was many things, but hardly the rogue his "calumniators," as he called them, branded him. Before he was thirty his fame as a speaker had propelled him from an obscure parish in Connecticut to the illustrious Park Street Congregational Church in Boston. The following year *Adventures in the Wilderness; Or, Camp-Life in the Adirondacks* was published, and he became an instant celebrity. For all his eloquence Murray lacked the clerical temperament: he was openly contemptuous of hypocrisy and the stultifying routine expected of a minister in his position. Each summer he fled the city to spend a month or two in the Adirondacks, and he insisted that every congregation owed its "dominie" a similar respite. "He will get more instructive spiritual material from such a trip," Murray wrote, "than from all the 'Sabbath-school festivals' and 'pastoral tea-parties' with which the poor, smiling creature was ever tormented. It is astonishing how much a loving, spiritually-minded people can bore their minister."

A worldly man, Murray had enormous energy, which he spun off on writing, lecturing, and traveling—to the detriment, some felt, of his ministerial duties. And there was another passion that squared poorly with his vocation: he revered good horseflesh almost as much as his Maker. He wrote a book entitled *The Perfect Horse,* and at the Connecticut farm where he'd been raised he set up a sophisticated breeding operation. As his nonclerical activities proliferated, Murray's relations with his parishioners became strained. At length he left to found a church and a weekly newspaper of his own. By 1877, as the historian Warder Cadbury has written, he had amassed "three houses, nine barns, nearly a dozen dogs, and some sixty horses." He even found time to design an improved buckboard, and it was this project that brought his downfall. Having invested everything in the manufacture and sale of his wagon, he was unable to cover his loans when they came due.

In a matter of weeks he lost everything. Isadora Murray shared her husband's love of the outdoors and in the early years had helped support him by teaching. What happened between the two isn't clear, but the marriage also dissolved. Mrs. Murray moved to Vienna and embarked on a new life, becoming the first American woman to be granted a degree in surgery there.

For a time Murray ranched in Texas, and later he surfaced in Montreal, running a restaurant. He remarried, began writing again, and took to the lecture circuit, where he earned enough money to buy back his Guilford farm. He died there in 1904.

There are striking parallels between Murray's life and that of W. W. Durant. Both were men of intelligence, energy, and a range of interests. Both achieved prominence and at the peak of their careers suffered abrupt and terrible reverses. Both divorced and married Canadian women with whom they found contentment. Both ended up in relative obscurity. Although the years of their greatest influence did not overlap, both men played key roles in the development of the Adirondacks. "More than any one man in Adirondack history," wrote William Chapman White, "Murray gets the credit for the widest popularization of the region. Before 1869 it would have been difficult to name fifty hotels in the entire Adirondack area; some were hotels in name only, rickety buildings with roofs against the weather. By 1875 there were more than two hundred, some with several hundred rooms and the latest improvements."

A paved road now leads to Buttermilk Falls, and well-worn trails honeycomb the woods around it. We ate lunch in a shady spot away from the stream of sightseers, then scrambled down the rocks to admire the forty-foot falls from below, as Sears did in 1883, "watching the dashing, foaming water and footing up the utter impossibility of any man or boat ever tumbling over those ragged boulders and coming out anything but corpse and kindling wood."

The day continued gloriously clear. A half-mile paddle, another half-mile carry, and a short stretch of river took us to the head of Long Lake, where we found a good campsite facing back up the Raquette. To our right a small bay was choked with water shield, the small oval pads favored by ducks, and across the river a great blue heron stalked patiently through a marsh, oblivious to the boat traffic a few feet away. We were back in the land of the internal combustion engine, and the transition felt almost violent, as if we had breached a membrane.

We swam and dozed on the baking rocks. It was August 30,

and fall was definitely on the way: the air freshened as soon as the sun dropped behind a ridge, and we knew the night would be chilly. Ravenous as usual, I had no trouble disposing of my soup, but my appetite deserted me when I tried my freeze-dried entrée, and I noticed that John wasn't exactly tucking in either. The bag said it was turkey, but the glutinous mass it produced tasted like cardboard. We raided our lunch bag and settled for sandwiches.

Back home, these hikers' meals had seemed a brilliant solution because I'd been working up to the day of our departure and had had no time for meal planning and shopping. They also solved several problems presented by our lack of space: they were compact, weighed only ounces, could be reconstituted with water, and took fifteen minutes or less to heat. I had bought about thirty packets, enough for the entire trip plus a few weather-bound days. Friends winced at my solution, but I paid no mind; I'd read somewhere that freeze-dried foods have improved significantly in the past few years, to the degree that they're now actually tolerable. Horse badordies. I wouldn't feed them to my dogs, and my dogs eat everything except lemons and coffee grounds. These entrées do have one virtue, John pointed out: there's no need to burn, bury, or hoist your leftovers. No animal would consider them food.

"As a rule, on a mountain tramp or a canoe cruise, I do not tote canned goods," Sears wrote in *Woodcraft*. "I carry my duffle in a light, pliable knapsack, and there is an aggravating antagonism between the uncompromising rims of a fruit-can and the knobs of my vertebrae, that twenty years of practice have utterly failed to reconcile." But from that day on we did tote canned goods, supplemented with pasta and rice and fresh vegetables. (In the years that followed I learned that you can dehydrate soups, ground meats, vegetables, and fruits at home. They offer all the benefits of freeze-dried food, and they retain most of their flavor.)

Sears was accustomed, in those pre–game law days, to living off the land, and in *Woodcraft* he shared his recipes. "I neither cook nor converse in French," he told his readers, "and I have come to know that the plainest cooking is the best." On the subject of "the universal flapjack" he was succinct: "I do not like it; I seldom make it; it is not good." He preferred johnny-cake and unleavened breads, and rhapsodized about strong Brazilian coffee and green or black tea. He explained how to make soups and stews, beans and potatoes, and how to dress and cook fish, quail, pigeon, duck, woodcock, ruffed grouse, venison, squirrel, rabbit, even "the fretful porcupine" ("very like spring lamb, only better"). Most game he parboiled and then fried, or he impaled the carcass on a stick angled over the fire and roasted it with a ribbon of pork fat tucked between the legs. For variety, birds could be wrapped in clay, covered with coals, and buried to cook overnight—but "usually," he admitted, "unless I have more than one bird, I get so blessed hungry that I can't wait for the above process." Sears's appetite, like ours, was dramatically heightened by life outdoors. "I eat more at one meal here in the forest than I eat at three when at home," he observed.

Even if the law had allowed us to hunt and fish at will, John and I would not have done so; neither of us likes to kill, and with supplies available in towns all along our route, why destroy something wild?

The morning air was so cold we needed a fire to loosen our fingers before packing up. Paddling slowly out into the lake we could see more signs of autumn, a faint blush on the hillsides, here and there a limb gone golden. Soon, on the east shore, we came abreast of Deerland, a collection of homes on the site of the Grove House, which had been open only a few days when Sears turned up in 1883. On the second page of the hotel's register, now at the Adirondack Museum, you can see his modest scrawl, "Geo. W. Sears, Wellsboro, Pa." The date was July 29, the same day a boy named Benito was born in Romagna to Rosa and Alessandro Mussolini.

The Grove House was owned by Dave Helms, a guide who seven years earlier had piggybacked W. W. Durant (who had a broken leg at the time) over the Marion River Carry to Raquette Lake on his first visit to the region. The Grove House site, Sears wrote, was "beautifully chosen, on a piney, breezy, sandy point." Many of those pines, massive now, still stand there. Opposite Deerland rises a mountain called Owl's Head, which Sears paddled past in 1881 and 1883. "Once, I would not have believed that I could pass 'Owl's Head' without ascending it to the uttermost peak," he had written, but his climbing days were over. Ahead of us stretched Long Lake, a fourteen-and-a-half-mile widening of the Raquette River, with its eponymous town about a third of the way down. From Deerland north, the shore is thick with houses, marinas, motels, and housekeeping cottages.

We were soon abreast of a sandy beach where the most famous Adirondack guide of all, Mitchell Sabattis, once lived. Sabattis (pronounced Sa-*bat*-is, probably a corruption of Saint-Jean Baptiste) was an Abenaki Indian whose gentle personality and mastery of woodcraft earned the respect of everyone he met. "In the woods he saw and heard and reasoned with a refinement that was uncanny," the historian Alfred Donaldson has written. "The stories of the big game he killed, of his coolness and resourcefulness in danger and dilemma, would fill a volume." Donaldson tells an affecting tale of Sabattis's renunciation of liquor and his founding of the town's Methodist church. During his aborted 1881 cruise Sears stayed at the Sabattis home. Today the property belongs to a motel.

The bridge that straddles the lake loomed above us, and a few minutes later we floated up to the state boat ramp. Both of us were looking forward to a hot shower, clean clothes, a soft, spacious bed (something wider than our twenty-three-inch sleeping pads), and a good meal. I had imagined that my first impulse would be to stuff red meat into my face, but oddly enough, we craved salad. On coming out of the woods Sears had the same appetites, longing "not for the fleshpots of Egypt, but for the vegetable gardens at home, green peas, so to speak; succotash, as it were; the early harvest apple; the sweet bough; the summer sweeting; the fresh tomato . . . "

The car we had left on our way to Old Forge was unmolested. We loaded it up, got a cabin at a lakefront motel, and took turns standing mindlessly under the scalding spray of the shower. The rest of the day was given over to the chores we would perform at the end of each leg: retrieving the other car (in this case a ninety-mile round trip), doing our laundry, grocery shopping, reloading packs. By the time we sat down to dinner an intractable fatigue had rendered us nearly speechless; five minutes after I tumbled into the king-sized bed I was muttering in my sleep.

6

LONG LAKE TO RAQUETTE FALLS

MY FAVORITE VIEW OF LONG LAKE stretches north from the bridge in the center of town. In the middle distance sits Round Island, "like a huge green cylinder, sunk there end-wise, in the waves," as Joel T. Headley described it in 1844. As your eye moves down the lake the dark green shores pale to blue, purple, and finally to gray. To Headley it was "one of the most beautiful sheets of water I ever floated over," set as it was in a "frame-work of mountains."

Not far from the bridge, in 1881, Sears encountered a young woman who, he said, "interested me more deeply than any human being had ever done on so short an acquaintance." He was landing the *Susan Nipper* when a girl passed by, humming a melody from an opera. "Suddenly she stepped up to the canoe, raised it by the stem, turned it to port and starboard, read the name, and said sharply, 'Humph! "Susan Nipper." Dickens. "Master Dombey is a permanency; Miss Edith is temporary."

Why don't you name her Miss Edith? She looks sufficiently temporary.'

"She was about the first one who had recognized the name, and I looked her over with more interest. Why, she was a woman! Hair and eyes like an Indian princess—weight and size like a girl of ten years. A thin, attenuated form, a bright glow in either cheek, and a sharp, intellectual expression, with the worn, womanly outlines, told the story." She begged Sears to give her a ride and he complied, making a nest for her in the bow and paddling her to the opposite shore, where he made her comfortable in a sunny spot. When she grew tired he returned her to her father, who was anxiously walking the beach. "She held out her thin little hand at parting, saying: 'I trust you will understand me? I am a dying girl. They let me do as I please now. I have left conventional fetters and forms behind, with a good deal more that I valued once—but no matter. Good-bye.'" Had her tuberculosis blighted a romance? Sears wondered.

The hamlet of Long Lake was one of the earliest settlements in the Adirondack interior but so cut off from the rest of the region, except by water, that years passed before the community took hold. The settlement's prospects were the subject of a genteel dispute in New York City newspapers between Joel T. Headley and the Reverend John Todd, a Congregational minister who had struggled to establish a church in Long Lake. Todd envisioned a magnificent agricultural future for the area; Headley passed through three years later and noted that several of the settlers had departed and their laboriously cleared holdings were reverting to forest. Long Lake's future, he asserted, lay not with farming but with tourism, and he was right.

Besides the beauty of its setting, Long Lake boasts another distinction, one it shares with Boonville. It was here that nineteenth-century guides developed and refined the handsome craft known as the Adirondack guideboat. A narrow, oar-driven design with short decks on both ends, the boat, usually about eighteen feet long, could hold two hunters, their gear, and a trophy buck, yet was light enough (eighty-odd pounds was light in the 1850s) for one man to handle on the carries. Sears conceded the speed, strength, and capacity of the guideboats but "I never did and never shall like the Long-Lakers," he wrote. "They are swift but frail, weak, cranky and tiresome to ride in." His demonstration of the efficacy of solo canoe travel likely contributed to the eclipse of this indigenous craft. "It was all very well," Paul Jamieson has observed, "for a native guide, who knew the country, to back into it as rower. The visiting explorer preferred to front the unknown as paddler."

Sears admired the country around Long Lake but did not care for the community itself. The place was "too civilized. Too many guides. Too much landlordism. Too much cost for the accommodations." Today the village center has migrated from the west to the east shore of the lake, and it is largely a service community for boaters, sportsmen, and tourists. Long Lake has an easygoing feel to it; the diner opens before dawn to feed its regulars, a revolving cast of men and women in windbreakers and gimme caps. In fall one roadhouse posts a cardboard sign that reads NO GUNS OR KNIVES IN RESTAURANT, and the counter talk at the local hamburger stand concerns the moose someone saw, the accidental shooting of a three-legged pet deer with a ribbon around its neck, and a repertoire of well-worn guiding tales ("So he keeps askin' me how far back to camp and I keep sayin', ''Bout twenty minutes.' This goes on all afternoon. Finally, the light's goin' and he taps me on the shoulder and asks again, and when I say it's about twenty minutes he gives me a real long look. Five minutes later we hit it. I never was so lost in my life. You know the place I'm talking about, Danny, that boggy patch behind the mountain? Next day I went back in to figure it out and damned if I didn't get lost again"). Above a door in the municipal office building a sign proclaims Town Justice. If you've ever lived in a small community, this will strike you as an oxymoron.

Having moved at a sustained dogtrot for five days, we were still bone tired on Saturday morning after eleven hours of sleep. We lingered over breakfast before driving thirty miles north to stash a car, and by the time we got back the overflow from the launch-area parking lot jammed both sides of the road. A line of cars with trailers waited to back down to the water, and as we shoved off, six canoes from Middlebury College were being loaded. It was Labor Day weekend.

The view down the lake was magnificent, hills and mountains on both sides and the jagged profile of the Seward Range straight ahead. It soon became clear that competition for campsites would be stiff: every one we passed was occupied, usually by a couple with a powerboat and enormous amounts of gear. The most desirable sites were the lean-tos (you can stay in them up to three nights), so I had expected them to be snapped up on Friday. Still, I had underestimated the sheer numbers of people using the lake.

The sky ahead was bright but to the southwest dark clouds were massing, and the wind was nudging our backs. Where would we stay? The bulk of the tent sites were clustered within three miles of town; beyond them there were only a few in the six and a half miles to the end of the lake, and even fewer on the Raquette River. Long before we'd planned to, we began searching for somewhere to stop. The only empty sites were those on sluggish backwaters, and they were smelly, littered, and buzzing with flies. I was beginning to panic when, in Landing Bay, our last chance for miles, we found a fire ring and a good flat spot for the tent tucked into a grove of pines and birches. Enormously pleased with ourselves for holding out, we threw our sleeping pads onto the pine needles and ate lunch in sybaritic splendor. The Northville–Lake Placid trail was only a few hundred feet away, and twice we were visited by hikers' dogs, who trotted over to see if they could wangle a handout. They certainly could; we missed our own mutts.

Landing Bay was the terminus of the very first trail to Long Lake from the east, and it was an abrupt terminus, according to Headley. In 1844 he emerged here after fifty miles on horseback through primeval forest: "The path as we approached the shore, had dwindled to a mere Indian-trail, and there entirely disappeared. With no road around, and no sign of life, save a solitary log hut on the farther side of the lake, we waded up and down the shore till stopped by the rocks . . . " A boy saw his party and rowed across the lake to fetch them. The next morning they swam their horses across.

We were learning the virtues of stopping early, not least of them the chance to contemplate our surroundings before darkness and fatigue drove us into the tent. That afternoon I took my binoculars down to the water, chose a comfortable rock, and surveyed the happy mayhem that is Long Lake on a holiday weekend. At one point I was tracking more than a dozen boats, even though Round Island, just to the south, hid a good stretch of the far shore. My attention was eventually caught by an odd tableau. A white-haired man in work clothes was steering a Zodiac, while a teenage boy in striped jersey and natty cap lounged in front of him, hugging a cooler. In their wake, attached by a painter, bobbed a green canoe. The boy faced straight ahead and seemed never to speak to his companion. Perhaps the motor was too loud; perhaps they had nothing to say. Was the young master being fetched home from an impetuous expedition by a family retainer? I watched for close to an hour as they chugged slowly along the opposite shore, past homes and docks and boathouses, disappearing behind the island and emerging far down the lake as a foreshortened speck. I was vaguely disappointed when they vanished around a point. It had become a lovely afternoon. The rain never materialized, yet a refractive light hung over the lake, as if a shower had cleansed the air.

We longed for the weekend to be over, for the summer people to haul out their docks, shutter their cottages, trailer their boats, and clog every highway leading down off the dome. By Tuesday morning, we told each other, we'd have the place pretty much to ourselves. Hell, maybe even by Monday; a lot of people would probably try to beat the rush.

The next morning we paddled north under lowering skies, the light a strange milky blue, the surface barely rippled. The few people abroad were mostly fishermen, who exchanged quiet pleasantries with us as we passed. When Sears left the Grove House, he paddled the *Sairy Gamp* to a spot three miles from the foot of the lake, where U.S. Senator Orville H. Platt had built a cabin. "I found Senator Platt in camp," he wrote, "and a pleasant visit, fish, venison with open bark camp and huge log fire in front go far to compensate for the almost daily soakings I have caught since leaving the Forge House."

It is not clear whether Sears had met Platt before, but no doubt he had heard about the senator who came to his beloved Adirondack "shanty" whenever he could get away from the capital. Platt was born in Washington, Connecticut, where W. H. H. Murray later preached, and he helped get Murray a better pulpit in Meriden. The two shared a passion for the outdoors (it may have been Platt who introduced Murray to the Adirondacks), and it was to the senator that Murray affectionately dedicated *Adventures in the Wilderness.* Every American writer is indebted to Platt. In 1891, after years of congressional stalemate, he engineered passage of the International Copyright Law that gave authors control over works published abroad. Until then, literary piracy was commonplace and unactionable.

I was unsure just where Platt's log cabin had stood, so when we were close, I pulled up to a dock where a young man stood cradling his morning coffee. I was only one cove short, he told me pleasantly; in fact, his place had been part of the original Platt lot. Around a point we paddled and into a shallow bay protected by a cobblestone breakwater. There was a good dock and a stairway leading up to a large house and outbuilding where a figure was visible working in the yard. As I drifted toward shore he straightened and hurried to the top of the stairs. He appeared to be in his sixties, with iron-gray hair and a heavy, square face. When I wished him good morning, he held his hands in front of him and flicked his fingers outward in the international Shove Off sign. The gesture froze the smile on my face.

"Excuse me," I said, trying to mollify him. "I'm doing some historical research and I'm looking for Senator Platt's old camp. Would this be it?"

Scowling, he came partway down the stairs. "Yes."

I tried again. "I'm sorry for disturbing you. I'm working on a book about a man who stayed here in the summer of 1883. I was just wondering whether any of these buildings date from that era."

"No," he said, drying his hands on a towel. "Platt's place was torn down."

"Oh, I see. Well, I didn't mean to bother you; it's just that I've been looking for this camp for some time. It's quite a historic spot."

"If you want to know about it, it's in that history of the Adirondacks."

We were considered trespassers even though we hadn't touched shore. Of course I should have found out his name beforehand and written a letter, but I hadn't anticipated this level of hostility. It hurt.

I began to backpaddle. "Thanks for your time, and sorry to have disturbed you. You have a lovely place here."

He started back up the stairs, then turned and called after me, "We've had a lot of trouble with vandalism."

Did he really believe that a middle-aged couple in tiny canoes had paddled six and a half miles to trash his place? Did he think we had crowbars concealed in our paddle shafts? Or was he simply justifying his antagonism? Whatever the reason, it was clear that Senator Platt's hospitality had not survived in this place. The French have a term—*esprit de l'escalier* ("staircase wit")—for those moments when you realize what you should have said. The rest of the way down the lake I brooded about the encounter and indulged in *esprit du canot.*

No one has come up with an explanation for the phenomenon, but the northern end of Long Lake has proved highly attractive to hermits. In the nineteenth century two of them lived on opposite shores. With a decided twinkle in his prose, Alfred Donaldson wondered "if two hermits can live on the same lake without forfeiting their integrity of title. Does the conjunction of two hermits on one spot precipitate a community, or does it merely augment a condition? And at what point in the density of neighbors does the evaporation of hermits begin?"

On the west shore lived Bowen, an erudite man whose cabin walls were lined with books. An agnostic, Bowen was often proselytized by a local churchman, to no effect. Ah, but when Bowen faced death, the believer predicted, he'd change his tune. At length the Dark Stranger, as Donaldson called him, lingered at Bowen's door and he sent for the churchman, who must have hurried down the lake with righteous glee in his heart. As it turned out, Bowen had summoned him only for "the satisfaction of telling him that . . . he had neither changed his mind nor lost his skepticism."

The hermit Harney arrived some years later. The more genial of the two, he farmed and sold milk to Senator Platt, among others. What ultimately made Harney odd was the fact that he wasn't really Harney at all. When a son arrived to take the aged man away, it was discovered that his name was Larmie Fournier.

In the twentieth century a third recluse lived in the area, but high in the mountains where the Cold River rises. Noah John Rondeau stretches the definition of a hermit, since from time to time he agreed to be flown out and put on display at the sportsmen's shows in New York and elsewhere, but he did live alone in some of the wildest country in the Adirondacks. His pronounced eccentricities endeared him to everyone except the local game officers, with whom he occasionally skirmished. He planted vegetables and flowers around his clearing and in warmer months shared his assemblage of huts and wigwams with passing hikers, many of whom became lifelong friends. He never finished his memoir of childhood in a French Canadian family (of his difficulty understanding a neighbor's conversation he wrote, "My English at that time was all in French"), but his diary chronicled the seasons with the grace of poetry:

"Aug. 10, 1947: Nasturtiums are at glorious best. Humming birds call to please the flowers."

"April 13, 1952: In Snow storm against gloomy sky, 4 robins pose in an Oak with breasts rounded out like ripening apples."

"Feb. 11, 1953: I watch the wind gather snow in its arms and whirl it in a spiral 20 feet high and then scatter it like vanishing smoke."

Rondeau was born July 6, 1883, the same week Sears claimed the *Sairy Gamp* at the Boonville freight depot.

At its northern end Long Lake becomes shallow and the character of the surrounding forest changes. Here the deep green of conifers gives way to the lighter tones of maples as the Raquette River resumes in a maze of alder-studded islands. One of the region's earliest thoroughfares, a military road hacked out between 1808 and 1812, passed through here, but from water level we could see no sign of a crossing place.

By the time we turned for a last spectacular look up the lake the motorboat traffic was picking up. "Just a few hundred yards and we'll be free!" I assured John. We glided over a sandbar, turned a bend, and the lake disappeared. Asylum. Now we were entering wilder country, where for mile after mile we would see no roads, no houses. There would be only the river, bearing placidly north through a broad valley.

Almost immediately we were overtaken by three men in solo canoes. Their choppy strokes marked them as racers in training for the annual Adirondack Canoe Classic, a ninety-mile scramble from Old Forge to Saranac Lake that in three days would cover roughly as much terrain as we would traverse in thirteen. They nodded hello and swept past as if we were anchored. No sooner had they disappeared than two powerboats (illegal in these waters, which are designated scenic) put the lie to my promise of peace. Each carried a man and several children; each left behind a miasma of blue smoke. Slowly they chugged past, dodging sandbars, while we dawdled to avoid their fumes. We had planned to paddle a mile or so up Cold River but jettisoned that idea when they turned off there. It would have been fun, because we had camped at a lean-to on the Cold on our first shakedown cruise, in early May.

In spring this had been a vastly different landscape, the Raquette in what Paul Jamieson calls "a glorious state of uncontainment" as snowmelt from the surrounding peaks swelled feeder streams. Here and there the river sprawled over its banks, creating an unearthly drowned wilderness that seemed to fill the valley. The water in the main channel bustled along with a remorseless, hissing drive, tinkling and gurgling around obstructions. Undermined red and silver maples had toppled over and were invisible but for a branch or two vibrating madly in the current. The air had been alive with the songs of wood thrushes and white-throated sparrows.

Now the water level was four or five feet lower, and the banks rose over our heads as we made our way between pungent mud flats lined with the carcasses of trees. The birds had raised their families and were for the most part silent. In spring, tree swallows had skimmed the surface; now dragonflies, miniature Vietnam-era Hueys, darted back and forth. One settled on my left breast and rode with me a while, sunlight scintillating off the lace of its wings. Waterbugs zigzagged just ahead of our bows, and the first spent leaves of the season twirled down to drift alongside us, a yellow and pink and orange flotilla bound for the Saint Lawrence. Just beyond the Cold River we grated over a sandbar and knew we were at last beyond the reach of outboards.

In the 1884 edition of *The Adirondacks: Illustrated,* the photographer and publicist Seneca Ray Stoddard remarked on the huge cedars that lined the banks and the sluggish motion of the flow. Here the Raquette seemed, he wrote, "more like a river of black glass than water." Today the forest is second-growth, but the dark river still glides smoothly over a sandy bed. I dropped back to revel in the stillness and the sensual pleasures of paddling, the swirling vortex left on the surface by each stroke, the dark bow wave streaming past me toward the stern, the soft splash of blade on water like a lone swimmer slapping through an empty pool. The day had turned glorious, cloudless and warm, and I thought of Sears and his wretched luck. Between Cold River and Raquette Falls, he reported, he ran into "a soaking rain that left me without a dry thread."

Soon we could hear rapids, and a weathered sign on a boulder in midstream warned of danger ahead. Raquette Falls is a mile and a quarter of rapids interrupted by two fifteen-foot drops. A jagged hunk of aluminum, the wrecked bow of a canoe, swung from a tree as a further admonishment. Here in 1882 stood a dam and a dock, part of W. W. Durant's ambitious transportation network. The eighteen-foot steamer *Buttercup* plied a route from the head of Long Lake to the falls, but not for long. Local guides resented the competition, and one night the boat was quietly scuttled.

In spring there was no landing to speak of, but now a broad beach lay revealed at the foot of the steep hillside. As we rigged our packframes two groups of daytrippers pulled in and several came over to chat. As they had done with the *Sairy Gamp* a century ago, they wanted to "lift her by the nose" to see how light she was. The conversation was the usual amiable chatter: Where'd you start? Where you headed? How long you think it'll take you? Boy, you really got the weather.

The mile-and-a-third carry around the falls is one of the oldest in the region, used in turn by Indians, white trappers and hunters, sportsmen, loggers, and tourists. The falls themselves aren't visible but their "comforting roar," as Raquette River historian Charles Bryan put it, drifts up to the trail, an undulating path that hugs the flank of Lookout Mountain. Lined in May with the demure blossoms of wood violets, spring beauties, and trout lilies, in autumn the path is dominated by the broad, burgundy-splashed leaves of witch hobble. The day was hot enough that I was thankful we would only have to portage it once. At the height of land I paused for a blow and thought longingly of the old days, when a pair of oxen hauled boats and gear over this carry. The drover was, oddly enough, the man who became the hermit Harney.

7

RAQUETTE FALLS TO STONY CREEK PONDS

TOWARD THE END OF EVERY LONG CARRY, a canoeist strains to spot the glint of water or the thinning of canopy that marks the end of the trail. What first greets the eye below Raquette Falls, however, is neither water nor sky but an Adirondack anomaly, a generous meadow of about a dozen acres in the midst of deep forest. In the Civil War era this clearing, sloping gently uphill from the river, held a lumber camp; when the loggers moved on, their cook and her husband stayed on to run an inn that became known as Mother Johnson's. Lucy Johnson, a homely, good-natured woman, became a northwoods immortal when W. H. H. Murray praised her pancakes and her forbearance in *Adventures in the Wilderness.* Murray and his guide had stumbled in famished, just before midnight. The imperturbable goodwife rolled out of bed, fired up her stove, and shoveled flapjacks into her guests until they begged for mercy.

Like most Adirondack hoteliers, Lucy and her husband, a man with the delightful name of Philander, took a dim view of fish and game laws. ("Mountain lamb," a menu mainstay throughout the region, was actually out-of-season venison.) In the 1874 edition of his guidebook, Seneca Ray Stoddard described a meal at Mother Johnson's:

"'What kind of a fish is that, Mrs. Johnson?' I inquired.

"'Well', said she, 'they don't have no name after the 15th of September. They are a good deal like trout, but it's against the law to catch trout after the fifteenth, you know.'"

The winter after Stoddard's visit, Mother Johnson died at her inn. Although she had asked to be buried in Long Lake, her request had to be deferred in the face of January realities: a frozen river, thigh-high snowdrifts, and miles of forest in every direction. The burial itself proved difficult enough. Harney had to snowshoe ten miles to find someone who could make a coffin, and then several miles farther to get the lumber. In the meantime a shallow grave was hacked out of the frozen earth on a knoll behind the inn. There was no real ceremony; besides the family only three mourners were present. The plan was to move her remains in the spring, when the river opened.

A mystery attends the final disposition of Lucy Johnson's remains. Some historians believe she still lies beneath her knoll, but there is no trace of her grave at the falls. There is, however, a marker in the Long Lake cemetery bearing her name, and it stands among other stones dating back to her era. (Her headstone is a curious affair. On one end of the small slab someone chiseled "Old Mrs. Johnson" and then thought better of it, turned it upside down, and chiseled "Mother Johnson." The original inscription is still visible at the grass line.) A married daughter ran the place for a while, and for the next forty-odd years a succession of other innkeepers came and went, although the house continued to be known as Johnson's. It was here, on or about August 1, 1883, that the bedraggled Sears fetched up, having covered the ten and a half miles from Senator Platt's camp.

After the First World War, Johnson's became a private residence. First in summer and then year-round, a New York City lawyer named George Morgan lived here with a library of two thousand volumes. The universally esteemed Morgan entertained friends and passing hikers as his money and health ran out, and in the fall of 1944 he was buried, like Mother Johnson, on a knoll near his house. A plaque on a boulder at the edge of the clearing commemorates his generosity of spirit. The clearing's final inhabitant was Charles Bryan, former president of the Pullman railroad car company and author. He and his wife, Mary, were summer residents; when he died the state acquired the parcel.

Fire and time have claimed the original structures, but a few weathered buildings, along with lean-tos and tent sites, hug the edge of the clearing. In summer a forest ranger is stationed here, his presence indicated by a sign with the legend Department of the Interior Outpost.

At the landing we found scores of swimmers and picnickers lounging on rocks, dogs and children splashing in the shallows, the air alive with shouts and happy screams. The six Middlebury canoes were arrayed at water's edge, along with four from a New Jersey outing club and assorted Old Town and aluminum models belonging to young couples. My map showed four lean-tos in the next seven miles but they would surely be occupied. It was time to start looking for a campsite. A canoe launched just ahead of us had to be lifted over a shallow ledge, but our boats cleared it with centimeters to spare, to the entertainment of nearby sunbathers. Around the first bend three tandem canoes idled in the current, waiting for a fourth.

At the next turn a patch of eroded bank laced with exposed roots indicated a campsite nearby, and we were pleased to see no canoe drawn up by the shore. Within minutes we'd investigated and taken possession of a fine spot, a piney bluff twenty feet above river level, screened by young hemlocks. The previous occupant had been what we call an otter. There are two kinds of canoe campers, an outdoor writer has proposed, dolphins and otters. Dolphins tend to talk about how fast they covered a given distance, otters about what a great time they had playing at a waterfall. Dolphins are always on the move; otters prefer to stay put and enjoy their surroundings. Otters lavish hours on their campsites, fashioning rustic shelves, tables, and chairs from the woody debris in the area. This one, bless him or her, had left a meticulous stack of wood graded by diameter, a log seat next to the fire ring, and a whittled stake-and-crosspole arrangement for hanging pots over the flames. I wish there were more of the otter in my makeup, but like John I seem programmed to plan, to move briskly on to the next task. I'm working on it.

There was a good deal of traffic on the river. Powerboats are permitted on the twenty-two miles of the Raquette between Tupper Lake and the falls, and this is a shame. The river is a narrow, peaceful waterway for most of its length. Motorboats violate more than the spirit of the place: they leave air, water, and noise pollution in their wakes, and they churn up the sandy bottom. We learned the hard way, with a clogged filter, to wait a while before trying to draw water.

The powerboat parade continued until dusk. The racers we'd seen at the foot of Long Lake sped by on their return trip, having covered god-knows-how-many miles since we'd last seen them. During a lull we heard a frenzied splashing on the river and discovered two mergansers pursuing a third. The pursuee had a small fish in its bill and was streaking over the surface like a cartoon roadrunner, its legs a blur. Up onto the bank they went, back into the water, around and around.

During another lull we heard the deep, unmusical *quork*s of a common raven issuing from a deep slough across the river. Ravens were once widely distributed, but in the last century man has so persecuted them that they have retreated to remote corners of the country. They are the largest members of the most intelligent avian species, the crow family, and are magnificent fliers, able to soar like a hawk or tumble and dive like a falcon. Blue-black in color, they have shaggy throat feathers and a wedge-shaped tail in flight. Ravens are far-ranging, rare, and usually solitary scavengers.

In his cheerfully obsessive way, the zoologist Bernd Heinrich spent four years studying these birds, lugging eight tons of meat deep into the Maine woods, riding out storms in the tops of swaying spruces, and risking frostbite as he waited, often in vain, in unheated blinds. His patience allowed him to hear an astonishing variety of raven calls, ranging from trills to knocks, and to witness a unique form of cooperative foraging in which certain birds "yell" when they find a carcass. The yelling is meant to attract other ravens, but the behavior may not be as altruistic as it appears: Heinrich theorizes that the yeller is recruiting a group large enough to overwhelm any resident adults, who can be expected to defend the food in their territory. Yellers are juveniles who appear to be more courageous than their peers, and this dominance probably earns them the choicest feeding spots and the best mates.

Our raven soon fell silent, and a chill descended the moment the sun slipped behind the trees, promising another clear, cold night. We crawled into our dome and fell asleep to the patter of hemlock needles hitting nylon. Just one more day, and this gorgeous playground would be all ours.

In the morning the interior of the tent was beaded with condensation, our mingled respiration clinging to the fabric. I ignored my aching bladder and snuggled deeper into my sleeping bag while John bustled around outside kindling a fire. On this day twenty-four years ago we were married. I was twenty-three, officially a spinster; John was thirty-four and divorced.

The Unitarian minister, filling in for a colleague, was so nervous his hands were shaking worse than my knees. A photograph taken just after the ceremony shows our young selves in the church courtyard, flanked by two smiling couples whose marriages soon foundered. I look at the two people we were and I see a lot of hair, a lot of illusions. Luckier than our friends, we grew and changed together, and after a quarter of a century would still rather spend time with each other than with anybody else.

Sears appears to have been less fortunate in his domestic affairs. Not until he was thirty-five did he submit to what he called the "predestined and necessary evil" of matrimony, choosing a twenty-four-year-old local girl named Mariette Butler. A few weeks afterward, in a pattern that would become familiar, he left her to head out west.* The long-suffering "Mrs. Nessmuk," as he referred to her in print, bore two daughters and a son, but if she harbored any illusions about a normal family life, they must soon have been blasted. Sears proved a spectacularly indifferent husband and father, decamping at the slightest excuse, often without leaving her the means to feed and clothe their children. More than once she was forced to turn to Sears's brother Charles for help. (When Sears traveled, he corresponded not with Mariette but with Charles.) The few published references to Mrs. Nessmuk refer only to the insurance she would collect if he drowned. In his writing, at least, Sears expressed more affection for his hunting dogs than for his family.

A settled existence, and the labor necessary to sustain it, always came second. Almost any opportunity to escape was seized, sometimes on the spur of the moment. A *Forest and Stream* reader from Denver wrote Sears to ask about hunting in

* The date of this trip is vague; it was either fall 1857 or 1858. But if it was the latter Sears still fails dismally as a helpmeet, since Mariette was about to deliver their first child.

the Wellsboro area, and on his arrival, in July 1882, decided to look up his hero. "Found him at work on a boot," Myron Reed recalled. "He rose from his seat [and] informed his brother that he should be absent a week or ten days. . . ." Autumn was his favorite season in the woods; like the Indians he had known as a child, he tended to abscond as soon as the leaves began dropping. In 1871 he served as editor of the local newspaper, the *Tioga County Agitator*—until October, when he resigned, he said, to lay in his winter supply of venison. "As for the dull, hard routine of daily work by which most of us must win our daily bread, I decided to strike against that," he once wrote. "One may work always, if he will: the lame and lazy will see to it that he has the chance. But successful hunting . . . can only be done for a few weeks at the proper time and season." Unluckily for Mrs. Nessmuk, something was always in season somewhere.

Sears seems to have found little comfort in his marriage. If, as his journal hints, he had contracted syphilis, we should not be too surprised; he had many opportunities to do so, both before and after his wedding day. A young seaman was exposed to casual sex at every port of call on whaling trips, and syphilis was common among the Chippewa and Saint Regis Indians with whom he consorted during hunting and trapping expeditions. Nor is there any reason to believe Sears remained celibate during two tours in Brazil; in fact, one of his nieces contended that he came home not with malaria, as he claimed, but with gonorrhea. A worldly and passionate man with an eye for beauty, he more than once mentions lost, dark-eyed loves in his poetry.

Two poems suggest that he and Mariette might have lost an infant son. If this was the case, his grief may have been such that he never again completely gave his heart to a child, for his lack of interest in the parental role was evident. His own upbringing had provided little paternal benevolence for him to emulate. His father seems to have been a difficult individual, and the relationship between the two was an unhappy one. Sears was not alone in his troubles with the old man; at one point the patriarch was estranged from most of his family. A streak of instability worsened with age, and eventually the elder Sears was committed to a mental hospital, where he died.

Sears was thirty-eight and the father of a baby boy when he advised men to indulge their sons' obsessions with certain longed-for objects—skates, say, or boats, or guns. No doubt he was recalling his own campaign to be allowed a rifle, and his father's lack of sympathy. A father, he wrote in *Porter's Spirit of the Times* in 1860, ought to do more than buy the object for his boy; he should "join him, and take an interest in *his* favorite pursuits, if you wish him to take an interest in yours. If you think it better to get up the starch and thwart him at every turn—do so by all means, and see if he do not learn—before he is sixteen—to 'circumwent the Gov'nor' to your entire satisfaction."

Whether Sears followed this humane advice isn't clear, but sadly, his own son, named for his brother Charles, proved a disappointment to him. It's tempting to speculate that his frequent and lengthy absences precluded a strong father-son bond, as did his passion for solitude (he seems not to have included his son on camping trips, even those near Wellsboro). It could not have been easy, being Sears's son in a community that viewed the father as rather shiftless and eccentric. Whatever the cause, Charles Sears was often at odds with his father. Sears's journals record nasty rows between the two, as well as his conviction that his son was worthless. Remembered by contemporaries as a bright and generous soul, Charlie worked as a logger and drank his earnings, ending his days as an indigent in the county home. Sears's daughters, Jennie and Margaret, seem to have found more happiness. Both married and moved away.

~~~
~~~

"Present for you," John said, depositing washcloth, towel, soap, and a bowl of steaming water beside my tent door. This was a gift indeed. There is no greater luxury in the woods than hot water. People who'd rather have root canals than wash dishes cheerfully volunteer for camp KP because nothing feels better than getting grubby hands warm and clean. Well, almost nothing.

It was ten o'clock when we launched, after a leisurely breakfast of pancakes and maple syrup, washed down with Puerto Rican espresso. The sun, just clearing Seward Mountain to the east, warmed the left bank while the right remained in chilly shadow. "For once I had dry weather and a pleasant trip," Sears wrote of this leg, "though the wind was high." It was soon gusty for us too, and for the first time since we left Old Forge it was out of the north, yet another reminder that autumn was beginning to assert itself. As we tired, the stretches of glassy water seemed to get shorter and the windswept ones closer together.

Wind behaves according to certain unalterable principles, but I have discovered several not included in standard texts—Chris's Law of Vector Intransigence, for example. This principle, familiar to all canoeists, can be stated simply: a given wind will change heading as often as a given boat does, thereby ensuring that the wind is always in the paddler's face. The stronger the wind, the more adroitly it will shift. My Law of Vector Intransigence also applies to campfires: a given wind will change direction as often as the cook does, with the result that the smoke is always in his or her face.

(Two other immutable laws had become evident. Chris's Law of Infernal Gravity holds that the article you need next, regardless of where it was originally placed, will migrate to the bottom of its bag. This is why most campers spend roughly eighty percent of their time removing the contents of their packs in order to find one item. And then there's the Law of

Magnetic Concavity: wherever the campsite, any cup or bowl left uncovered will attract two pine needles, one twist tie, one twig, one fly, and several curls of ash. How these substances find their target is an enduring mystery.)

The river meandered northward between low banks, extensive marshes stretching away on both sides. The terrain was swampier than it had been above the falls, and the river itself had a languid, distinctively southern feel. "In this mountain region," wrote an Albany newspaperman named S. H. Hammond, "one would look for a rapid, roaring stream, . . . [but] this river, save in a single locality, flows along with a deep and steady current,—winding around wooded points, and stretching in long reaches through an unbroken wilderness, the shores lined with forests of gigantic growth, or natural meadows. The appearance along the shores is that of a country beautifully level, and were it not for the tall peaks standing out against the sky . . . one would think that he was in a region like the Mississippi valley . . . " That was in 1854. Within ten years Hammond's "forests of gigantic growth" were succumbing to the lumbermen. First to go were softwoods hundreds of years old: white pine, then black spruce, hemlock, white cedar, and balsam fir. Softwoods went first because they float, and could easily be borne to the mills by spring freshets. The heavier hardwoods—maple, beech, birch, and cherry—survived until roads and railways reached into the interior.

Still, the Raquette remained a lovely river. In 1899 a state politician named Martin Van Buren Ives pronounced this section "enchantingly beautiful. For long distances the boat passes over shallows, whose sandy bottoms resemble pure gold, importing to the water an amber-like shade, but as the water deepens its color changes to red, and still deeper, to black. Nearly all this level of the river has interval banks covered with soft maple and elm trees, whose branches in some places nearly span the stream, thereby well nigh shutting out the noonday sun. . . ."

Today the Raquette is lined with red and silver maples and occasionally a stand of white pine or a corridor of balsam fir. Along the banks cardinal flowers and wood asters were blooming. At one bend a spotted sandpiper strutted on a mudflat like a wind-up toy, and near a venerable tree known as the Halfway Pine, a flock of magnolia warblers disputed ownership of a green caterpillar.

Traffic on the river had fallen off dramatically. After two hours we were passed by a couple in a heavily loaded tripping canoe. They were utterly competent, their paddles stroking quickly and smoothly. The woman was tanned and handsome; her companion, also dark, with a bushy black beard, could have passed for a voyageur. As we exchanged hellos the woman shipped her paddle and twisted around to pick up a bundle. A tiny fist poked out as she settled it in her lap.

"Wow, you're brave!" I said as they glided by.

She flashed a radiant smile. "Nah, he's a great camper. Port-a-baby."

Ten yards beyond us she slipped her blouse off one shoulder and cradled Port-a-baby to nurse, sending a wave of sixties nostalgia through me.

Not long thereafter we swung right, into the mouth of Stony Creek. In May, this had been a lake with outcroppings of stunted trees here and there; now we found a twisting little stream lined with grasses that rose over our heads. The name Stony Creek is obviously an Adirondack joke; where the bottom was visible it was resolutely sandy. The stream was only a little broader than the width of our paddles and so shallow our blades were continually befouled with aquatic plants. To clear them we learned to twirl our paddle shafts backward, the way you'd unroll spaghetti from a fork.

"Of all the crooked streams it has been my fortune to see or traverse," Headley wrote, "this certainly will bear the palm. So sharp are the angles, that in turning them the boat seems to swing on its bow as on a pivot, and comes round with a swirling sound. A snake in motion is a straight line compared to it. In one place it is only three rods across a neck of land to the creek again, while following the channel, it is a mile to the same point."

There were two beaver dams in the mile and three quarters to Stony Creek Ponds, and we had been on the water long enough that it felt good to stand up on them to pull our boats across. Beaver were scarce in the Adirondacks in Sears's time, a consequence of overtrapping in the eighteenth and nineteenth centuries. This must have taken some doing: beaver are profilic creatures, and originally they numbered in the millions here, yet by 1895, when protection was enacted, only about ten animals remained in the region. Recovery was so slow that stocks had to be imported. In the winter of 1904 seven Canadian beaver were brought to Old Forge and held for release in the spring. (The person who tended them was Ned Ball, who twenty-one years earlier had carried the *Sairy Gamp* over the last three and a half miles of the Brown's Tract Road.) Eventually thirty more beaver were released, and by 1920 there were estimated to be more than twenty thousand. By 1925 state-approved trapping had caused another population crash, but thereafter a more judicious policy evolved.

The beaver restoration was more successful than two other programs undertaken in the same era. In March 1902 five wapiti (known here as elk) were released near the Fulton Chain, but the animals were hopelessly tame; they hung around settlements cadging handouts from residents. One day that fall someone gunned down all five as they browsed peaceably in the woods. That same year three Canadian moose were brought in, but they too had become imprinted on humans, so much so that they could only be lured out of their crates with offerings of sugar. As Joseph Grady reported, "It required the employment of strategy on the part of the resourceful Ned [Ball] and

Harry [Radford] to coax them into the fringe of forest, and additional strategy for the strategists to escape without being detected and followed." All told, about fifteen moose were liberated, but one by one they were picked off, for sport or for their meat.

The force behind both the moose and beaver restorations was a bumptious young fellow named Harry V. Radford, who wrote editorials, raised money, hectored politicians, and personally attended most of the liberation ceremonies. At eighteen Radford started a magazine called *Woods and Waters* to champion the Adirondacks he had loved since boyhood. Based in New York City, the magazine prospered under his editorship, and by the time he folded it in 1906 its circulation was a respectable twenty thousand. Such was his ardor for the mountains that he earned the sobriquet "Adirondack Harry," a reference to the original popularizer of the region, "Adirondack" Murray, whose friend and hagiographer he became. (A few years later Radford and a companion were killed by Eskimos after an argument at Bathurst Inlet, in the far north.)

Sears had pushed through to First Stony Creek Pond, where he stopped for lunch before making the mile-long Indian Carry to Upper Saranac Lake. We turned off at Third Pond, a pretty little lakelet with homes along its western shore. One of these belonged to friends, who had offered their guest room as headquarters for the northern leg of our trip. Every few days we would turn up here to shower, wash our clothes, raid the refrigerator, and generally comport ourselves like college kids home for a long weekend. We beached our boats at their landing and hefted our packs for the short climb to the house. As we passed the garden we picked cherry tomatoes hot from the sun and crammed them into our mouths.

UPPER SARANAC LAKE TO SPITFIRE LAKE

BY THE TIME SEARS REACHED UPPER SARANAC LAKE, in midafternoon, its waters were choppy, "altogether too rough," he concluded, "for the *Sairy.*" He killed time talking with the guides at Corey's Lodge while he waited for the small steamer, probably the *Mosquito,* that bustled twice daily around the lake. He was tired, he admitted, but he was defensive about hitching a ride. "I had already paddled more than the distance from side to side of the wilderness, and if it looked like dodging to avoid water on which the canoe could not live, so be it."

The steamer zigzagged from landing to landing, disorienting Sears so thoroughly that he "found the sun setting in the east—a vexatious thing to a woodsman. Missing one of the turns of the boat, I was turned myself. I straightened myself out by shutting both eyes and letting a muscular guide whirl me around half a dozen times promiscuously, then setting the compass without looking at the sun; then, being right on the cardinal points, I took a general average of the landscape. This brought me right."

Upper Saranac Lake is eight miles long and shaped like an hourglass, with a narrows halfway up. The lake occupies part of an ancient oval basin surrounded by mountain peaks, yet of this spectacular scenery Sears had almost nothing to say. This perfunctory reaction, which would be repeated on Tupper Lake, was no doubt the result of the way he traveled. The steamer, with its noise and congenial human cargo, insulated him from his surroundings. It also carried him through the landscape much faster than the *Sairy* could, which meant he saw far less. Instead of a place to be explored and experienced, Upper Saranac Lake was merely an interval between hotels.

We set out early in the day, while the lake was still tranquil. Not a soul was astir, and the sky was a light, luminous blue. We had not gone far when we noticed the algae bloom that earlier in the summer had erupted here and migrated far to the northeast, through Middle and Lower Saranac lakes. What caused the imbalance has yet to be resolved. Some residents blamed the state transportation department, which had removed a nearby beaver dam and allowed an influx of nutrient-rich water; others mentioned contamination from wastes emitted by the state fish hatchery at the head of the lake. A third possibility was septic system leakage: there are plenty of antiquated systems among the five hundred-odd camps along the shoreline. Whatever triggered the bloom, the effect was an unpleasant cast to the water, like weak coffee diluted with milk. It was peculiar to see my paddle tips vanish in murk a few inches below the surface.

Chapel Island, near the put-in, is only a little larger than the church that clings to its rocky back. On Sunday mornings in summer, boats of all sizes and shapes converge at its dock for interdenominational services (the church is nominally Presbyterian). The building dates only to the mid-1950s, when the original 1889 chapel went up in flames. We landed, walked around it, admiring the rustic white-birch cross in front and peering through the windows at pine walls and pews, a smaller birch cross behind the altar, the light streaming in through clear glass windows. A bright, airy space, it was unpretentious and oddly moving.

We headed off to the northeast, where a long bay funnels down to the lake's outlet. In the last century the stream of tourists entering the Adirondacks from the east diverged here, parties heading north toward Paul Smith's, south to Long and Raquette lakes, or west to Tupper Lake. Beyond the rapids at the end of the bay there was once a hotel called Bartlett's, a place renowned as much for its proprietor's short fuse as for its meals. Sears's steamer stopped at Bartlett's landing, and there the *Sairy* created a sensation among the guests. "I think that not less than fifty people had a turn at lifting her," Sears reported. "Then they wanted to see her go. So I took off boots and coat, got in, and paddled out into the lake, where there was a swell that made her dance like a cork." Near the outlet today, just off the north shore, you can still see two substantial wooden cribs filled with rocks. Set about nine feet apart and well preserved, these footings may well have supported Bartlett's dock. I drifted and indulged myself, imagining the afternoon light, the watchers onshore, the *Sairy* bobbing in the swell.

Returning up the bay we were met by a broadsiding southwest wind that kept us dodging from island to island until we cleared a headland and turned due north. Then we fairly flew, our paddle blades catching the breeze, the waves tossing us forward and breaking with a hiss beside us. The lake was alive with herring gulls tilting lazily overhead and congregating on white-stained rocks; Gull Bay and Gull Point attested to their long residence on Upper Saranac.

Our map showed four campsites at the southern tip of Buck Island, just beyond the narrows. The westernmost one was especially attractive, its fire ring and tent site tucked into the woods, a broad prow of ledge, perfect for sunset-watching, jutting into the lake, but before settling in we decided to reconnoiter the lean-to deep in Saginaw Bay, where there would be less traffic. Saginaw's state-owned shoreline was soothingly empty but the lean-to had been removed to let the site recover from years of hard use. A nearby tent site was beset by flies.*

We had been gone only half an hour but in that time the wind had intensified. It was stiff going back to the open lake, where conditions were worse thanks to the wind tunnel of the narrows. It took all my strength to get across the strait to the island, where a surprise awaited. As if by magic, the two easternmost campsites had been claimed, and when we fought our way around the tip we saw that the third had also been taken. Our favorite was hidden beyond a small cove but since it was the best, it was probably occupied too. Where had these people come from? Didn't they know it was after Labor Day? We were suddenly tired, hungry, and dispirited. *Waaaaahhhhh!*

My depression turned to anger at the wind, and I began to paddle savagely, teeth gritted, shoulders aching, water swirling around my calves. John fell steadily behind. While I could see no boat drawn up at our cove, I refused to give in to hope: they had probably landed on the far side of the point. Steep waves slapping directly onshore made alighting tricky, but we stumbled up the bank to find no one there. Almost giddy with relief, we dragged our wet sleeping pads onto the ledge and wolfed chicken-spread-and-cucumber sandwiches and oranges. When we could eat no more we moved back into the woods, set up the tent, and fell deeply asleep.

* Flies, biting or otherwise, never bothered Sears, who made his own insect repellent from tar, pennyroyal, and castor oil. When starting into the woods, he explained, he applied "a good, substantial glaze, which I am not fool enough to destroy by any weak leaning to soap and towels." Olfactory speculation is irresistible: was Sears a solo traveler by choice, or was his person so pungent that no one could be persuaded to accompany him?

Clouds were massing in the west when we woke; there would be no gorgeous sunset after all. I settled down on the ledge with the binoculars to survey the scene. The powerboat activity was about a quarter of what it had been last week, most of it headed for the state campgrounds in Fish Creek Ponds, directly west of us. At suppertime the traffic all but stopped and I was blindsided by the beauty of the place, the lake a giant meniscus trembling in a hushed green basin.

The journalist S. H. Hammond was dazzled by Upper Saranac in the late 1840s. "The beauty of the scenery around these lakes, to be appreciated, must be seen," he wrote. "More than that, it must be seen by those who have a taste for the woods—who love to be sometimes alone, beyond the hum of the thousand voices, . . . to be away, among nature's unshorn, as well as unadorned loveliness; to hear her unawed by the sights and sounds of civilization, talking (as my guide termed it) to herself. They must be men of patience and some nerve, who are, for the sake of the pleasure, willing to submit to some privation, to encounter some weariness, and much discomfort."

Discomfort was mine the next morning when I slipped on a log and was pitched unceremoniously into the cove, smashing an elbow, jamming a finger, and tearing open my shin. (More than a year later I still felt pain when I straightened my arm, and the scar on my leg remained even longer, emblems of a day whose gloomy dawn proved an omen.) With the previous day's battle fresh in our minds, we raced through breakfast and made our way, under lowering skies, up the west side of the lake, setting a direct course from point to point. A peninsula and an island gradually detached themselves from the surrounding shores, and we threaded between them and into Back Bay. In Sears's day there had been a four-mile "draw carry"—a horse-drawn wagon hauling boats and gear—from here to Big Clear Pond (now Lake Clear) and a shorter one from Big Clear to Upper Saint Regis Lake. Both have been obliterated, the former by a highway, the latter by forest, so we would drive those sections.

As we hauled out we discussed our options. Lake Clear was small enough that it would take a couple of hours at most, but rain was threatening and both of us were sore, I from my log-rolling, John from a chronic shoulder inflammation. At some point in the trip he had planned to dash home and pay the bills, and this seemed as good a time as any. We drove back to our headquarters.

While John packed, I called my office and learned that I no longer had a job; *New England Monthly* was dead. In six and a half years it had won unprecedented back-to-back National Magazine Awards for general excellence, but it had failed to turn a profit. Although I had known when I left home that the situation was perilous, I was unprepared for the speed of the denouement; the office would close before I got back. The end was like a death in the family, with no ceremony to mark the loss.

Unless you've worked on a magazine it's hard to understand how labor intensive the process is and how difficult it can be to put together even one good issue. For *NEM*'s first four and a half years I served as managing editor, and my involvement was total: I bought our office furniture (used), chose a typesetting system (hey, nobody's perfect), and hired our first typesetter and copyeditor. Marooned in the publishing no-man's-land of western Massachusetts, our mostly young staff tended to hang out together after work; many friendships and three marriages resulted. It's still not clear which was worse, our office parties or our softball team.

Our quarters in an old brass mill were cramped and usually stifling. The ceilings leaked water and fine grit, and on hot evenings gnats got through the screens and were incorporated into layouts. Until it was found floating belly-up one morning, the fact-checking department had a pet fish called TK, and the official ban on dogs in the office was routinely ignored. Dress was casual, editorial meetings anarchic (one was conducted entirely in falsetto). Two of my favorite moments:

Woman on the phone to a gentleman of a certain age: "Hello, Mister Watkins? My name is Cathy Harding; I'm a fact-checker for *New England Monthly* magazine. . . . No, Mr. Watkins, not hat-checker, *fact*-checker."

An uncharacteristic lull settles over the cavernous room that houses editorial staff. In the hush our first and most devoted fact-checker's voice booms out, "I'd just like to check that spelling: is that B-U-C-K-Y? B-E-A-V-E-R?"

Three days later we were lugging our boats along a discreet fishermen's path to the eastern shore of Lake Clear. The day was bright and chilly, but not as bad as the ones Sears encountered in the summer of 1883, when unseasonable cold settled over the entire Northeast. On August 4 of that year New Hampshire's *Concord Monitor* noted that many families were cutting short their vacations and those who stuck it out at White Mountain resorts "are reported to sit huddled around the fires, and not venturing out of doors without thick overcoats."

Our arrival at a wide beach surprised about fifty common mergansers, who erupted en masse and half-ran, half-flew over the surface until they were safely offshore. Like loons, mergansers have wings that are essentially a compromise between the mechanics needed for flight and for underwater maneuvering. Unable to spring straight into the air like mallards, which have more wing surface, mergansers must skitter awkwardly over the water, particularly on windless days, to gain sufficient speed to get airborne.

Lake Clear is essentially round, and small enough that most of it was visible from the beach. Houses and cottages line the south and east shores, where the highway provides access. To the northwest looms Saint Regis Mountain. Since we could not camp on the lake (you can now, thanks to a state purchase), we had brought no gear, and our unweighted boats felt preternaturally responsive. This became less pleasant as the wind picked up and began nosing us around, a phenomenon known as weathervaning. After the murk of Upper Saranac the water seemed transparent, but then, it always has. "One can look away down into its depths, and see the white pebbles on its gravelly bottom, twenty or thirty feet beneath him," S. H. Hammond observed in 1854.

Here Sears once again had rotten luck, getting soaked in a squall as he paddled from the west shore to Joe Baker's camp. He huddled by the cookstove all evening and then, to his irritation, was forced to lay over another day while a steady rain drummed on the roof. "I relieved the tedium," he reported, "by playing the mouth organ for Joe's children, talking to anybody who would listen, and baking my mouth with five-cent cigars." Happily, August 6 dawned bright and cold, and Baker's horses took him over the muddy, two-mile Saint Germain Carry to Upper Saint Regis Lake.

Ten years after Sears's visit, the Mohawk and Malone Railway (later the New York Central) pushed through and ignited a local boom, a process that was repeated throughout the Adirondacks in those years. "Lakes which had been one to two days' travel from the nearest railroad found themselves within sight of the new line," wrote historian Harold K. Hochschild. "Remote forest retreats blossomed into thriving summer resorts." In 1906, when Paul Smith built an electric railroad to connect his resort to the main line, the Saint Germain Carry fell out of use. Now the railroads are also dead, but they are not yet gone. The New York Central's rusting rails are visible between Lake Clear's south shore and the highway, and Paul Smith's line can be deduced from the ghostly right-of-way that dodges back and forth across the highway heading north.*

We paddled past a phalanx of cottages to the northeast shore, where Baker's camp stood. (Baker was born Joseph Boulanger, but Americans couldn't get their tongues around that.) Over the years the Baker property metamorphosed into the four-story Lake Clear Inn, now no more than a hole in the lakeside foliage. Continuing our counterclockwise tour, we made for the western side of the lake, where one summer in the 1930s Albert Einstein occupied a cottage. (When he was a boy, local historian John J. Duquette saw Einstein sailing a catboat on a nearby lake. He and a couple of friends swam out, hoping for an autograph. "Go 'way," said the great man.)

From the middle of the lake, away from the screening shoreline vegetation, we saw what a nineteenth-century tourist would have termed a sublime prospect. The horizon was ringed with peaks, a circle of water encircled by mountains, continuity made manifest. Bobbing beneath the bright blue vault of the sky, I could have been centered in an enormous paperweight.

It was dark the next morning when we grabbed breakfast and dropped a car at Little Clear Pond, where we planned to emerge in three days. This was the last leg of our northward journey, our turnaround point at Paul Smith's College. By the time we reached Upper Saint Regis Lake, the sky had bright-

* While Sears objected to many of the technological advances of his day, he appreciated railroads, particularly the one beside Pine Creek, west of Wellsboro, where he liked to camp. "On the whole, I rather like it," he wrote in 1884. "A train does not stop to go marauding about my camp, nosing around to steal whisky and loose duffle, as the old-time logger did. And I cannot see that the railroad interferes with the game or fish. . . . Moreover, when I am ready to break camp I can step on to a car, take a cushioned seat, and in an hour or two be at my own door. Only four years ago this would have called for an exhaustive, all-day, up-and-down tramp with a heavy load."

ened and tatters of mist were curling off the water. Saint Regis Mountain, a constant presence now, bulked up in the west. Once again we were alone on the water.

Upper Saint Regis is the southernmost of three interconnected lakes, and boasts the most elegant real estate on our route. Thousands of acres in this area were once owned by Paul Smith, who sold lots to longtime guests of his hotel, most of them millionaires. Among the early residents were the yachtsman Frederick W. Vanderbilt, the journalist Whitelaw Reid, and the financier Anson Phelps Stokes. The camps many of these families built began as tent colonies, with separate units for sleeping, dining, games, and so on, and evolved into permanent structures built with understated taste. Far more modest than the Great Camps to the south, they demonstrate Old Money's preference for comfort rather than show. Because these properties have been passed down from generation to generation, there is little of the subdivision that has cluttered other lakefronts. Camps here are tucked discreetly into the woods and set at some distance from one another, which gives the place a subdued elegance.

The substantial boathouses sprinkled around the shores shelter lovingly preserved sailboats, canoes, and guideboats. So genteel is Upper Saint Regis that it has its own sailing club, founded in 1897 by summering New York Yacht Club members, and its own sailboat, the Idem class, a dozen of which were built to race on these waters. (*Idem* is Latin for "the same"; all boats shared one design to ensure that the skill of their crews would prevail.) Several other one-design classes also compete under the Saint Regis Yacht Club banner, and Upper Saint Regis and adjacent Spitfire Lake are dotted with turn markers.

It was only two weeks before Sears paddled through Upper Saint Regis that Anson Phelps Stokes moved his family from New York to Birch Island for the summer. In *Camp Chronicles,* his daughter Mildred Phelps Stokes Hooker recalled the Gilded Age on the lake: a bejeweled woman and tuxedoed partner paddling their canoe to a dinner party, Sunday morning boat races to church, lean-to parties, the White House chef brought in to help out. "When father had our little log playhouse built as a surprise, it was 'Goldilocks Hall,'" Mrs. Hooker reported, "and when he first led us to it there was a bear looking out of the window. That same bear is old now, and tame, and Alice has taught him to stand in her living cabin and hold umbrellas."

My favorite among this grande dame's stories concerns another bear, a trained female who was performing at Paul Smith's hotel. One day she slipped her tether and wandered off into the woods. Her owner was understandably agitated: the bear was his livelihood, but more than that, she had been raised in captivity and knew nothing of survival in the wild. Fearing that she would starve, he assembled a search party. Men fanned out through the woods, and at length one of them came upon his quarry in a clearing. She was all alone, assiduously performing her routine in the hope of being fed. I can see it now, the shambling waltz, the pirouette, the somersault, the bow, the silent spruces, the baffled creature starting over again.

We paddled the eastern shore and at one house counted eleven boats strewn around a dock. A little farther along stood a water mansion, a massive boathouse with five bays below and two stories of living quarters above. The building was contemporary, but it echoed the Great Camp style so successfully it might have been there for a century. Smoke curled lazily from its chimney as a man in a dressing gown—Jay Gatsby?—leaned on a verandah railing with his mug of coffee.

On a point nearby stood a handsome wooden pagoda belonging to the camp Frederick Vanderbilt bought in 1902. The Vanderbilts had just returned from the Far East and were smitten with all things oriental. To remodel their camp they hired the Asian crew that had just built the Japanese village at the Pan-American Exposition in Buffalo. But the Vanderbilts didn't stop there, Mrs. Hooker reported: "They not only had the cabins Japanized, they dressed all their maids in kimonas! They had taken over a stout English maid of Mother's and she nearly died of embarrassment when she had to appear before us in this odd new uniform."

A short, narrow channel (locally a "slough," pronounced *slew*) led us to Spitfire Lake, where the chockablock far shore was an abrupt return to Adirondack reality. Near the entrance lay a small atoll bearing a plaque identifying it as Rabbit Island. Here the pioneer tuberculosis researcher Edward Livingston Trudeau kept a colony of rabbits to study the effects of environment on the disease. Another Paul Smith client who liked the area so much he bought land from his host, Trudeau was so debilitated by TB when he visited in 1873 that it appeared he might die at Smith's hotel. (A guide who carried him upstairs to his room remarked that he weighed no more than a lambskin.) But the fresh air agreed with him, and a year after Sears paddled past Rabbit Island, Trudeau established the country's first private, nonprofit sanatorium in nearby Saranac Lake. Thousands sought a cure there, including Robert Louis Stevenson, Eugene O'Neill, and Branch Rickey. The revered doctor died in 1915 but the sanatorium continued until 1954 when, thanks in part to its own research, drug therapy replaced older regimens.

The wind was rising, wrinkling the waves and tugging at our paddle blades. Sears had worse problems here, when a "flawy" wind drove him ashore and forced him to bushwhack to the outlet. Still, it was a relief to slip into the protection of the marsh that separates Spitfire from Lower Saint Regis. Just one more lake—a small one, at that—and we'd reach Paul Smith's College. From there our bows would turn south, and with any luck the winds would make their autumnal shift to the north to speed us along. Belatedly I realized that this was a special morning. Why hadn't I thought to bring a split of champagne?

9
TURNAROUND

IT MUST HAVE BEEN A WONDERFUL MOMENT, in the nineteenth century, when one emerged from the slough to Lower Saint Regis Lake and found arrayed on the far shore the rambling white frame buildings of Paul Smith's hotel. The most fashionable hostelry in the Adirondacks, from the very first it was a playground for the elite, from presidents (Cleveland, Harrison, Theodore Roosevelt, and Coolidge) to celebrities (P. T. Barnum) to the lower-profile powers who financed and guided American business. According to W. H. H. Murray, Paul Smith's was "the St. James of the wilderness. Here Saratoga trunks and Saratoga belles are known. Here they have civilized 'hops,' and that modern prolongation of the ancient war-whoop modified and improved, called 'operatic singing,' in the parlors." To S. R. Stoddard the place was "an astonishing mixture of fish and fashion, pianos and puppies, Brussels carpeting and cowhide boots."

Formally the Saint Regis House but seldom called that, Paul

Smith's opened in 1859 as a woodland retreat for wealthy hunters and their families, and for many years its ambience was resolutely primitive, its amenities including neither bellboys nor indoor bathrooms. Originally the building had seventeen bedrooms, but like nacre around a grain of sand, ells and floors and annexes and cottages accreted until, by the early 1900s, 225 units had materialized. Scattered around the main complex were a garden, stables, a boathouse with sleeping quarters for sixty guides, a casino with bowling alley and billiards (and a direct wire to the New York Stock Exchange), a smithy, woodworking and electrical shops, a laundry, icehouse, staff dormitories, a four-story warehouse, a sawmill and planing mill, an office, and a store. Until 1912, when the electric railroad took over, a fleet of stagecoaches connected the hotel with the outside world. ("Coaches arrive every day," Sears wrote, "quite after the style of fifty years ago. Full inside, six on top; guard playing a loony tune on a preposterously long tin horn.") Paul Smith's had its own post office and telegraph and, eventually, a telephone exchange. In later years Smith built water-powered generators to service his empire and neighboring towns.

By day the guests fanned out on strolls or hikes (climbing Saint Regis Mountain was de rigueur) or took to the water with their guides for fishing, hunting, picnicking, and botanizing. "When evening comes at Paul Smith's," wrote A. Judd Northrup, "the long parlor is brilliantly lighted. At the piano is seated a lady in elegant summer costume. . . . By her side . . . stand men of faultless attire and foreign speech. . . . There are social games, sober family gatherings and flirtations in the nooks and corners, and in the office letter-writing and newspaper reading. . . . Meanwhile, the long verandah is crowded with easy chairs, and the fragrant Havana mingles its perfume with the aroma of balsam and spruce and pine. . . . At ten o'clock everybody goes to bed."

Presiding over all this activity was the genius of the place,

Apollos A. Smith, who in his youth had served his affluent patrons as a guide. The term most often applied to Smith, usually with some admiration, is "shrewd." He believed he had been "born smart" and that formal education made fools of men. Early on, he understood the value of land and set about acquiring thousands of acres of surrounding woodland, which he parceled out to favored guests. His real estate operations were breathtaking in their canniness. In one transaction he acquired thirteen thousand acres for twenty thousand dollars, then turned around and sold five acres of it for the same figure. It didn't hurt that he was the only game in town: once he had sold his well-heeled clients their lots, his sawmill provided the lumber to build their camps and his store the supplies to run them. By all accounts, Smith was a charmer. He loved a good story and was renowned for a quick and sly wit. Whatever their station, he treated everyone the same way, with a kind of amused tolerance. While Smith held court on the verandah, his wife, Lydia, made the place work. She handled all behind-the-scenes management.

The hotel was expensive, but its exclusivity, coupled with its proprietor's irreverence, was part of its appeal. The three-dollar-per-day charge for a room (children and servants half price) was only the opening wedge in the business of separating guests from their green, an art so refined by the host that he was soon a wealthy man himself. One widely circulated tale concerns a pair of boots—or a barrel of flour, whichever you prefer. A clerk in the hotel store confessed that someone had come in that day and charged the item, but in the flurry of business he had forgotten who it was. Smith's solution: add the item to everyone's bill; most would never notice, and if someone complained the charge could be removed. (Only two protests were registered.) Smith died in 1912 but the hotel continued under a son's direction until it burned to the ground in 1930.

~~~
~~~

When Sears paddled out of the slough, in August 1883, the hotel was still relatively modest in scale. It was only a mile from the inlet, but getting the *Sairy Gamp* across the lake proved something of an adventure. Again the northeast wind drove Sears ashore, this time at Peter's Rock, a broad granite point named for Mitchell Sabattis's father. Sears was close enough to the hotel to watch couples promenading and children playing, but he was hopelessly windbound. "So I amused myself," he reported, "by putting a board shanty which stands on the rocky point in order, picking blueberries, cutting wild grass and making believe I was going to camp all night within one hundred and fifty rods of a first-class hotel." An attempted crossing late in the afternoon nearly capsized him, and he decided to wait for evening, when the wind would drop. He had been seen, however, and soon two guides rowed over to give him a tow. Despite his embarrassment he accepted, he said, because the hotel's guests were "anxious to see the little canoe and the little old woodsman who had paddled and carried her over 118 miles." Among the admirers was Paul Smith himself, who entertained his latest arrival with tales of his guiding days and, according to Sears, fell in love with the *Sairy Gamp*.

As you emerge from the marsh today, the view is of the assorted wood and brick buildings of Paul Smith's College, a small two-year school established with the old man's legacy. It's ironic that Smith, who liked to say "There's no fool like an educated fool," should have ended up bankrolling a college, but the school's original specialties, forestry and hotel administration, were businesses he understood well.

Our northernmost lake greeted us, as it had Sears, with a dancing chop, but its water was as murky as Upper Saranac's had been. From Peter's Rock we were able to see why Sears had been so frustrated: the north shore is tantalizingly near. Under way once more, our problem proved the opposite of his, the wind chivvying us along from behind and driving us headlong into the stacked waves at the shore. In the foamy wrack at water's edge a small catfish lay on its side, gills barely moving. John nudged it back into the water and watched it float woozily off.

We scrambled up the bank and exchanged high fives and a kiss. A year ago I had driven in and stood here, wondering whether this day would actually come and imagining the rush of accomplishment we'd feel after paddling and portaging ninety-odd miles. The moment wasn't quite the triumph I'd envisioned, no Mormon Tabernacle Choir, no throng of admiring onlookers. My bladder was full, my fanny numb. Okay, strike the choir and crowds; I'd settle for a cup of coffee.

Reconnoitering the campus, we found the snack bar closed, the library dark, the place as deserted as if a smart bomb had fallen. We had forgotten that it was Sunday. We found a log drawn up at the waterfront and sat down to contemplate a view that thousands of rusticators have enjoyed. In 1860 a journalist named W. C. Prime visited Paul Smith's and described an echo from the far shore: "The distance over and back requires about ten seconds, and hence a long bugle note . . . may be given on the piazza, and a few seconds of silence follow, and then out of the distant forest, across the lake, the notes come back with a sweetness that can not be imagined." No one today seems to know about this phenomenon. Perhaps the echo was stilled when the giant white pines were logged off, but I have my own theory. I think it died the day the stagecoaches stopped rolling up to the door with their corny fanfare. I like to imagine the last note of the final loony tune, as Sears called it, hanging over the lake forever.

Prime's visit was full of nostalgia. "One who has in former years lived much in the woods," he observed, "forms a stronger attachment for that life than a man ever forms for any other. . . . I walked down to the beach, and, pushing off one of the canoe-like boats, paddled away into the moonlight on the water, and then lay still, listening to the old familiar sounds—the wind, the short yelp of a dreaming hound in some camp, the rush of a hungry trout seeking his food . . . and constantly that laugh of the loon, varied now and then by his long, mournful cry."

The voice of the north woods also beguiled Theodore Roosevelt, who as a boy made several trips to Paul Smith's. A myopic child, he had compensated by developing an acute ear for birdsong, and by the time the eighteen-year-old Teddy arrived with a Harvard friend in June of 1877, he was an accomplished naturalist. The notes from this and previous journeys resulted in his first contribution to natural history, *The Summer Birds of the Adirondacks in Franklin County, N.Y.*, in which he listed ninety-seven species, some rare, that he had seen in the area.

The two weeks Roosevelt spent here in 1877 proved a revelation. His previous visits had all been in August, when birds were scarce and mostly silent. Now they were everywhere, their plumage as bright as it would be all year, their songs lasting late into the evening. Among his notes was this description of an encounter with a hermit thrush:

> Its song, which is uttered until the middle of August, is very beautiful and peculiar to itself; . . . there is a weird, sad beauty in it which attracts the attention of the most unobserving, and once heard it can never be forgotten. It sings in the early dawn, at sunset, and if cloudy often through the entire day. I have even heard it at night. Perhaps the sweetest bird music I have ever listened to was uttered by a hermit thrush. It was while hunting deer on a small lake in the heart of the wilderness; the night was dark, for the moon had not yet risen, but there were clouds, and as we moved over the surface of the water with the perfect silence so strange and almost oppressive to the novice in this sport, I could distinguish dimly the outlines of the gloomy and impenetrable pine forests by which we were surrounded. We had been out for two or three hours but had seen nothing; once we

> heard a tree fall with a dull, heavy crash, and two or three times the harsh hooting of an owl had been answered by the unholy laughter of a loon from the bosom of the lake, but otherwise nothing had occurred to break the death-like stillness of the night; not even a breath of air stirred among the tops of the tall pine trees. Wearied by our unsuccess we at last turned homeward when suddenly the quiet was broken by the song of a hermit thrush; louder and clearer it sang from the depths of the grim and rugged woods, until the sweet, sad music seemed to fill the very air and to conquer for the moment the gloom of the night; then it died away and ceased as suddenly as it had begun. Perhaps the song would have seemed less sweet in the daytime, but uttered as it was, with such surroundings, sounding so strange and so beautiful amid these grand but desolate wilds, I shall never forget it.

Six years later, while Paul Smith was regaling Sears with the choicest of his well-worn yarns, Roosevelt had just returned to Long Island from the Richfield Springs resort he so thoroughly detested. His summer had been, he said, a "nightmare," but things were bound to get better. His wife, Alice, was pregnant with their first child, and his reelection to a third term in the New York Assembly that fall seemed assured. Yet six months later his world was shattered. His wife and his mother, the two people he most loved, died on the same day, Alice of Bright's disease after delivering a daughter, his mother of typhoid fever.

The boy who was enthralled by a hermit thrush was vice president in September 1901, when he returned to the Adirondacks to climb Mount Marcy. While descending he learned that the assassinated McKinley was dying, and by the time he reached North Creek, after a harrowing nighttime gallop, he was president. Roosevelt went on to become one of this country's most influential conservationists. His lifelong appreciation of wilderness, it could be argued, was born here, at Lower Saint Regis Lake.

We sat on our log and ate apples as the wind bulled around us. An overcast was creeping across the sky to the southwest. It was too late in the year for the fluting of thrushes, but we could still experience some of the things Roosevelt did in 1877. Cloud shadows still chase each other down the flanks of Saint Regis Mountain, and waves still rhythmically slap the shore. A few massive white pines give voice to the breeze, and across the way Peter's Rock slopes gently down to the water the way it did one, two, many centuries ago.

> TROY, N.Y., Aug. 8.—Joseph L. Newell, the well-known Adirondack Mountain guide, was drowned yesterday near Paul Smith's, in the Adirondacks, by the upsetting of a boat. It is supposed he was attacked with heart disease. He had been guiding A. E. Douglass, of New-York, who fell into the pond when the boat upset, but swam ashore.
>
> *NEW-YORK TIMES*
> AUGUST 9, 1883

It was a fine evening at Paul Smith's. Sears was standing in front of the hotel, talking with some guides, when a boat raced from the outlet to the beach. As Sears recounted the scene, the newcomer strode up to the group with the tidings:

"Boys, Joe Newell's drowned."

"Where? When? How?" were the hurried questions.

"In Follensby, Jr. [Pond]. Two hours ago; fell out of his boat somehow and tangled up in the lily-pads."

There was silence and soberness among the guides. Finally one remarked, "Somebody ought to tell his wife."

"Jim, you go up and tell her."

"I—I can't. I've got to wash my boat and take my party up the lake. Why don't you go?"

"Wouldn't do it for a hundred dollars. Let the clerk send a boy."

Two days later, at 4:30 A.M., Sears slipped the *Sairy Gamp* into the water for her journey south. Only the night watchman was present to see him disappear into the gloom. That same day, in Wickes, Montana, Chester Gillette was born, a boy whose destiny was to drown his girl in a lonely cove on an Adirondack lake.

In Sears's time, as now, a popular day trip called the Seven Carries linked Paul Smith's with Upper Saranac Lake. Instead of trying a new route, however, Sears retraced his steps to Joe Baker's, on Big Clear Pond, and then enlisted a young man to help him with the half-mile carry to Little Clear. Why did he pass up a chance to see something different? I suspect the idea of seven portages, even short ones, was more than a man in his condition could face. To us the Seven Carries sounded far too romantic to bypass. We would tackle it tomorrow; today, since rain was predicted, we would shoot for the only lean-to on Upper Saint Regis.

We left our turnaround point unceremoniously, fighting our way out of the shallows toward the slough. In the twisting, marshy channel the wind was riffling the surface with wonderful patterns, tweeds, seersuckers, herringbones, corduroys. Emerging into Upper Saint Regis was like stepping into a wind tunnel and presented us with the usual dilemma: hugging the shore was safer, but the turbulence there was harder to handle.

Directly in front of us lay Birch Island, where in July 1883 Anson Phelps Stokes and his family were living in tents. Of the nine children, the most intriguing was Graham. On April 6, 1905, page one of the *New York Times* carried the headline "J. G. PHELPS STOKES TO WED YOUNG JEWESS." The woman in question was Rose Pastor, a socialist writer and labor organizer with green eyes and a mane of titian hair. She was a working-class girl who had spent fourteen hours a day rolling cigars and surreptitiously reading books concealed under her apron. Her poetry attracted notice, and in time she became a columnist for the *Jewish Daily News.*

While Rose's milieu was the tenement, the Phelps Stokeses shuttled, according to the season, from a mansion on Murray Hill to a summer home on Connecticut's Long Island shore to a hundred-room castle in Lenox, Massachusetts. In *"The Rest of Us,"* Stephen Birmingham tells of one of the boys wiring his mother at Lenox, ARRIVING THIS EVENING WITH CROWD OF NINETY-SIX MEN, to which she replied MANY GUESTS ALREADY HERE. HAVE ONLY ROOM FOR FIFTY. A Yale graduate who sailed and played tennis and belonged to all the right clubs, Graham had developed a social conscience and was working, as he would for many years, at the University Settlement House on the Lower East Side and living nearby. Sent to interview him, Rose fell in love, and her feelings were reciprocated. The fiancées were besieged by the press, and Rose became the Jewish Cinderella.

To her credit, she never forgot her working-class roots. She campaigned, spoke, marched, and demonstrated on behalf of labor and women's issues, and was badly beaten for her beliefs. Tried for sedition during the First World War, she eventually helped found the American Communist party. What was remarkable about the marriage was not so much that it occurred as that it lasted twenty years, as Rose became increasingly radical and Graham increasingly conservative. They were divorced in 1925.

After a short but difficult pull to the west, we rounded a point and put the wind squarely at our backs. Now we were able to look around and enjoy the muted opulence of Upper Saint Regis. The handsomest of these camps bring to mind the world E. L. Doctorow created in *Loon Lake,* a world of private railroad cars and seaplanes and mahogany runabouts, of cavernous stables and boathouses and hangars, of tennis courts and sailboats and bridle trails, all of it maintained by legions of servants for owners who appear for a few weeks each year.

We might have been the only people alive as we made our way up North Bay, a cul-de-sac of still, black water. The lean-to sat far up a slope, in a stand of yellow birch and hemlock, and it was unoccupied. Our timing couldn't have been better: a gentle rain began as we hauled our boats onto the bank and humped our gear up the hill. A routed sign announced that the shelter had been built by Rec. 242 (a Paul Smith's College class?) in the summer of 1974. Nice job, 242, particularly the waist-high shelf that made food preparation so easy. Obviously a student hangout, the lean-to walls were covered with sexual graffiti and sophomoric wit (another oxymoron).

In midafternoon we fell asleep, lulled by a light rain pattering on the roof, and were wakened by the chippering of red squirrels and the *yank-yank* of red-breasted nuthatches. From time to time the quiet was broken by loon laughter echoing down the bay. We brewed tea and relished the warmth curling into our bodies. The season was indeed changing.

The intermittent rain continued. I had fantasized, before we set out, that we would lounge beside a snapping fire late into the evening, talking, thinking, listening to the night sounds. This never happened. There is no comfortable place to lounge in the woods: stumps and logs and lean-to floors, even softened with a life jacket, soon tire the back and numb the backside. Moreover, it took too many ergs, after a day of paddling and portaging, to gather enough wood for dinner, dishwashing, and extended navel-gazing. We found that once our chores were done, unconsciousness was not far behind. As the days grew shorter we were sleeping longer, about eleven hours a night. A cumulative fatigue was seeping into our bones, as if nature was preparing us for winter. Our notion of time was changing, too. The day of the week and the date had become irrelevant; what mattered were the number of hours of daylight remaining each afternoon.

Our turnaround may have been anticlimactic, but once we'd swung our bows to the south, something inside both of us clicked over. For one thing, we began to relax. Autumn had emptied the Adirondacks and there was no need to fret over getting a campsite. Also, it was now clear that we could manage the physical demands of the trip. In many ways, the pressure was off. Coinciding with this relaxation of sphincters, and perhaps directly related to it, was our realization that the world we were inhabiting was essentially benign and far more beautiful than we had dreamed. We began to experience a rising bubble of delight in our surroundings, and the longer we stayed out, the less inclination we had to return to what we jokingly referred to as the real world.

UPPER SAINT REGIS LAKE TO INDIAN CARRY

A SHORT PADDLE down the west side of the bay took us to Topridge, largest of the Upper Saint Regis camps, once owned by the cereal heiress Marjorie Merriweather Post. When her father committed suicide in 1914, Mrs. Post inherited twenty million dollars and the company that became General Foods. A woman whose wealth outstripped her taste, Post's major preoccupations were entertaining and trying to spend a virtually inexhaustible legacy. At various times she owned the largest private yacht in the world, the 350-foot *Sea Cloud* (crew of seventy-two) and the largest private aircraft, a Viscount turboprop. Post had four husbands, among them the dashing financier E. F. Hutton and Ambassador to the Soviet Union Joseph Davies.

One of her estates was Mar-A-Lago, the Palm Beach showplace acquired in the 1980s by Donald Trump. Awash with marble and Spanish tile, tapestries and spurious coats of arms, the mansion was a breathtaking farrago of styles. An apocryphal but delicious story told by Post biographer William Wright is that when Harry Thaw, who killed Stanford White, saw Mar-A-Lago for the first time he said, "My God, I shot the wrong architect." My favorite Post tale took place in Washington during the Second World War, when Mrs. P. was rolling bandages for the Red Cross. One day she leaned over to the woman next to her and said, "Tell me, what time is it, dear? They forgot to wind my watch this morning."

The sixty-odd buildings of Camp Topridge are scattered along a steep esker. From the water you can see very little beyond a massive boathouse whose roof is supported by whole tree trunks and the rails of a funicular built to whisk guests up the ridge. At peak occupancy the camp employed about eighty-five staff, including seven full-time guides and a man who sat all day whittling artistically curled kindling for the guest cottages. A full-sized replica of a Russian dacha, complete with tile stove, was used for evening square dances.

Guests would be flown on Post's plane from Washington or New York to the airstrip near Saranac Lake. Limos took them to her private dock, where a launch waited to take them to camp. Life at Topridge was highly organized: guests were expected to appear promptly for meals, to dress for dinner, and to stay reasonably sober. There was plenty to do: tennis, hiking, fishing, swimming, sailing, rowing, and canoeing. There were first-run movies and dinners served on rafts in the middle of the lake, with courses sent out by relays of boats. If nothing else appealed, a group might fly to Boston for a meal. A standard outing was something called a carry, in which guests were taken across the lake in guideboats and then led along a trail to a nearby pond. Each person was encouraged to get into the portaging spirit by carrying some small item—a frying pan, blanket, or hamper—to the picnic ground, where the guides prepared a meal. A specialty of these al fresco offerings was an infarctial concoction called Adirondack pie, mounds of pancakes layered with maple sugar and then drenched in maple syrup.

The last gala weekend was held in 1972; when the mistress of Topridge died the following year, the property was given to the State of New York, which had no real use for it. Empty for years, it was bought in 1985 for less than a million dollars by Roger Jakubowski, a former arm-wrestling promoter who had made his fortune selling hot dogs at the New Jersey shore. A collective frisson may have swept the Upper Saint Regis colony at the idea of a brash, fast-talking arriviste as master of Topridge, but there were also inescapable parallels between the old and new owners. Both of their fortunes derived from the food business. Both transcended a limited education to invent themselves in the American tradition. Both had generous egos and voracious appetites for acquisition. And if Jakubowski's origins were not exactly *Social Register* material, neither were Post's: her father once peddled suspenders door-to-door.*

Topridge was deserted as we paddled past. A skeleton staff now looks after the place, yet things looked spruce enough. The boathouse was immaculate, with red geraniums spilling from waterside planters, and a sailboat, *Hot Dog* lettered on its transom, bobbing in one of the slips.

The day was cool, with a low ceiling that hid the lookout tower atop Saint Regis Mountain. Soon I was joined by a monarch butterfly, which zigzagged along just above my head and kept pace with the *Sairy Damp*. We had seen them over every lake, a tide of orange and black pulsing southward, hitching rides on thermals to ease a journey that for some of them stretches twenty-five hundred miles, all the way from Canada to

* Eventually even the master of Topridge fell victim to the national recession. In the spring of 1993 a New Jersey bank foreclosed on Jakubowski, seeking $1.5 million owed on his mortgage. The 207-acre estate and its furnishings were offered at public auction in April, but no buyer stepped forward.

a winter roost on a fir tree in the mountains of Mexico. From time to time this one looped off to the east, but to my surprise it kept reappearing. I was sorry when it fluttered off ahead, leaving me to my thoughts and the *plip-plop, plip-plop* of my paddling.

We meandered along the shore, lusting after a succession of camps. I was passing a shingle-style masterpiece when a gust of music spilled down the lawn and across the water. It was a classical piece I didn't recognize, heavy on strings. I rested my paddle on the gunwales, closed my eyes, and rode the gentle swell as the sound flowed over me. It was the first music I'd heard since we left Old Forge, and it betokened a magical day.

The small white sign marking the start of the Seven Carries was easy to find, the first portage only two hundred feet long. A yellow Lab rushed from a nearby house to bark and feint at us and then, his job done, sidled up for petting and a smooch. So short were the carries on this route—the longest only six-tenths of a mile, most considerably less—that our pack-frame routine made no sense. Instead we doubled the carries, toting one boat at a time, right-side-up, with the lightest gear left inside.

The six chain ponds we traversed—Bog, Bear, Little Long, Green, Saint Regis, and Little Clear—have distinctly different characters. Some are tiny, some are lake-sized; some have green water, some black. They lie close together but in typical Adirondack fashion apportion their waters into three separate drainages, the first three into the Middle Branch of the Saint Regis River, the next two into the West Branch, the last into the Saranac system.

Aside from hydrology, what makes this region special is a ban on motorized traffic. In the 1970s, as adjacent areas like Fish Creek Ponds were being overrun and degraded, the state designated this the Saint Regis Canoe Area and restricted use of its fifty-eight lakes and ponds to canoeing and kayaking, fishing, snowshoeing, cross-country skiing, and temporary camping.

Paul Jamieson knew the region in the old days, when people snowmobiled here, flew in outboard motors for summer boating, and lived in permanent tent-platform camps. Now, he writes, the integrity of the place has reasserted itself, and "the new silence in this pocket-sized wilderness is wonderful." Indeed it is; it's a sanctuary, and we wondered why there aren't more of them in the park. In our day and a half there we saw one other traveler. This was as close as we would come to the world George Sears saw on much of his trip.

On tiny Bog Pond, the water was dark with the acids of decomposing plant matter. Beyond a small patch of open water lay the eponymous bog with a narrow passage snaking through banks lined with leatherleaf, bog rosemary, and cottongrass. Halfway across Bear Pond, I leaned out of my boat to pluck a stem from a raft of pink amphibious smartweed. Little Long Pond, highest in elevation, is dumbbell-shaped and surrounded by giant white pines. So quiet and wild was this spot that we could easily imagine an osprey or an eagle dropping out of the sky. Unable to tear ourselves away, we sat by the shore for half an hour and watched a green frog watch us. Next came Green Pond, small, round, and unexceptional, no islands or points to add interest. Within minutes we had cut across its northwest corner and were well along the two-hundred-yard trail to Saint Regis, largest of the six.

A big fellow in his late thirties was paddling a handsome wooden strip canoe toward the put-in as we launched. His broad-brimmed hat and tan fishing vest made him look vaguely official, but he turned out to be a tourist like us. We admired his boat and wished him luck; he was off to try his tackle on another lake. My map showed nine tent sites and one lean-to here, and while we assumed the fisherman was using the latter, we decided to check it out anyway. On the shores and islands stood enormous white pines whose limbs and bent tops, trained by the prevailing winds, all pointed to the northeast. They represented a new horticultural form, I decided: giant bonsai.

The lean-to was deserted, its graffiti first-rate.

8/24/88

KRISTEN SAID YES!

AND MADE

ME HAPPY!

IN REMEBRENCE OF A WONDERFUL BREAKFAST

6/7/82

FISHING VERY BAD. WEATHER GOOD.

THE BUGS ATE ME ALIVE.

Hey, what did you expect in June?

We again gave ourselves the afternoon off and happily settled in. The act of taking possession of a camp, strewing your gear around and arranging things according to your own sense of order, gives you a proprietary feeling for a place, and idling away some time there helps even more. While John paddled off to explore the far shore, I lounged by the water with binoculars. Directly before me Saint Regis Mountain disappeared into the clouds. The air was still, the water glassy. Nothing moved.

Wop-wop-wop-wop-wop-WOP-WOP-WOP-WOP-WOP-WOP-WOP.

Whaaaa?

A large yellow helicopter appeared from the east and passed almost directly overhead. This was puzzling; the state prohibits low-level flights here.

Wop-wop-wop-wop-wop-WOP-WOP-WOP-WOP-WOP-WOP-WOP. Twenty minutes later it reappeared, headed in the opposite direction. I could make out several figures inside the open cargo door. Most likely it belonged to the Department of Environmental Conservation; perhaps this crew was restocking a pond, replacing a privy, or repairing a lean-to.

Peace returned at suppertime. I was lolling under a pine at water's edge when in the blessed stillness I heard a different kind of droning. I looked straight up and noticed for the first time that thousands of insects—wasps or bees of some kind—were harvesting a clear nectar from the tips of the boughs. The tree sang with their labors. A little later the fisherman rounded the point to the east, beached his canoe, and disappeared into the woods. Soon we saw smoke and the glow of a campfire. I hoped he'd been lucky and was even now frying his catch.

Dusk drew us back to the shore, where we found the magic we'd experienced at Forked Lake: the hush, the deepening colors, the solid comfort of mountain and forest. A Zen garden writ large, John called it, with water in place of raked sand. We sprawled on pine duff, absorbed in our thoughts.

Fifteen yards in front of us two loons popped up and John laughed delightedly.

"What?"

"Well," he said, "I'd just told myself, 'If you were ever going to get a message from the Creator, this would be the time.' And then I thought, 'Oh, *right!* God doesn't speak; God draws pictures.' I was admiring this picture, and—boop! loons."

We had retired and were half asleep when from close by came the sound of beaver tail meeting water, followed by another slap, then another. The rhythmic whacks continued around the point and faded down the bay. Perhaps we were being rebuked for our no-doubt smelly presence, or perhaps Canada's national rodent was saluting an expatriate. I imagined Harry Radford, patron saint of Adirondack beaver, smiling with me.

Morning brought clear skies and a view of the full, imposing bulk of the mountain. We left reluctantly, paddling down the outlet bay to a plank dock thrown across the ooze of a marsh. For this longish carry we rigged boats to packs, and soon we were emerging on the shore of Little Clear Pond. Having looped to the west, we were now rejoining Sears's route. "If I wanted to go into camp for a week or two for fishing and hunting," he wrote, "I have no ground I would prefer to the pleasant, lonely banks of Little Clear Pond. It is well stocked with both lake and brook trout. And a young [man] who helped me on the carry said, 'Lake trout have been taken here weighing twenty-five pounds.'" The youth told Sears that brookies were scarcer than lake trout because the spring holes were full of ochre paint, which they disliked. Ochre paint? said Sears. Yup, said the boy, and went on to talk about deer.

Ochre paint? Well, sort of. Rust-colored deposits do form in some of these lakes; that's how Ochre Pond, not far to the northwest, got its name. The process is entirely natural, the action of iron bacteria on groundwater.*

We failed to find any ochre seepages, but all the same we enjoyed Little Clear. The lakelet is relatively pristine because fishing and camping are forbidden on its shores and islands; its waters are used by the state fish hatchery located on the outlet stream. We navigated the western shore, threaded our way between a pair of islands, and much too soon found ourselves at the boat ramp.

~~~

* John Brown, of Schenectady, a chemist and Saint Regis Canoe Area aficionado, offers this explanation. "Anaerobic groundwater, especially if charged with carbon dioxide or acid bog leachate, can dissolve a little of the iron present in the rocks and take it into solution as a ferrous (Fe++) salt. When this sort of iron-laced, anaerobic water reaches the surface and meets atmospheric oxygen, an environment is created that permits the flourishing of *aerobic* 'iron bacteria.' These peculiar microbes live on nothing but Fe++, oxygen, and carbon dioxide, which they convert to organic matter just as plants do. The product of this reaction is a hydrated ferric (Fe+++) oxide, which forms a flocculant orangish precipitate. You can often see this around springs or seepages where iron-rich water gets to the surface. Once accumulated, the chemical composition of the hydrated oxide gradually changes to a series of less hydrated forms having a variety of colors. Thus, paint pigments ranging from ochre to brown to classic barn red could all arise from the aging of the original deposits over the course of geologic time."
~~~

I believe Sears again resorted to the steamer on Upper Saranac Lake, for once more he was silent about this spectacular three-hour paddle. If so, his choice is understandable: by the time he reached the lake he had traveled twelve and a half miles, about six of them overland. Before him lay roughly seven miles of wind-scoured lake, a three-mile draw over the Sweeney Carry, and a fifteen-mile steamer trip to the head of Tupper Lake—all told, about a thirty-five-mile day. As it was, he reached his hotel in time for supper.

He would have caught the steamer at the Prospect House, whose proprietor, Ed Derby, had had a harrowing encounter the previous year. While driving his carriage to town one day, he heard cries for help issuing from the woods and discovered that a large bear had treed a guide. He grabbed his revolver and crept close enough to shoot the animal in the shoulder and head. This act served only to enrage the bear, which whirled and charged him. Derby stood his ground long enough to get off two more shots and then, noting that they had not produced the desired effect, precipitated his 230 pounds in the direction of his carriage. At this point his horses elected to remain noncombatants and departed without him.

Adrenaline is a wonderful thing: he managed to pull himself into a tree, and when the bear climbed after him emptied his revolver into it. But adrenaline is a wonderful thing for a bear, too; the animal kept coming. Derby now tried his knife, hanging with one hand while slashing at his assailant, who slashed back. Both contestants had managed to inflict several gashes when the limb from which Derby depended detached itself, leaving him on the ground with a sprained shoulder and no resolution to his problem. The bear dropped to earth and again charged; as it rose to its full height Derby plunged his knife into its heart and ended the skirmish.

The bear may have exacted a slower revenge, for the following year, on a business trip to New York City, Derby collapsed and died. But his hotel grew, prospered, and became the Saranac Inn, another mammoth clapboard community that lasted long after its contemporaries were only memories. In the early 1960s it closed, its 276 rooms left to squirrels and mice and paper wasps. A desultory salvage operation was in progress in June 1978 when it burned to the ground, leaving a gaping hole that remains to this day.

Upper Saranac was glassy when we set out at dawn, the eastern sky a preposterous shade of orange-pink above the mountains. We had not gone far when I saw, off to the left, the distinctive jagged profiles of three common loons. These were likely young of the year, congregating for their migration to the Atlantic, where they remain for two or more years until they reach sexual maturity. In the meantime, the adults return each spring to their territorial lakes to raise, if all goes well, two chicks. Best known for calls that sound like maniacal laughter, loons are the oldest birds in North America but still largely mysterious. There's so much we don't know about them: why adults and young migrate separately; how the young find their way to the ocean the first time; exactly where specific populations winter, and whether they move around; or even how returning loons time their arrival to coincide precisely with ice-out.

Like the diving ducks, loons have evolved relatively small, tapered wings. These propel them through the air at seventy-five miles an hour and through water at similarly remarkable speeds. The loon's streamlined shape is enhanced by legs set far back on the torso, almost at the tail. What's graceful underwater, however, becomes less so on land, where their gait is an ungainly shuffle. Heavy, solid bones and deflatable air sacs allow the loon to sink like a rock and to plunge as deep as 240 feet, which is why this bird is also called the great northern diver.

I had seen my first loons a few weeks before, in the Lake Temagami region of northern Ontario. On our first morning I went swimming before breakfast and noticed one fifty yards in front of me. *Hoo!* it said. *Hoo!* I said back. It dove and surfaced twenty-five feet away. *Hoo!* we both said, whereupon it again disappeared. When it bobbed up it was ten feet away and swimming in my direction, its ruby eyes intent on me. Had I said something reprehensible? Was it going to attack me with its murderous beak? Never since have I been so close to a loon, close enough to see every feather on its handsome black head. I admired its snowy chest, the striped necklace of Native American legend,* the spotted wings and back that camouflage it in gentle waves. We treaded water and stared at each other for what seemed like minutes, and then it was gone. I'm a good mimic, and on that trip I perfected two loon calls, the hoot and the tremolo, or laughter. I no longer use the latter, however; it's a distress call, and loons have enough problems without my alarming them.

Sears was paddling the *Sairy Gamp* on a lake southwest of here when, he reported, a loon "settled within ten rods of the canoe, raised himself on hind legs (they are very hind, and he has no others), turned his white, clean breast to me and gave me his best weird, strange song. Clearer than a clarion, sweeter than a flute, loud enough to be heard for miles. Never, as my soul lives, will I draw a bead on a loon. He is the very spirit of the wildwoods. Fisherman he may be. He catches his daily food after his nature. . . . Don't, please don't, emulate Adirondack Murray and waste two dozen cartridges in the attempt to demolish a loon."

* Many nations tell versions of this story. A blind boy sits beside a lake crying because he will never see the birds and animals his people describe to him. Loon hears his sobbing, draws near, and, taking pity, invites the boy to ride on his back. With the child's arms around his neck, they plunge to the bottom of the lake, and when they surface, the boy can make out dim shapes. Again and again they dive, and each time the boy's sight improves, until at last he sees the world with sparkling clarity. To thank Loon, he and his mother make a fine strand of shells and drape it around the bird's neck, where it turns into the pattern of striped feathers Loon wears to this day.

The young George Sears, undated.
(Courtesy of The Adirondack Museum)

Undated visiting card image of Sears, probably 1870s *(Courtesy of Charles Brumley)*

Sears poses for *Forest Runes* frontispiece, late 1886.

The *Sairy Gamp*:
nine feet long, twenty-six inches wide, ten and a half pounds.
(Photograph by Peter Lemon)

Forked Lake House.
(Courtesy of The Adirondack Museum)

Grove House, Long Lake;
proprietor Dave Helms *(left)* with guideboat.
(Courtesy of The Adirondack Museum)

Mother Johnson's, Raquette Falls.
(Courtesy of The Adirondack Museum)

Departure, Paul Smith's Hotel, 1880.
(Courtesy of The Adirondack Museum)

Ned Buntline's Farm on Eagle Lake;
Blue Mountain in background.
(Courtesy of The Adirondack Museum)

Alvah Dunning, circa 1891.
(Courtesy of The Adirondack Museum)

Arnold's, formerly Herreshoff Manor; "quite a tragical place."
(Courtesy of The Adirondack Museum)

The *Sairy Gamp* (left) meets the *Sairy Damp*.
(Photograph by Jim Meehan)

Day One, launch at Old Forge waterfront, in fog.
(Photograph by John Jerome)

Rising wind on Forked Lake.
(Photograph by John Jerome)

John at the foot of Long Lake.
(Photograph by Christine Jerome)

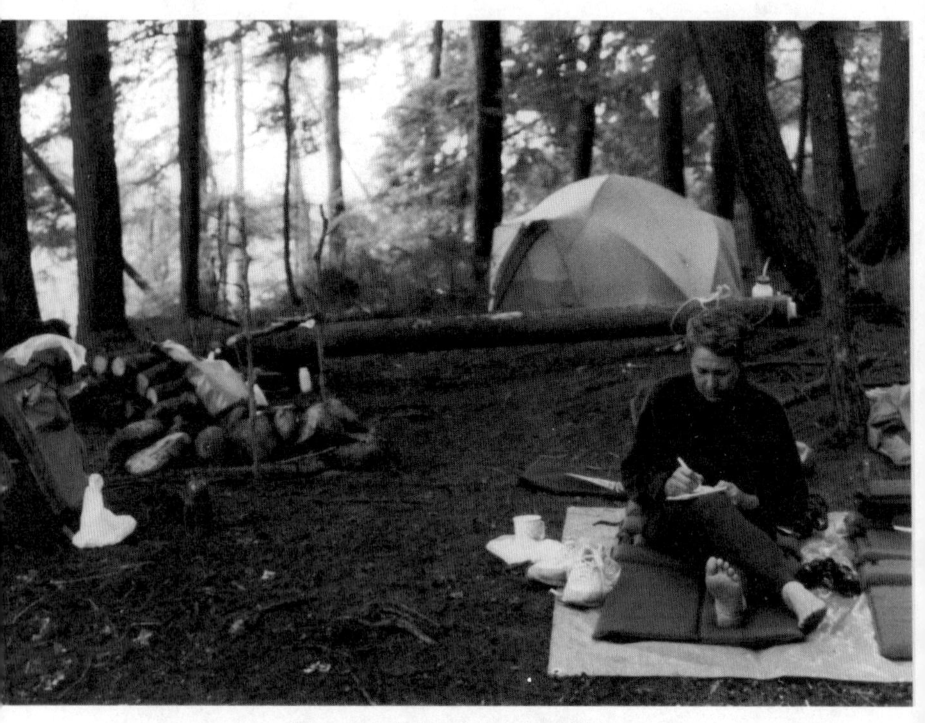

In camp, below Raquette Falls.
(Photograph by John Jerome)

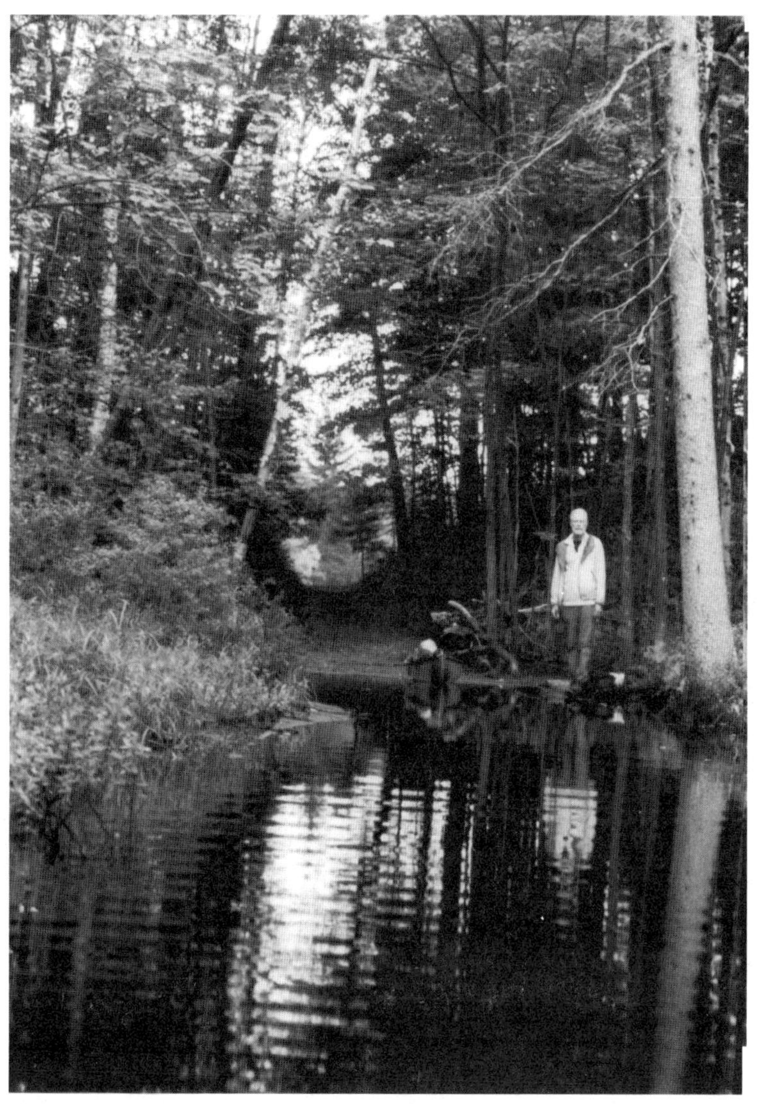

Carry from Bog Pond to Bear Pond, St. Regis Canoe Area.
(Photograph by Christine Jerome)

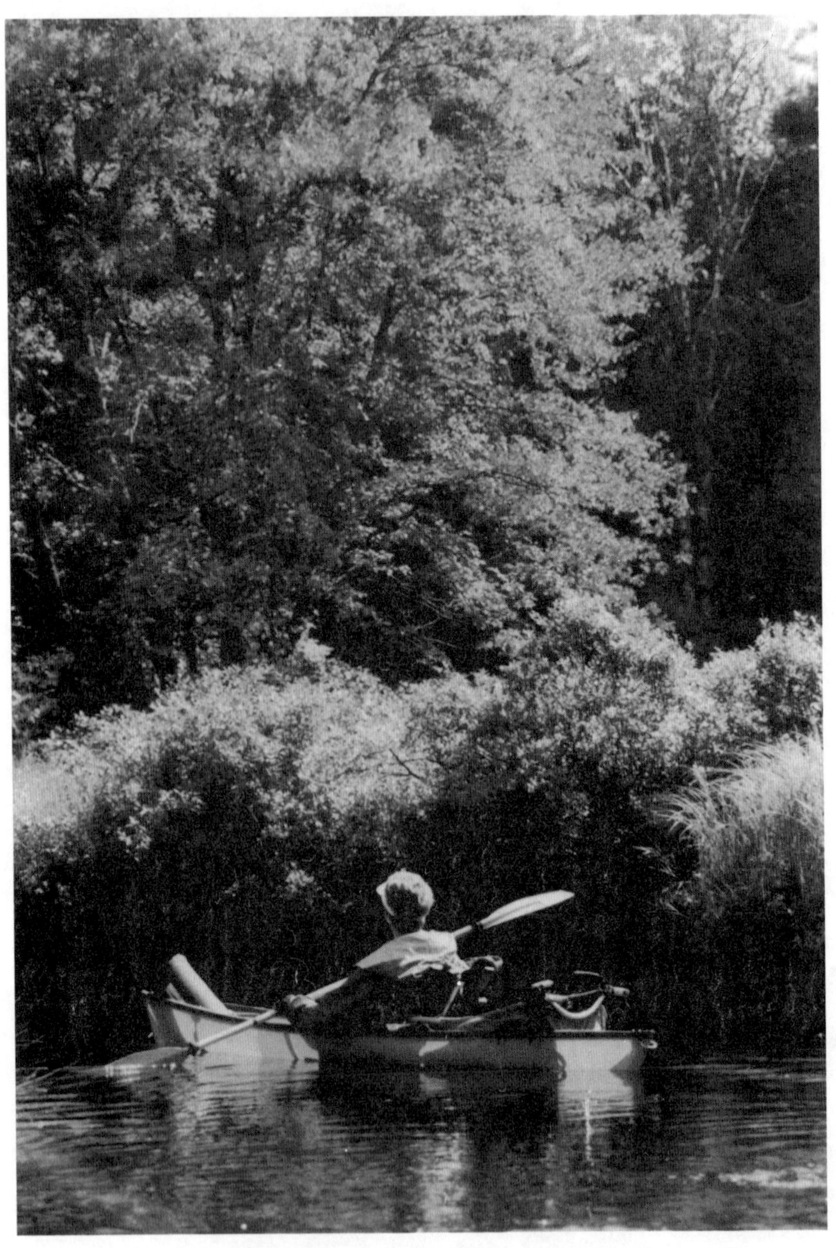

Paddling down Stony Creek in September.
(Photograph by John Jerome)

Canoes rigged to packs.
(Photograph by John Jerome)

Carry from Eighth Lake to Seventh Lake, Fulton Chain.
(Photograph by John Jerome)

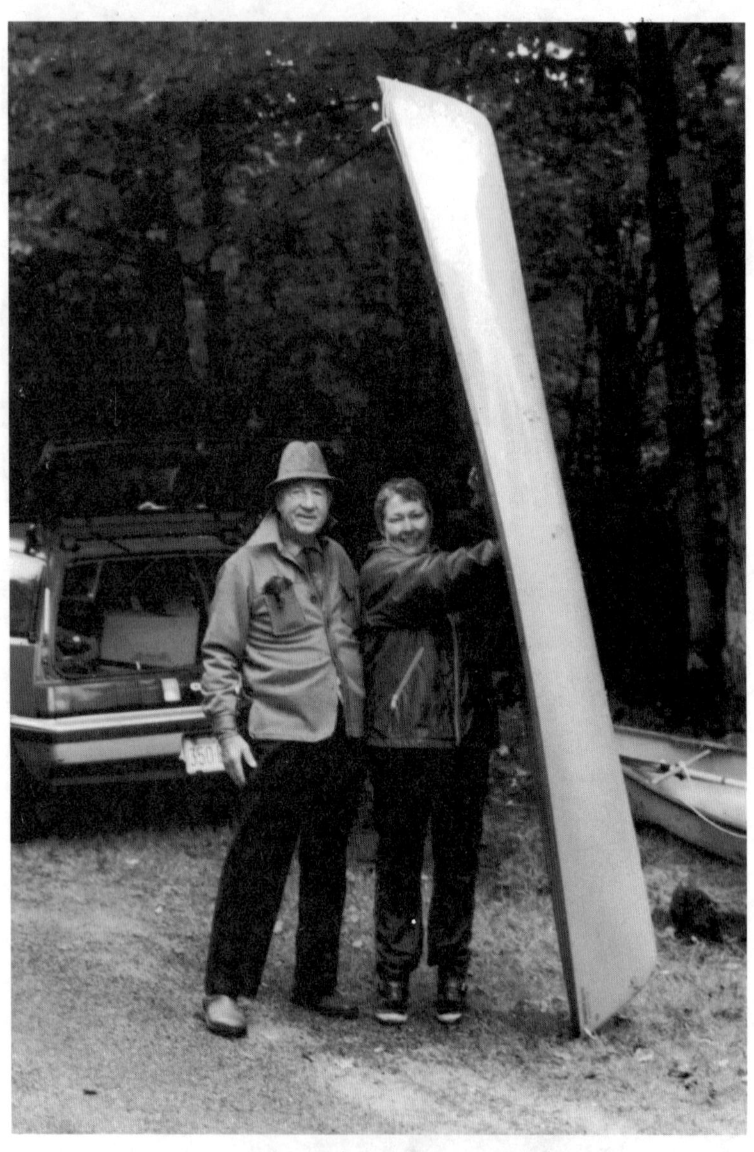

With Herm Albright at final take-out, Minnehaha.
(Photograph by John Jerome)

But shooting loons was great sport in the nineteenth century; their ability to disappear in an instant and surface far away made them challenging targets, and their skill at fishing invited persecution by human anglers, who saw them as competition. Although they were protected from gunners by 1918, their numbers have never rebounded and it seems unlikely that they ever will. The modern world offers different but no less lethal challenges to their survival: oil spills, mercury pollution in the Great Lakes, lead poisoning from ingested fishing lures, dwindling food stocks in acidified lakes, entrapment in fishing nets, loss of habitat from shoreline development, and harassment by boaters.

We canoeists like to think of ourselves as less intrusive than motorboaters, but to loons we probably represent the greater threat. More than most birds, they require privacy while brooding and raising their young. Barely able to walk on land, they build their nests right at water's edge in secluded coves and backwaters—the very places canoeists like to poke around in. In a strategy that might have been devised by Walt Disney, the fuzzy chicks often ride on their parents' backs for warmth and protection. When threatened, adults perform dazzling displays, standing up like penguins and racing across the water while their young flee to shelter in the shallows. During this separation a chick is vulnerable to attack by snapping turtles and larger fish, so if you care about loons, give adults with chicks a wide berth.

Over the past century, the common loon has responded to human encroachment by moving ever farther north. In New York State alone, biologist Judith McIntyre has determined that roughly thirty-five percent of the lakes that once hosted nesting loons have been abandoned in the last forty to seventy years. Adirondack populations, while diminished, appear relatively stable at somewhere between 216 and 270 breeding pairs. This may well change. The state's fiscal disarray has prevented it from buying and protecting choice wilderness lands just as lumber companies and private estates are putting them on the market. When these parcels fall into the hands of second-home developers, shorelines and islands sprout cottages, boathouses, and docks, and the loons fade away. In my tent at night I hear their eerie wails, hoots, yodels, and tremolos, and wonder how long this miracle can last.

We stroked slowly down the west side of Upper Saranac, past Green Bay, Moss Rock Point, Little Square Bay, Butternut Point. Far to the south, a motorboat tore silently across the lake four feet above the surface, an illusion created by humidity and refraction. By the time we were abreast of Buck Island, where we'd camped on our way north, the southwest wind had risen and John's face had tightened in pain. When he was in his late forties, he had taken up the competitive swimming he'd abandoned in college. He'd done very well in masters' competition, but the intense training eventually damaged his shoulders, and paddling aggravated the injury. Even the cortisone shot he'd taken on his recent dash home hadn't helped for long. For the next few days he was mostly a receding figure as he opted for the straightest line to each take-out. I could do nothing for him, so I poked along on my own, peeking discreetly through the greenery at a succession of Great Camps.

The character of the lake changed considerably in the thirty-odd years between Sears's visit and T. Morris Longstreth's. "At the end of every vista," Longstreth wrote, "there is a 'no trespassing' sign, actual or implied. . . . Saranac is no longer a part of the wilderness; it is a pleasure-land of great beauty. If you recognize this at the outset, there will be no disappointment. There is plenty of wilderness elsewhere, and one must not begrudge, but congratulate the millionaires upon their architects. Nature has been educated to perfect taste. The lake is eight miles long, and unless you try to find a place for your tent, you would never guess how expensive."

It would be pleasant to report that in the egalitarian north woods there was less anti-Semitism than elsewhere, but in the latter part of the nineteenth century discrimination was widespread. Private associations and hotels in the Adirondacks routinely turned away Jews ("Hebrews will knock vainly for admission" ran one dictum). Most egregious was the Lake Placid Club, founded by Melvil Dewey, father of the decimal library system and advocate of simplified spelling. His club declined to admit—or even entertain as a guest—anyone against whom there might be "physical, moral, social or race objection." This included all consumptives and Jews, "even when of unusual personal qualifications."

Understandably, Jewish families felt more comfortable in clubs and compounds of their own. When W. W. Durant was squeezed for funds in the 1890s, he sold his Upper Saranac holdings to several New York families who proceeded to build Great Camps along the southwest shore. Otto Kahn's Bull Point enclave is gone, but Adolph Lewisohn's place at Prospect Point still stands, as does Isaac N. Seligman's Fish Rock Camp and Julius Bache's Wenonah. All four men belonged to the great German Jewish families chronicled by Stephen Birmingham in *"Our Crowd,"* a breezy saga of the itinerant peddlers and small-scale retailers who rose to found some of the country's most powerful merchant and investment banking houses.

My favorite of these Jewish patriarchs is Adolph Lewisohn, whose ingenuity in the copper business made a fortune. The first of his generation to become a playboy, he lived on an extravagant scale, throwing parties at his four estates, shuttling back and forth to Europe, and supporting legions of servants, friends, and hangers-on. He did exactly as he pleased; when a son warned that he was spending his capital he responded with

Lewisohnian logic, "Who made it?" In his seventies he took up lieder singing and in his eighties, tap dancing. On his eighty-ninth birthday he partied until 3:00 A.M.

When Sears passed this way, a lone cabin marked the start of the Sweeney Carry, a well-worn trail to the Raquette River that cut about twelve miles off the route Sears had taken through Stony Creek Ponds. The spot where the cabin stood now belongs to a resort called the Wawbeek, and the northern half of the carry path has disappeared. We would take a more roundabout route and reenter the Raquette where we'd left it nine days before.

As I paddled past an island, a great blue heron uttered a disgruntled croak and flapped slowly away. I was headed for the foot of the lake, where on his way north Sears had caught his steamer at Corey's Rustic Lodge. Jesse Corey was the first white settler on Upper Saranac, although generations of Indians had built their summer encampments on the site he appropriated. The spot where he erected his hotel in 1850 lay at the north end of a mile-long barrier that separates the Saranac and Raquette watersheds. Geologists theorize that ten thousand years ago the retreating glacier deposited this narrow dam, diverting the Saranac River into a new, easterly drainage. (Another of these deposits, at Blue Mountain Lake, is thought to have turned those waters from the Hudson River system into the Raquette.)

Rustic Lodge anchored the north end of the Indian Carry, which in those days cut directly across the glacial barrier on its way to Stony Creek Ponds. In the 1890s, however, the property passed into private hands, and the new owners built a nine-hole golf course (on the meadow where the Indians were said to have planted corn) and razed the inn to make way for a mansion with thirty rooms, nineteen fireplaces, and a spectacular view of the lake. To gain some privacy, the family paid the state to move its highway away from the lakeshore, and the north half of the carry was rerouted to the edge of the property. The latter move did not sit well with local guides, whose fathers and grandfathers had been accustomed to taking the shortest way across. In 1912 they registered their disapproval by vandalizing the gate blocking the old trail, but the gate stayed put. In the early 1970s new owners were about to proceed with a large-scale development when a new regulatory body, the Adirondack Park Agency, denied a permit. Although a few homes have been tucked into the woods, the property has been saved from condoization.

Bobbing just offshore, I tried to find traces of the old carry road—"the Times Square of the woods," as Paul Jamieson puts it—over which Louis Agassiz, Ralph Waldo Emerson, James Russell Lowell, the Honorable Amelia Murray, and hosts of others once traveled. I settled on a faint grassy lane lined with old white pines, but whether this was really the trail was hard to tell. All along my route I strained for glimpses of the old carries and buildings, but in almost every case they have vanished utterly. While the historian in me was disappointed, the environmentalist rejoiced to see how quickly nature can obliterate our works. One seedling takes hold, then another, and a road reverts to forest. Weeds push up flagstones, moss colonizes a shingle roof, wind and rain splinter clapboard walls. Floors sag, joists dry into powder, sills warp, nails fall, and soon there are only wild blackberries nodding in sunny cellar holes.

11

INDIAN CARRY TO BOG RIVER

The Indian Carry follows half a mile of flat gravel road to Route 3. Until recently canoeists had to walk west along the highway, traffic whizzing by their elbows, to a paved road leading to Stony Creek Ponds, but in 1990 this unpleasant leg was replaced by a more direct path through the woods. The new trail was dedicated to Paul Jamieson, dean of Adirondack writers and emeritus professor of English at St. Lawrence University. (Not long after our trip I asked Paul if he'd gone over to take a look at the dedication plaque beside the highway. "Yes, I have," he said with a grin. "I wanted to see it before it got defaced.")

A tall, spare man who likes nothing more than, as Philip Roth put it, "turning sentences around," Jamieson has written and edited a fine body of regional literature. He has also devoted his energies to river corridor preservation, and his efforts have resulted in state acquisition of several beautiful parcels. As the years went by, however, he grew impatient with piecemeal approaches to the problem, and turned to the broader issue of navigation rights. For more than twenty years now he has waged a one-man campaign to reopen miles of waterways to the public.

There was a time when all Adirondack rivers were considered public highways and canoeists could travel hundreds of miles without impediment. But in the latter part of the nineteenth century, as wealthy individuals bought large parcels of wilderness, they closed them—and the waters that flowed through them—to the public. Barriers were thrown across rivers, and anyone who ventured beyond them was prosecuted. Private landowners were supported in their policing by law enforcement and conservation officials, and in the twentieth century the practice of posting rivers has continued on lands owned by paper companies and sporting clubs.

"It is ironic," Jamieson wrote in a 1988 article for *Adirondack Life,* "that Adirondack rivers, once they leave Park boundaries, are fully open to navigation but are wholly or partially closed inside the Park, which was dedicated in 1892 to 'the free use of all the people for their health and pleasure.'" In the rest of New York State and throughout New England, common law ensures public right of passage on navigable rivers. "Private ownership of shore and riverbed does not extend to the moving water," Jamieson pointed out; moreover, in the rest of the country, boaters have the right to put in and take out at public parks and bridges, and to use the shore when necessary to bypass dams and obstructions. After years of his polite but persistent lobbying, the Department of Environmental Conservation recently reviewed state navigation regulations and decided Jamieson was right. Thanks to him new routes should soon be opened up and older ones can begin to recover from overuse. (The *Sairy Gamp* followed the most heavily traveled route of all, what Jamieson calls "the trunk line.")

The new carry path undulated gently through a mixed hardwood forest and ended at a tidy landing on the largest of the

Stony Creek ponds. These waters were once known as the Spectacle Ponds, but since several other Adirondack lakelets bore this name, these were styled for the stream that joined them. (In the last century place names were commonly repeated from district to district. "Take Stoddard's map," Sears wrote. "You will find nine 'Clear Ponds,' seven 'Mud Ponds,' six 'Long Ponds,' six 'Wolf Ponds,' four 'Rock Ponds,' several 'Round Ponds,' etc., etc." Some repetition stands to this day: the Saint Regis Canoe Area boasts two Little Long Ponds only seven miles apart.) The small island in Second Pond was visited circa 1853 by S. H. Hammond, who found "thousands of [turtle] eggs, some on the surface and some buried in the sand." I thought I'd have a look, but a No Trespassing sign discouraged me from landing. The owners needn't have worried; the sun had brought out clouds of biting flies, and their atoll was being strenuously defended.

A narrow channel led to Third Pond (or First, if you're traveling south), where in 1883 the Hiawatha House stood. It was here that the hermit Harney had come to get a coffin made for Mother Johnson, and here Sears paused for lunch on his way north, before taking the Indian Carry to Upper Saranac. Strategically located as it was, this spot sheltered travelers long before Sears's era, although not always in comfort. In the early 1850s Hammond spent a night here, accepting his host's feather bed only to discover that he was not its only occupant. "Towards morning," he reported, "I awoke, with hundreds of fleas, and bed-bugs fast hold of me, and as many more, travelling in different directions over my bare flesh. . . . If a bed-bug or flea, would eat and lay down, I could bear them; but after feasting upon my blood, to make a highway of my body to travel round on, is a thing I can't stand." A few years later, on his way to the Philosophers' Camp, the eminent Judge Ebenezer Rockwood Hoar bedded down in the loft and was besieged all night by mosquitoes and midges. Three successive Hiawatha Houses overlooked First Pond, and two of them (possibly all three) burned. Adirondack histories are full of photographs of hotels and their smoldering ruins. Fire was used for everything—heating, cooking, lighting—but even so, the dependability of these conflagrations is striking. Almost every hotel Sears stopped at eventually burned.

At the far side of Third Pond, two channels lie side by side. One, I knew, was Stony Creek, the other Ampersand Brook, but which was which? "So near together are the inlet and outlet," Joel Headley wrote, "that one can stand on the point of land made by the two streams, and without moving from his place, fish in both." John had long since paddled off with the map, so I ventured left. Within ten feet my mistake was obvious; the aquatic grasses were bending toward me, which meant I was heading upstream, not down, and this could only be Ampersand.

It had been only nine days since we'd pulled up Stony Creek, yet now the visual spectrum had shifted. The grasses had faded from green to gold, and the leaves of the swamp maples were red and pink. It was a joy to be moving with the current, heeling around one turn after another under a bright sun, pausing only to pull the *Sairy Damp* over beaver dams. I caught up with John, and for the last mile we paddled in tandem.

The lean-to at the Raquette River was unoccupied, its graffiti the best of the trip. My favorites:

DID YOU EVER WAKE UP TO THE SOUNDS
OF YOUR PARENTS MAKING LOVE
AND GUESS FROM THEIR CRIES YOU WERE LISTENING
TO A FIGHT; WELL YOU KNOW
HATE'S JUST THE LAST THING THEY'RE THINKING OF
THEY'RE ONLY TRYING TO MAKE IT THRU THE NIGHT

HAD THE TIME OF MY LIFE
WITH THE GIRL OF MY DREAMS

A NINE MILE SKID ON A TEN MILE RIDE
HOT AS A PISTOL BUT COOL INSIDE

8/8/85
WE BAD
KEVIN - HEATHER
GERARD - MARION
MD - NY

FOURTH DAY STILL NO LUCK
LOOKS LIKE RAIN
HEADING OUT ALL HUNG OVER

YUPPIE PIGS
MUST DIE!

The lean-to is accessible from a road, and in the packed earth by the fire ring we found evidence of hard and not particularly thoughtful use: broken glass, unburned garbage, cigarette butts, twist ties. Wherever we camped, there were twist ties—paper ones, plastic ones, long ones, red, blue, yellow, and white ones, striped ones. The camp litter of the nineties, they are as ubiquitous as pop rings used to be. I always picked them up; almost everything we used was bagged in the event of a capsize, and they came in handy. As the trip wore on and the tangle in my pocket grew, I felt obscurely empowered. I was the twist tie queen, Our Lady of Perpetual Closure.

It had been a thirteen-mile day—probably fourteen for me, with side trips. In midafternoon we gave in and drifted to sleep to the nattering of chickadees and the faint voices of campers setting up nearby. At dusk, when we went down to the river to watch the light fade, we found that our neighbors had had the same idea. While the men pottered around the beach the women began singing, at first tentatively, then with shy warbles of harmony. "By the Light of the Silvery Moon" they sang, then "Home on the Range," "Shine On, Shine On, Harvest Moon," and for a finale, "Down By the Old Mill Stream" ("Not the river but the stream"). In the night came a second concert, barred owls calling to each other *Who cooks for you? Who cooks for you-ahhh?*

The singers departed just before we did. Not wanting to run up behind them, we took our time in the lingering chill and let the river do most of the work. The Raquette bore north for half a mile and then swung abruptly west at Axton, where a public boat launch was all but hidden in a plantation of evergreens. Axton ("Axe-town") was once an experimental silviculture operation managed by the Cornell School of Forestry, with a hotel, a store, a windmill, and several outbuildings on a slope that is now densely forested. In *Durand Camp,* Howard Wells remembered a 1907 visit to the Forester's Hotel: "I can recall Cousin Jennie saying to the proprietor that it seemed as though [her] sheets had been used. 'Yes,' he replied, 'they were used, but he was a nice young man.'"

For the next sixteen and a half miles the river is a maze of sweeping bends and deep backwaters lined with red and silver maples. As the current ferried us along I tried to envision the scene long ago, when the Raquette passed through what Charles Bryan described as "the finest forest in eastern North America," a hallway of deciduous and coniferous giants whose canopy formed an arch ninety feet above the water.

When William Stillman took his friends to the Philosophers' Camp on Follensby Pond, the loggers had not yet descended. "The scene, like the company," he wrote late in his life, "exists no longer. There is a river which still flows where the other flowed; but, like the water that has passed its rapids and the guests that have gone the way of all those who have lived, it is something different. Then it was a deep, mysterious stream meandering through unbroken forests, walled up on either side in green shade, the trees of centuries leaning over to welcome and shelter the voyager, flowing silently in great sweeps of dark water, with, at long intervals, a lagoon setting back into the wider forest around, enameled with pond lilies and sagittaria, and the refuge of undisturbed waterfowl and browsing deer."

The end came in 1870, when lumbermen built a dam at Setting Pole Rapids, below Tupper Lake, so they could float logs to the mills. The dam raised the river ten feet for a distance of almost thirty miles, all the way back to Raquette Falls. As millions of trees drowned and decayed, the Raquette became a putrid mess. It was "not the stream to linger on," Sears wrote, which is why he took the shortcut from Upper Saranac and then caught a steamer to "get down and out in the quickest possible time." So vociferous was the outcry at the devastation that the dam was eventually lowered, but the landscape never regained its former glory. Still, what remains feels satisfyingly wild, and the monotony of maples is here and there broken by a stand of pine.

The outlet of Follensby Pond appeared at one of the many bends where the river twisted back on itself. Off limits to the public for many years, the pond is the centerpiece of a private preserve of some 14,400 acres that the state has targeted for purchase. It has long had an option to buy the property, with its historic (and happily, undeveloped) lake and many miles of Raquette River frontage, but in this case too, fiscal disarray has prevented it from acting. Like Whitney Park, the Follensby Pond parcel is coveted by conservationists for the quality of its wilderness. It was here that young bald eagles were fledged in the early 1980s.

We waited in the shallows until the motorboat we had heard

droning from afar had left us rocking in its wake, and then paddled on to the broad backwater known as Trombley Landing. Here, at the southern end of the Sweeney Carry, Sears caught his steamer, either the *Altamont* or the *Forester*. The old trail still exists as a fire road disappearing to the north through a grove of spruce. At the easternmost lean-to we were entertained by a series of inscriptions commemorating the annual visits of Rogers, *père et fils*, and their dog Zig Zag. I was shoving off when I heard a familiar piping, *Old Sam Peabody, Peabody, Peabody*—the only white-throated sparrow we would hear on our trip. In spring these inconspicuous birds had sung us down the river, all the way from Long Lake, with a call Teddy Roosevelt pronounced "singularly sweet and plaintive."

Twice we saw squirrels—one red, one large gray—swimming across the sluggish current. Farther along, the highway came into view, retreated, and then passed a few yards from the water. Our sense of solitude dissipated completely as a row of houses and docks hove into view. Yet what we lost in solitude, we gained in bird life. When the naturalist John Burroughs visited the Adirondacks during the Civil War he came expecting to find the woods full of rare and new species. This proved not to be the case. "The birds," he noted, "for the most part prefer the vicinity of settlements and clearings, and it was at such places that I saw the greatest number and variety." Here, at the eastern end of the community of Tupper Lake, we saw more species than anywhere else on the river: ducks, herons, hawks, sandpipers, nuthatches, blue jays, kingfishers, warblers, woodpeckers.

We had worried about finding our way through the infamous Oxbow but needn't have; the channel was clearly marked. In no time we passed under a bridge and were through the shortcut to Simon Pond. Directly ahead rose Mount Morris, its flanks striped with ski runs. We kept to the marshy north shore and discovered a flock of Canada geese hidden in the reeds. They were asleep, save for one black-headed sentry scanning the horizon.

In the Northeast, we see two populations of Canada geese. One is migratory, the other overwinters wherever there is open water and enough forage for them to survive. The latter group are becoming pests in some communities, their droppings befouling parks and golf courses. The former, like most long-range migrants, are having a hard time. Development of subarctic regions (such as Hydro-Quebec's massive power project on James Bay) is decimating traditional breeding areas, while loss of habitat is accelerating all along the Eastern Flyway, which means they're increasingly hard-pressed to find places, like the marsh on Simon Pond, where they can feed and sleep in peace.

To me, wild geese represent gallantry itself. In the fall small bands of them drop like lengths of heavy chain onto the pond beside our house. (I once counted 126 birds on our third-of-an-acre puddle.) The groups that arrive in the morning depart at five or so; often as not another flight will come in half an hour later, to spend the night. I love to get up in the dark and watch their ghostly forms drifting in ranks, heads heavy on their backs, a lone sentinel moving among them. Their leave-taking is a tremendous occasion. First they grow restless, swimming back and forth, tossing their heads, fanning their wings. Next they align themselves in rows, facing into the wind. Suddenly one bird rears forward and begins running across the surface, great wings beating. In a second they're all moving, the pond churned white, the hillside throwing back their cries. They stream above, around, and through a windbreak of Lombardy poplars and out over the valley. When the heaving water stills, the pond seems unimaginably empty.

In the channel where the Raquette enters Tupper Lake an old man was tacking to and fro in an aluminum boat. It was a homemade rig with clear plastic sheets for sails and a paddle for a rudder, and although he was getting nowhere, he was having a hell of a good time.

"Wish I had one of those rigs," I told him as I passed by.

He smiled sheepishly. "Sometimes it works pretty good," he said.

The marsh thinned as the lake opened up, and soon the state launch area appeared on our left. It had been one of our longest paddles, seventeen miles, and it was all we could do to clamber up the concrete ramp. In the parking lot our singing neighbors were slinging their gear into a van.

From the launch area at Moody, Tupper Lake doglegs six and a half miles south, its eastern shore built up, a series of islands marching down its center. We arose in the dark and postponed breakfast to get on the water early. By the time we had deposited a car at the southern end, the sky was a dramatic pastiche of blue patches and swatches of clouds. A gentle swell lapped at the ramp. The forecast was for a blustery morning, with a chance of rain later in the day.

"Think we ought to wait till tomorrow?" I asked John.

That morning we had moved out of our friends' house and made our good-byes. In silence we pondered the prospect of killing a day, possibly two if a big front was coming in.

"Ah, let's knock this sucker off," John finally replied.

"Yeah, let's. We can always scoot over to the far shore if it really starts to blow."

Hubris. We set out jauntily enough along the east shore and then cut between Birch and Bluff islands through a stiffening chop. A nacreous haze softened the mountains to the east and gave the long vista down the lake a painterly shimmer. There is often a peculiarly beautiful quality to the light on Tupper Lake. One day I saw a scene so striking I stopped my car to take it in. The sun was setting behind layers of black clouds, and between the strata there was a slice of clear sky. For just a moment the light blazed forth and illuminated a narrow strip of shoreline. Everywhere else darkness had fallen, but this ten-mile-long frieze glowed bright orange, as if a celestial finger had pointed *there* and transformed an unremarkable ribbon of lakefront into something sublime.

S. H. Hammond paddled Tupper one morning in the late 1840s and was puzzled by "a distant roaring, not like a waterfall, or far-off thunder, but partaking of both." As the light strengthened he saw "vast flocks of wild pigeons, winging their way in different directions across the lake, but all appearing to have a common starting-point in the forest . . . We had no difficulty in finding it, for the thundering sound of those vast flocks, as they started from their perches, led us on. About half a mile from the lake we came to the outer edge of the roost. Hundreds of thousands of pigeons, had flown away that morning, and yet there were hundreds of thousands, and perhaps many millions, old and young, there yet. It covered acres and acres . . ." The crush of roosting birds was so great that huge limbs crashed to earth under their weight and the ground was thick with droppings. Hammond's party robbed several nests of their young for breakfast.

Hammond's wild pigeons were passenger pigeons, long-tailed birds with slate-blue heads and iridescent plumage that glowed gold, violet, or reddish-purple, depending on the light. In 1866 an observer in Ontario saw a spring flight that stretched a mile in width and some three hundred miles in length. Highly communal, in fact, fatally so, flocks of passenger pigeons roamed the eastern and midwestern forests, feeding on beechnuts and acorns. They began to decline as their habitat disappeared, when millions of acres of woodlands were cleared for farming. At the same time, Americans conceived an almost inexhaustible taste for their flesh.

In an 1882 *Forest and Stream* article entitled "Outrage on the Innocents," Nessmuk described what was happening all over the country: hunters descended on a roost to the west of Wellsboro before the birds could even finish building their nests. Roost trees were hacked down, birds were smoked out with sulphur, and "three hundred nets are daily spread in a pigeon roost only three miles long by about half a mile in width," he reported. Those not sold for food were used as targets in trap-shooting tournaments. "It is the same old criminal trick of heartless brutality that has pained and disgusted every humane sportsman and lover of nature for the past fifty years," Sears wrote, proposing stiff laws, but he was too late. Flocks fragmented and ceased roosting and breeding; efforts to breed them in captivity were seldom successful. On September 1, 1914, the last passenger pigeon in existence, a female named Martha, died in the Cincinnati zoo.

On the far side of Bluff Island we visited the Devil's Pulpit, a granite cliff that plunges one hundred sheer feet into the water. By this time the swell was rocking my boat hard enough that I had trouble taking a picture. We decided to sprint down to County Line Island, just to our south, and then over to the west shore at the narrowest spot. This proved a mistake; as I should have known, the strait was a wind tunnel. When I resorted to tacking, the gap between my boat and John's widened until I found myself alone and pitching wildly. The wind was lifting trails of spume off the whitecaps and whipping them into my lap. By the time I caught up with John on the far shore I had turned peevish. "Do you think you could stay closer to me?" I said. "It was really hairy out there."

He was sorry; he'd been concentrating on getting across himself, and hadn't noticed until it was too late how far apart we'd drifted. I was becoming chilled from the water sloshing around my legs. The few cottages along this stretch were shuttered, and we could see no other boats on the lake. At last we found a cove of sorts, a slight indentation in the shoreline, where I could bail out. Timing my moves between slamming waves, I managed to get out and unload the *Sairy.* Twice in the next hour I had to repeat this procedure as conditions deteriorated. Now there was no question of going back; the center of the lake was seething with whitecaps.

A longer canoe can span the troughs between steep waves, but a nine-footer pitches headlong into them, its open bow exposed to the next roller. As we fought our way along the deserted shore, there were times when I was sure I would founder, and fear climbed up my throat. I cursed myself for the stupid overconfidence that had got us into this situation. The gusts were often so strong we could make no progress at all, but eventually fatigue made us wise. We learned to rest during the worst blasts, to paddle in the lulls, and to read the etching on the waves that meant another surge was imminent. For once I wished I had a single paddle that I could feather. Our double blades, angled for comfort, were being tugged so hard they nearly flew out of our numbed hands.

Foot by hard-earned foot we pulled our way south, toward the nearest wind shelter, in Black Bay. As we reached it and turned down this arm a new problem arose. The waves here were jumbled but for the most part hitting us broadside, and they were threatening to swamp my left gunwale. Desperation is a marvelous teacher: I discovered that if I rolled my fanny and tipped my boat up left, I could gain several inches of freeboard and blunt the force of the waves. Now I was glad that my canoe, unlike her namesake, had no keel. The rounded hull made her easy to tilt, although the maneuver required some delicacy, since too vigorous a roll would submerge the opposite gunwale. At any rate, my discovery got me safely into calmer water.

In spite of our exhaustion we bypassed a swampy-looking campsite in favor of the lean-to at the head of the bay, where there might be a picnic table to cook on. It was a crushing disappointment when we drew close enough to make out figures moving around and a powerboat moored by the shore. I suggested that we cross to the north shore and find a patch of sun;

I wanted to dry my pants and warm my bones. I even thought I saw a flattish rock among the rubble, but when I turned around John had pulled his canoe onto a low granite shelf and was unloading the food bag.

"Don't you want to get over there into the sun?" I asked. "It'll be a lot nicer."

"This is fine," he said. "The wind'll dry your pants in no time."

I unloaded in a sulk, turfing my gear onto the rock and slamming the *Sairy* over onto her gunwales to drain. John moved about imperturbably, setting up the stove for coffee and laying out bowls and spoons. When I muttered that I was freezing he offered his own dry clothes. Declining as curtly as I could, I ransacked my pack for dry underwear and sweatpants, and by the time I'd changed and drunk half my coffee I was coming around. As we talked I learned what I ought to have seen, that by the time we entered the bay John's shoulders were enraged and every stroke had become an agony. He had simply been unable to go farther. I felt very, very small and apologized for my ill humor, an apology that was instantly accepted. It occurred to me, not for the first time, that I had married a saint.

Forty minutes later, when we crept out of the bay and were again slammed by the wind, nothing had changed, and yet something had. Taking on fuel had certainly helped, but there'd been a shift in attitude as well. We knew what we were facing, and we were confident of our boats and ourselves. We tackled the final two miles with something approaching glee, ducking into each bay for a few minutes of rest before fighting our way around the next headland. Several times we laughed out loud as a walloping gust actually drove us backward. I was reminded of Longstreth's battle on this same lake in the early 1900s in which "every moment was a sparkling uncertainty."

At Warren Point we passed the site of the Tupper Lake

House, where the steamer deposited Sears that long-ago day in time for supper. The hotel had changed hands the year before he turned up, a hunting accident having claimed the life of its proprietor, W. W. Graves. In the nineteenth century, the practice of hounding was widespread in the Adirondacks. Packs of dogs were set loose to chase deer to the lakes where they instinctively fled for safety. Men stationed in boats could easily overtake the swimming animals and shoot them, slit their throats, or brain them with an oar. Deer rarely survived these encounters, but on a fall day at nearby Horseshoe Lake, one beat the odds.

According to a Plattsburgh newspaper, "A large buck being driven in, Mr. Graves attempted to drive it near the shore that his son might shoot it. Mr. Graves had the deer by the tail, and was pounding him on the head with an oar, when suddenly [the deer] turned and swam under the boat, capsizing it. The boat being old and leaking, he could not right it, but thought he could get ashore by taking hold of the dog's tail, and being towed, but the dog, instead of swimming, would turn and get on Mr. G.'s shoulders. He then tried to swim ashore, but could not reach it. The water was very cold, and he quite warm from his tussle with the deer. When near the shore he told his little son he could swim no farther, and bid him 'good bye,' telling him to bid his mother and little sisters the same, and sank to the bottom. The water where he sank is not over 10 or 12 ft. deep, and very clear. His little son could see his face when he was sinking, until near the bottom."

Hounding (also called floating) was finally outlawed as unsporting, as was jacking, in which, under cover of darkness, hunters drifted up to feeding deer, mesmerized them with a lantern, and then picked them off. Although he occasionally joined hounding parties and does not seem to have felt any qualms about the practice, Sears preferred still-hunting. As a loner and dedicated loafer, he was best suited to settling down near a game trail and waiting for his quarry to appear. His weapon of choice was a "single-barrelled, hair-triggered" Billinghurst muzzleloader, a hopelessly old-fashioned choice to those who used breechloaders. He had tried all kinds of rifles, including models offered by Sharps, Winchester, Maynard, Spencer, and Remington, but all of them were unsatisfactory in some way. There was no such thing as a perfect gun, he once wrote; what was effective for chipmunks would not work for grizzlies. Nor should there be an all-purpose firearm: game was scarce enough as it was.

He freely admitted that he had done more than his share to bring this about. "With my hand on my mouth, and my mouth in the dust, I admit that I shot thirty-six deer in a season. I deserved to be hung for it. . . . Why should I ever have killed a deer that I did not need for immediate use? Why, in the name of heaven, was I looking for market prices and quotations? Well, I was young. I knew no better. Today, the mother doe or the spotted fawn can pass me on a runway as safely as my own mother."

Trapping had been even more exciting than hunting; in hunting you had the chase and then one shot, but tending a trapline was like holding thirty or forty tickets in a daily lottery. But he no longer trapped either, although he'd been highly successful with muskrats: "When I remember that I have murdered more than 5,000 of these bright-eyed innocents and stretched their skins for an average of twenty cents each, I am quite prepared for the gospel of evolution. I shouldn't be surprised to know that a few thousand years back my ancestors wore hair instead of cassimere and lived mostly in trees."

At the foot of the lake, beneath an arched bridge, the Bog River enters, foaming impressively over smooth granite benches. We floated as close to the falls as we dared and felt our hulls vibrating to their rumble. It had, we agreed, been quite a ride: what should have taken three hours at the outside had taken five.

~~~

Exhilarated by our battle with Tupper, we surprised ourselves by electing to continue up the Bog River. It was only one o'clock, we'd had a late breakfast, and neither of us had any interest in trying to kill the afternoon in town. The surrounding forest would protect us from the wind, we reasoned, and although we'd be working against the current on our way up, it was only two miles of flatwater to the turnaround at Round Lake Outlet. We launched in a shallow, overgrown channel to the right of the falls. Within minutes the rumble of the cascades had given way to the silence of a marsh. Two bends later, we found ourselves in a different landscape, a corridor of dark spruce. "It is a narrow stream," Joel Headley declared, "possessing no beauty, and awakens anything but pleasant feelings as it winds its sluggish way through the silent forest." I found it quite beautiful.

A belted kingfisher showed us the way, looping down the river, perching, then swooping ahead again, all the while scolding us with its sharp rattle. It's easy, at the first flash of plumage, to mistake a kingfisher for a blue jay, since both have blue and white feathers. Kingfishers, though, have a distinctive shape, with short tails and oversized heads. They also sport white collars and a spiky crest that gives them, like common mergansers, an air of perpetual surprise. Of course they are wonderful fishers, plunging headfirst into the water after prey. They are excavators as well, burrowing deep into riverbanks to hide their nests. "The halcyon or kingfisher is a good guide when you go to the woods," John Burroughs observed. "He will not insure smooth water or fair weather, but he knows every stream and lake like a book, and will take you to the wildest and most unfrequented places. . . . He loves the sound of a waterfall, and will sit a long time on a dry limb overhanging the pool below it, and, forgetting his occupation, brood upon his own memories and fancies."
~~~

In an hour we had reached the Bog's junction with Round Lake Outlet. The way south was blocked first by rapids and a deep gorge, and thereafter by the northern boundary of Whitney Park. A century ago canoeists could go on to Round Pond and Little Tupper Lake, and from there in three directions, to the Fulton Chain, to Forked Lake, or to Long Lake. The last of these three, the Slim Ponds route, was the one Sears chose, but it has been closed by the Whitney family since the turn of the century.

We squatted on rocks beside the rapids and ate our lunch. The return trip, with the wind and current at our backs, was considerably faster, and this was just as well: as we neared the falls we could hear mutters of thunder in the west.

When I closed my eyes that night I again felt my boat rocking beneath me, my inner ear not yet reconciled to the land. About two o'clock I was awakened by the sound of drumming rain and worried about leaks in the tent. It was several moments before I realized that the rain was pounding on a motel roof in Long Lake. Feeling wonderfully snug, I rolled over and burrowed back under the covers.

BLUE MOUNTAIN LAKE TO EAGLE LAKE

THE FOLLOWING DAY DAWNED RAINY, cold, and windy. Remarkably enough, it was the first time we'd been forced to wait out the weather, but neither of us really minded: our adventure on Tupper had tired us out. We had paddled roughly 136 miles in seventeen days, an average of eight miles a day—not much for a tandem canoe, but a respectable pace for a nine-footer. We spent the morning doing chores and that afternoon moved into a cabin near Blue Mountain Lake, our headquarters for the rest of the trip.

I had hoped to get permission from Whitney Industries, the timber company that operates Whitney Park, to follow Sears's route through Stony Pond and Big and Little Slim ponds. Failing that, I hoped to be allowed to spend a few hours touring Little Tupper Lake, which Sears had declared one of the finest in the region, "gamy as the gamiest, clear as the clearest." I'd heard that the company occasionally made exceptions to its ban on travel, so I had written Whitney management explaining my project and asking permission to paddle through its holdings. My letter failed to elicit a reply.

My disappointment at having to abandon Sears's itinerary stemmed partly from my desire for symmetry in our trips and partly from the fact that this was (and still is) the least developed part of his route. He had responded enthusiastically to its charms. One day he saw a bear swimming across Stony Pond; the following night he stayed at Big Slim (the only night he camped out on his trip) and caught a fourteen-inch trout for his dinner. He passed several days at the small hotel operated by Pliny Robbins on Little Tupper Lake, and as usual, the *Sairy* stirred a good deal of interest. When he at last managed to tear himself away, he returned to Dave Helms's Grove House, at the head of Long Lake, and from there retraced his earlier route up the Raquette River to Forked Lake and on to Raquette Lake. We would get to Raquette a different way, by duplicating Sears's 1880 trip from Blue Mountain Lake through the Eckford Chain.

In 1874 the only habitation on Blue Mountain Lake had been a rough cabin; six years later, when Sears visited it, the place had been utterly transformed. By 1880 Thomas C. Durant's Adirondack Railroad was shuttling loads of tourists from Saratoga Springs to North Creek, where they were met by stagecoaches from Blue Mountain Lake hotels. Another stream of vacationers converged on Blue Mountain Lake from the southwest, via steamer. Sears was aghast at what he found. The lake, he noted, was "a very clear and beautiful sheet of water . . . [that] has often been called the gem of the wilderness. But its days of natural wildness are gone forever. There are three large hotels on its banks filled to overflowing with guests. . . . All luxuries of the season are to be found at the hotels, and billiards, croquet, boating, lounging through the groves, singing and piano-playing give the shores of the lake quite a Long Branchy air." In addition to the hotels there were numerous boarding-houses clustered around the waterfront and private camps on all the scenic points.

He found every room taken. At the Blue Mountain Lake House people were appropriating sofas and chairs in the lobby, and by 11:30 the dining room floor was filling up. "I succeeded in getting a short lounge with a back-breaking bend in nearly the middle of it," Sears grumped, "but could not get so much as a cotton sheet in the way of bedding."

More development was to come. Two years after his visit the Prospect House, owned by a Durant relative, opened its doors. A six-story structure of three hundred rooms, it was "merely a gaunt, ungainly pile of piazzas and windows" from the outside, Donaldson wrote, but inside "it contained the latest refinements in comfort and convenience." These included a steam-operated elevator, an electric bell system, running water and steam heat throughout, a telegraph office, and an innovative two-story outhouse. The Prospect House was the first hotel in the world with electric lighting in every room, run off a generator designed by Edison himself.

On rainy days, guests could amuse themselves at the shooting range, the bowling alley, or the billiards room. Management made sure there was always something to do:

> This is tournament week at the Prospect House. The sports begin to-morrow with a guides' boat-race of two miles, in Adirondack canoes. On Wednesday the games will be for the benefit of the colored employes of the house. The programme includes a sack-race, a tug of war, climbing the greased pole, walking the inclined plane, and a tub-race, a prize of $10 being offered to the winner in each contest. On Thursday we are to have a carnival on the lake, and on Friday the tournament will close with a gentlemen's and ladies' shooting match, the gentlemen shooting at 100 and the ladies at 50 yards.

New-York Times
August 9, 1883

The following week was given over to a different kind of contest when a group met at the hotel to begin dealing with the environmental abuses that had aroused Nessmuk's ire. "On the 12th of this month," Sears told *Forest and Stream*'s readers, "Verplanck Colvin meets a commission at Blue Mountain to report on the expediency of preserving this grand region as a State park. May their counsels be guided by good common sense and humanitarian principles, and no politics, log-rolling, or hippodroming allowed the slightest consideration."

This was perhaps too much to ask, but in the end Colvin and his cause prevailed. Two years later a law created the state Forest Preserve, and in 1892 the Adirondack Park, incorporating all state and private holdings within the Blue Line, came into being. When illegal timber cutting and other abuses continued, a constitutional amendment was passed in 1894 to strengthen protection for Forest Preserve lands. They would be "forever kept as wild forest lands," the amendment read. "They shall not be leased, sold or exchanged, or be taken by any corporation, public or private, nor shall the timber thereon be sold, removed or destroyed."*

* The "forever wild" legislation preserved state lands within the park but offered no protection for the roughly sixty percent in private hands. The democratization of travel in the twentieth century brought unforeseen pressures in the form of strip development, theme parks, and uncontrolled building. In the late 1960s Governor Nelson Rockefeller appointed a commission (eventually headed by historian Harold K. Hochschild) to study the problem; its recommendations led, over strenuous local opposition, to the creation of the Adirondack Park Agency (APA), which was charged with formulating and administering regionwide zoning regulations. In 1973, when the APA's land-use plan became law, Rockefeller exulted, "The Adirondacks are preserved forever."

Well, not quite. In spite of the APA's efforts, pressures continued to mount. Between 1980 and 1990 applications for building permits rose 316 percent; sales of subdivided property increased 704 percent between 1982 and 1988. The agency was overwhelmed as the real estate market boomed. Then a new threat materialized when paper companies, squeezed by changing economic realities, found it more profitable to sell off huge tracts to second-home developers than to log them. Many of these parcels offered good recreation potential and were thus of interest to the state, but New York's acquisition machinery was cumbersome. It took months for the bureaucracy to act, while developers could produce cash within days.

In 1989 the state lost a choice piece of wilderness in just this way (part of it was

Sears dutifully paddled around the lake and then climbed Blue Mountain. The view was fine, he reported, although he could make out only about half of the twenty-eight lakes he'd been told he should see: "As to mountain peaks, the number was rather confusing than satisfying. They ran together and over and by each other in a manner to throw an ordinary mind into a state of temporary imbecility." Like many other Adirondack summits, the peak bore evidence of Colvin's survey party, which had been there seven years before. In addition to a rickety ladder nailed between two spruces and the signal staff, "one entire summit had been slashed [to open a sight line], and the dead, decaying trees, lying just as they fell, were not pleasant to look upon."

A seminal yet ambiguous figure in Adirondack history, Verplanck Colvin was a lawyer by training, but like Sears he had a habit of disappearing into the woods. During his roamings he discovered that the maps of his time were as often wrong as right and brought the matter to the legislature's attention. In 1872 the assembly appointed him to conduct a systematic survey of the region, and for the next twenty-eight years, often at his own expense, he and his crews crisscrossed the Adirondack

---

subsequently reacquired, but at a markup). The fiasco prompted Governor Mario Cuomo to appoint yet another committee, headed by National Audubon Society president Peter A. A. Berle, to recommend new safeguards for the park. Even before the Commission on the Adirondacks in the Twenty-first Century submitted its report, interest groups were lining up to oppose it. The commission came up with 245 recommendations, some sweeping (a proposed moratorium on shoreline development), some trivial. Most of my friends inside the park had trouble with individual recommendations but supported the intent of the document. Their voices, however, were largely drowned out by those of developers, real estate agents, a few powerful legislators, and special interest groups. At first Cuomo ignored the document; then he shelved it and substituted compromise legislation that failed to pass the legislature. (In July 1993, the legislature passed a precariously financed bill that may result in some land acquisitions, but it also killed a measure to restrict shoreline and backcountry development in the park.) Berle's committee did what it was asked to do: it took the long view, even though doing so was bound to be unpopular. For lack of political courage a critical opportunity for reform has been lost. Perhaps political courage is another oxymoron.

interior, measuring mountains and running lines through unknown territory. The reports he submitted to the assembly, which were widely disseminated, were equal parts scientific observation, adventure writing, and travelogue. It was one of Colvin's reports that lured Sears to the Adirondacks in the first place. Forty years later, Colvin's words mesmerized a boy named Bob Marshall, who went on to found the Wilderness Society.

Colvin lobbied for preservation of the Adirondacks on utilitarian grounds. In his view the forests should be exploited by the state, rather than individuals; in this way New York City's water supplies could be protected. Colvin had a gift for colossal schemes: some were visionary, some cuckoo. His proposal for an aqueduct to divert the headwaters of the Hudson directly to New York City enraged Sears, who predicted that such a scheme would "change the entire character and status of the Wilderness in a manner that guides and landlords have yet to learn." Anybody "with as much brains as a hen-turkey," Nessmuk fumed, could see the consequences of this idea.

Colvin's conviction that woods and waters were placed on earth for man's use was incompatible with his love of unspoiled wilderness, but as Philip Terrie has so eloquently observed, in this he was a product of his time. He never fully grasped the contradictions inherent in his twin beliefs in progress and private enterprise, although, as his beloved mountains succumbed to the axe, he was made wistful by the denudation. In 1900 he was forcibly retired when the United States Geological Survey assumed surveying responsibilities. He became a bitter, dejected figure around Albany, prowling the streets and talking to himself. One day he fell on an icy road and hit his head. The blow literally knocked him senseless; he died in an asylum in 1920.

Sears would be far more comfortable with the Blue Mountain Lake we found 110 years after his visit. The gargantuan hotels are all gone, and the scale of the community is now in harmony with its surroundings. While development is relatively dense on the south and east shores, where the highway passes by, the overall feeling of the place is intimate, an intimacy exaggerated by the bulk of the mountain that rises beside the lake. I have seen Blue Mountain from many angles, far and near, and in the way of mountains it never looks the same. It is not a high peak, only thirty-seven-hundred-odd feet, but it seems distinctly Japanese—benign, dreaming, timeless.

It was a chilly Sunday morning when, bundled up in long johns and layers of sweaters, we ventured onto the lake. Above us the mountaintop was obscured by racing clouds, but the lake's surface was barely riffled. From the western shore we paddled counterclockwise through a cluster of islands, pausing to enjoy the sound of a church bell pealing faintly across the water. At Long Island, an osprey swooped out of a tree directly in front of us. Minutes later a loon flew over so low we could hear the air hissing through its wings with a sound like heavy breathing.

By the time we reached the eastern shore, waves were pummeling the village beach. We continued our circle, passing a gaggle of prim housekeeping cottages where the Prospect House stood. The lake was kicking up, and the cold seeping through the hull was chilling my outstretched legs. The air temperature was about fifty, but with the wind in our faces it might have been twenty degrees lower. My open-fingered paddling gloves were wet, my hands numb. Relief came at last in the sheltered channel to Eagle Lake, where we passed under the bridge W. W. Durant built in honor of his father. In true Durant style it was meticulously crafted, its heavy stone abutments topped by rustic wooden rails. Hidden underneath, where only boaters could see it, a bronze plaque extolled the accomplishments of Durant *père*.

Blue Mountain, Eagle, and Utowana lakes comprise the Eckford Chain, which was named for an early shipbuilder-cum-surveyor. All these waters have borne other names: Blue, for instance, was originally Tallow Lake, and later Clinch Lake; Eagle was once named Janet Lake. When Sears came through Eagle Lake in 1880 he saw "an old settled farm house on the northern shore . . . which being the only imitation of a farm on the [Eckford Chain] usually induces inquiry. You will be told that long before the grand rush of tourists and the advent of costly hotels this place was cleared and occupied by 'Ned Buntline.' Here he secluded himself during a part at least of every year for many seasons; here he did his literary work, and the place is, and probably always will be, known as the 'Ned Buntline Farm.'"

If the terms "scumbag" and "sleazeball" had been in vogue in the nineteenth century, they would certainly have been applied to Edward Zane Carroll Judson, aka Ned Buntline, in whose defense I have found not a single word. In the course of a long and scurrilous career he fought a dozen duels and killed a man in one; was unsuccessfully hanged; deserted from the army; had six or seven "wives," sometimes two or more at a time; was jailed three times, once for inciting a riot that killed twenty-three people in New York City; founded a xenophobic political party; and claimed to have discovered, although he merely latched on to, Buffalo Bill Cody. When he wasn't drunk he gave temperance lectures, and when he wasn't lecturing he was churning out some of the worst pulp fiction of the era, serials with titles like *Elfrida, the Red Rover's Daughter* and *Mortimer Monk, the Hunchback Millionaire.*

In 1856 he saw the Adirondacks for the first time and the following year settled into a log cabin on Eagle Lake (then known as Round Lake, presumably because, in the Adirondack tradition, it was not). The property, called Hog's Nose, had belonged to the abolitionist Gerrit Smith and may have been a stop on the Underground Railroad. Judson renamed it Eagle's

Nest and celebrated it in a poem entitled "My Wildwood Home," which was widely anthologized and set to music. The writer lived on Eagle Lake for five years, feuding with his neighbor Alvah Dunning,* churning out his shoddy *oeuvre,* and getting knee-walking drunk on his infrequent trips to civilization. In Glens Falls he is best remembered for the day he rode his pony through the door of a saloon and up to the bar.

He married eighteen-year-old Eva Gardiner and took her to Eagle's Nest, but within a year she died in childbirth, along with her baby. Mother and child were buried next to his cabin. Judson soon found a successor, but when this one saw the shanty Judson had represented as a wilderness palace, her husband had to hide her shoes to keep her from fleeing. In 1862 the "legend in his own mind," as journalist Elizabeth Folwell has dubbed him, went off to the Civil War, never to return to his Adirondack holdings. Mustered out two years later as a private, he thereafter passed himself off as a colonel. Eventually he sold his wildwood home and bought a place in the Catskills.

The property remained a farm for some time, with fields of hay, hops, rye, and vegetables, and cows pastured across the lake, in grassy patches in the woods. Photographs show an extensive clearing, a haybarn, an icehouse, and the farmhouse Judson built to replace his log cabin. As was common in that era, the house also took in paying guests. In time, W. W. Durant acquired considerable acreage in the area, including the Buntline farm. Durant had plans for the property, and since "a constant desecration of her grave was inevitable," he had Eva Gardiner and her infant moved to the cemetery in Blue Mountain Lake. The boulder that marks the site is now all but hidden by shrubs, but you can still read the plaque Durant provided.

* Judson supported strict game laws; Dunning, who had always lived off the land, killed what and when he pleased. The two disagreed about everything. Judson took to calling Dunning an "amaroogian," an insult whose meaning was evident only to its author.

In 1899 Durant began transforming the farm into the Eagle's Nest Country Club, with a nine-hole golf course and a clubhouse with a restaurant run by a Delmonico's chef. The club opened the following year, but it was doomed from the start by Durant's accelerating financial difficulties. In 1904 foreclosure stripped him of Eagle's Nest and all adjacent lands, the last shreds of his empire.

The property, now shorn of the possessive *'s* and known as Eagle Nest, was sold to a group of New Yorkers who continued it as a private club for a time, then bought parcels and built their own homes on the lake. In 1910 Arthur H. Sulzberger, publisher of the *New York Times,* stayed there, and so did a six-year-old named J. Robert Oppenheimer. Original property owners included the diplomat Henry Morgenthau, Sr., and Berthold Hochschild, chairman of the American Metal Company, the international mining firm that became AMAX. The Hochschilds took over the clubhouse property, where Berthold's son, Harold, spent his boyhood summers. A short, stocky figure with a will of iron, Harold grew up with a fondness for boxing, horseback riding, and swimming. Three times in his forties he swam the six-mile length of the Eckford Chain, and for most of his life, a daily ritual was a swim across Eagle Lake and back.

Harold succeeded his father in the company and was almost fifty when he married forty-one-year-old Mary Marquand, by all accounts a warm, compassionate woman with a gift for painting and landscape gardening. The two were happy together, unusually so, spending summers at Eagle Nest and winters at homes in Manhattan and, later, New Jersey. The Hochschilds were generous hosts. On weekends friends and business associates were flown up from New York by Harold's brother-in-law, the dashing Russian émigré Boris Sergievsky, in a Grumman Mallard. Harold being a man of unvarying routines, activities were organized—swimming, waterskiing, horseback riding, tennis, golf, hiking, sailing. Russian cooks presided in the kitchen, and one wing of the clubhouse was allotted to servants. There were always servants—maids, governesses, chauffeurs, stablemen, groundskeepers. Harold loved the region, and later in his life wrote the acclaimed central Adirondack history *Township 34*. He also founded the Adirondack Museum, where the *Sairy Gamp* resides.

Harold and Mary's only child was Adam, born in 1942. The boy adored his mother but his relationship with his father, a distant, formal presence, was wary at best; at worst it made him physically ill. Adam loved the days at Eagle Nest, except when the man he called Father, the man he seemed unable to please, arrived for the weekend. He dreaded the interviews in which his father chastised him for normal high spirits or small social missteps. His father was embarrassed by private displays of emotion and mortified by public ones; the affection came from Mary.

Shielded by the insulation of money, Adam went to good schools and traveled widely with his parents. But he was a sensitive and observant child, and as he matured he became increasingly uncomfortable with his family's wealth. Inspection tours of the company's holdings in Africa and elsewhere revealed a troubling dichotomy between his privileged life and the lot of the miners whose labor perpetuated it. A summer working for a South African newspaper sealed his commitment to social justice. Surrounded by the stark contrasts of apartheid, the starving black children in shanty towns, the affluent whites with their vacation homes at the shore, he realized that he could never take his father's place, not in the boardroom, not at Eagle Nest. In the kind of irony usually reserved for fiction, Adam turned his back on his comfortable world to become a radical journalist for *Ramparts* magazine and after that, founder of *Mother Jones.* The struggle to become his own person was a formidable one, but Adam prevailed. *Half the Way Home* is a vivid memoir of life at Eagle Nest and his efforts to come to terms with his father.

If the son turned out to be an independent thinker, he most likely inherited the trait from Harold, who was a supporter of black majority rule in Africa long before such a stand was fashionable among members of his caste. Harold was also a maverick in his opposition to the war in Vietnam and his support of George McGovern. Toward the end of his life, particularly after Mary died and there was no one to run interference between the two, his relationship with Adam mellowed considerably. He died in 1981 and was buried beside Mary in the Blue Mountain Lake cemetery, not far from Eva Gardiner. Although Adam loved Eagle Nest, he had for many years felt it was wrong for one family to own such a place. In 1982 the property was turned into an artists' colony and conference center devoted to social justice and environmental issues.

Numbed to the bone, we paddled slowly down Eagle Lake to our cottage. That afternoon we dropped a car at Inlet and on the way back tried to catch a forecast. What we heard was not encouraging: overnight temperatures in the thirties, winds ten to twenty-five miles an hour, flurries possible. Chastened by our experience on Tupper, we resigned ourselves to another layover day. Autumn was now well advanced, the birches all yellow, the maples splendid in orange and red. Leaves covered the ground. A coffee-table book in our cottage reminded me that in the west, stagecoaches were still being robbed in 1882.

As promised, Monday was cold and blustery enough to keep us indoors, reading and sleeping. Bored, I calculated the distance we'd come and again reworked our itinerary. The schedule I'd concocted before we left home had us finishing up that very day; according to an amended version drawn up in midtrip we should have been back at Eighth Lake by now. We were behind, but only a bit. My final plan called for shorter stints over the remaining distance. When I explained that this would add another day, John hooted.

"You're dragging your feet, aren't you? You don't want it to end."

I was taken aback. "No, no. It's not that. I'm just trying to make this last part easier. There's no point in killing ourselves to save a day."

"You don't want it to e-end, you don't want it to e-end," he sang.

Okay, he's not *always* a saint. But he was right. For weeks I'd been obsessed with putting miles behind us. Now we'd turned a corner, and I found myself in no hurry to finish. I liked our life. The days had settled into a comfortable rhythm of paddling and carrying, paddling and cooking, paddling and sleeping. Then too, I had become addicted to having my senses ravished on a regular basis. Best of all were early mornings, the world silent except for the calls of birds and the gurgle of my paddle. Afternoons brought the sweet scent of shaded water, the hypnotic rocking of gentle swells. Sometimes the world we moved through seemed like a dream, an endless corridor of lakes and rivers down which the two of us paddled, day after day, suspended in time.

Only the advancing season reminded us that time was indeed passing. And as all canoe trippers discover, the longer we stayed out, the harder it was to face reentry.

EAGLE LAKE TO EIGHTH LAKE

THAT NIGHT A KILLING FROST settled over the North Country, and in the morning most of the remaining leaves on the maples were spiraling down to the lawn. It would be an uncomfortable morning on the water, but a warming trend was predicted for the rest of the week, so we decided we might as well go. Having lingered over coffee to let the sun clear Blue Ridge, we loaded up and set off down Eagle Lake. Half an hour later, as we exited the winding channel to Utowana, a rising wind drove us to the shelter of the north shore.

There is one camp on Utowana, accessible only by plane or boat. A row of deserted deck chairs faced the morning sun, a forgotten towel on one of them fluttering in the breeze. The Baekeland camp was bought in 1923 by the wife of Leo Hendrik Baekeland, father of the plastics revolution and inventor of Bakelite, the miracle substance found in everything from radio consoles to Art Deco jewelry to a still-classified role in the atomic bomb. The Belgian-born Leo, who also invented Velox photographic paper, had a son named George Washington Baekeland. George's son was named Brooks, and Brooks's son was Tony.

Even as a boy there were signs that Tony was a lonely and disturbed child. When he summered at the camp on Utowana, his cousins felt uncomfortable around him, and by his late teens he had been expelled from several elite schools. Discreetly homosexual, he had some talent as an artist and as a writer but seemed unable to focus on either craft for very long. His mother, Barbara, was a social climber, his father an adventurer. After they divorced, Tony and his mother lived a nomadic existence at chic European resorts as Tony continued his long, sad descent into paranoid schizophrenia. One day, in anguish, he confessed to an acquaintance that he was sleeping with his mother; soon afterward, at the age of twenty-six, he killed Barbara with a kitchen knife after a violent argument in the London apartment they shared. There followed eight years in mental hospitals, but the gradual improvement doctors saw was illusory: not long after his release he attacked his grandmother, also with a knife. While being held on Rikers Island Tony committed suicide by suffocating himself with a plastic bag, a product his great-grandfather had made possible.

The west end of Utowana is shallow and filled with stumps, evidence of drowning caused by the dam W. W. Durant built there to float his steamboats. As we nosed into the channel leading to the take-out, a flock of ducks—unidentifiable in the glare of the sun—wheeled up from the marsh. Remnants of the lively past of the Marion River Carry can still be seen by the landing: the splintered skeleton of the dock where the double-decked *Tuscarora* collected its passengers, and railroad ties moldering in the dirt of the half-mile trail. The Marion River Railroad that Durant built was the world's shortest standard-gauge line and perhaps its smallest, consisting of a locomotive and three former streetcars. Part of Durant's plan to bring the affluent all the way from Fifth Avenue to his country club dock, the line opened in 1900 and ran for twenty-nine years.

It was pleasant to scuff along the shady path, our loads creaking and jingling, the Marion River dashing over its narrow, rocky bed beside us. Where the carry crosses the river, we discovered that we were just able to float our boats off a gravel bar, so we saved ourselves the final quarter mile of trekking. Once out of the shallows, we found ourselves gliding down a ribbon of water scarcely wider than our paddles. Slowed now and then by beaver dams, the river twisted through a marsh, alders rising above our heads and every few yards an animal trail emerging from the vegetation. Beds of pickerelweed had been crumpled to the waterline by the previous night's frost, and along the banks warped ferns stood cinnamon-red among tawny grasses. As the valley opened up the river broadened, but its course remained delightfully erratic, "crooked as a wounded snake," Sears would have said.

The wider water brought the wind into play, and we were forced to pull harder through stretches of ruffles and ripples. Along the way we played tag with two great blue herons, whose dull gray plumage and long, woody beaks make them look like pieces of driftwood stuck endwise in the marsh. They wade through the shallows with a professorial hunch, lifting one foot ever so slowly, holding it immobile, and with infinite care placing it farther ahead in the muck. From time to time they freeze, still-hunting just as Sears did, until the activity around them resumes. There follows a lightning-fast strike, a silver gleam in the beak, a convulsion of the impossibly long neck, and the dignified perambulation commences once more. Izaak Walton on stilts.

Because they are so large, great blues were easy targets in the nineteenth century. Their massive nests, built in the tops of dead trees "like a saucer on the head of a cane," as A. Judd Northrup put it, also rendered them dangerously conspicuous.

In the 1870s, when Northrup visited a rookery near Cranberry Lake, he noted that the herons "had a way of standing up on their nests, like sentinels, and, when shot at, slowly sinking down until they were invisible." The one he picked off fell a hundred feet to the ground "with a tremendous thump and splash . . . It measured, from tip to tip of its wings, five and a half feet, and, from beak to toes, four and a half feet. It was a vile smelling wretch, and after being duly inspected at camp nobody had the slightest desire to bring it home as a specimen for the taxidermist's skill."*

In the 1800s herons all over the country were killed for their plumes, and because, like other fishing species, they competed with human anglers. In the Adirondacks, their greatest problems occurred in the late 1800s, when logging and forest fires set by passing locomotives decimated a million acres of habitat. The precipitous decline of beaver stocks also hurt them, since beaver dams create wetlands and improve conditions for fish; fewer beaver meant less food. Today great blues are back. We saw them all along our route, in almost every marsh and river.

* People thought nothing, in the nineteenth century, of shooting birds and animals merely to get a closer look. At Tupper Lake in the mid-1850s, S. H. Hammond killed a large "black fox" because he couldn't see it well enough to identify it. By itself this casual killing would not have significantly reduced populations, but when it was combined with years of systematic overhunting whole species disappeared. The larger the target, the quicker the extirpation: thus the moose were soon gone (hunting them, someone once wrote, is about as sporting as shooting parked cars), to be followed by the timber wolf, the cougar (panther in these parts, or painter, or mountain lion, or catamount, or eastern puma), and the lynx.

Protection came too late for some species, but others have rebounded. Bear and deer are plentiful today, and the bobcat has made a good comeback. About thirty moose have now wandered into the park from neighboring states. The Department of Environmental Conservation is studying the feasibility of reintroducing wolves and cougars, and a lynx restoration project is well under way, although mortality from cars has been higher than expected. A new species, the coyote, has infiltrated the Adirondacks and much of the Northeast. Persecuted by farmers and deer hunters, coyotes nevertheless perform a useful role as scavengers and cullers, weeding out weak animals to ensure the health of the herd. On winter evenings their melodious howls ring through the woods and remind me that we haven't come that far from the cave.

We lunched on a sunny rock and continued down the Marion, through rafts of fragrant white water lilies. More delicate than the waxy yellow bullhead lilies, these have whorls of petals and a clean, soapy scent. Now and then my paddle tip flipped a lily pad, exposing the startling red underside. At last the river broadened into a long bay, and our boats were dancing on the swell of Raquette Lake.

"Hey, there's a nice campsite," I said to John. Nestled in a stand of white pines, it sat high on a bluff overlooking the bay.

"Let's just go down to the end and see what the lake looks like," he suggested. "We can always come back if we decide it's too rough."

The bay was heaving gently as we made our way west. We stroked past a few cottages, rounded the headland, and turned north. On our left lay Osprey Island and dead ahead, beyond another bay, our destination at Tioga Point, where my map showed a group campsite with fifteen lean-tos. Too late we realized we'd been misled by the wind shadow behind Osprey, or perhaps we'd simply hit a lull. We were well past the island when the full force of the west wind hit us and the water became unmanageably choppy. *How does this happen so fast?* I wondered as a succession of rollers slammed into my side and set me yawing and pitching. The center of the lake was now visible, and it was alive with whitecaps trailing tatters of spume. Turning was impossible, so I tried to use John's canoe as a windbreak but couldn't get close enough without fouling his paddle. One by one I tried all my tricks—tacking, rolling up on my side, letting the boat have her head—yet after five minutes of grim pulling, Tioga Point seemed no closer. I found myself wondering whether there were people on shore watching our struggle and shaking their heads over fools in small boats. Had I come all this way to be drowned? What did Raquette Lake have against me?

By the time we staggered out of the surf on Tioga's broad beach even *my* shoulders were aching, and as usual I was wet to the waist. The eroded bank looked impossibly steep, but up we went, manhandling our packs, grunting with every step. We dumped our gear at the nearest lean-to and then stopped to study the short crossing that had turned so mean. From this slight elevation it didn't seem half so threatening. Too exhausted to unpack, we unrolled our sleeping pads on a sunny hillside, pulled out the plugs, and watched stupidly as each compartment inflated. Wet or not, they were irresistible. We flopped down and lay blissfully in the quiet, the scent of pine needles in our nostrils, our skin soaking up the late-afternoon warmth. When the sun slid behind the trees the sharpening air drove us to our chores. The campsite was deserted save for one other couple who had chosen a lean-to farther out on the point.

We had now rejoined the *Sairy Gamp*'s route. On his northern leg Sears had stopped here to inspect Ike Kenwell's Raquette Lake House and duly plugged it. He was especially pleased that the hotel maintained a lean-to. "The open bark camp," he wrote, "with its fragrant bed of browse and rousing fire in front at night is a delightful woodland affair that should always be a part of the wilderness hotel." Four years later Kenwell's followed precedent and burned.

At dinnertime a female mallard waddled up the bank and strutted around us, making soft noises deep in her throat. We admired the teal-blue speculum on her wing but resisted the impulse to feed her; the Meals on Keels program, I told her, was over for the season. She disappeared down the bank but in a few minutes was back. More dulcet noises, more beseeching looks. When John squatted she hustled over to worry his outstretched finger with her bill. Four times she appeared, before leaving for good.

Morris Longstreth observed that while July and August are the conventional months for camping, September is really the best: "In September dark comes earlier, which is a disadvantage, but there are no clotted showers, no days of hazy heat, no insects. . . . Once or twice the mercury falls below the freezing point, and you have new intimacies with your fire." That evening we certainly became chummy with ours. As the sky cleared and the bottom dropped out of the thermometer, we realized we'd be warmer in the tent than bedding down in the lean-to. We'd now been out twenty-three days; with the sun rising later and setting earlier each day, we'd lost about an hour of light. By 7:30 cold and dark had driven us into our dome, but we had no trouble settling down, a riptide of fatigue bearing us off to unconsciousness.

Sears, fortified by innumerable cups of green tea, would probably have stayed awake. "I have certainly spent much more than one hundred days in small, narrow [tents] alone during the 'dark days before Christmas,' when there was more than fifteen hours of darkness to be got over each twenty-four hours," he claimed, "and the time never yet seemed long nor hung heavily on my hands for a single hour." My hat's off to him; the man had a rich interior life. Had he bivouacked on Tioga Point, he would have smoked and mused and perhaps versified. My favorite Nessmuk poem is his record of a solitary night, year unknown:

NEW YEAR'S EVE IN CAMP.

Mercury 10° Below Zero, Northwest Gale.

The winds are out in force to-night, the clouds, in light brigades,
Are charging from the mountain tops across the everglades.
There is a fierceness in the air—a dull, unearthly light—
The Frost-king in his whitest crown rides on the storm to-night.
Far down the gorge of Otter Run I hear the sullen roar
Of rifted snows and pattering sleet, among the branches hoar.
The giant hemlocks wag their heads against the midnight sky,
The melancholy pine trees moan, the cedars make reply.

The oaks and sugar maples toss their frozen arms in air,
The elms and beeches bow their heads, and shriek as in despair.
Scant shield to-night for flesh and blood is feather, hair, or fur:
From north to south, for many a mile, there is no life astir.
The gaudy jay with painted crest has stowed his plumes away,
The sneaking wolf forbears to howl, the mountain cat to prey.
The deer has sought the laurel brake, her form the timid hare,
The shaggy bear is in his den, the panther in his lair.
From east to west, from north to south, for twenty miles around,
To-night no track shall dint the shroud that wraps the frozen
ground.

I sit and listen to the storm that roars and swells aloof,
Watching the fitful shadows play against the rustic roof,
And as I blow an idle cloud to while the hours away,
I croon an old-time ditty, in the minor key of A.

And from the embers beams a face most exquisitely fair—
The maiden face of one I knew—no matter when or where,
A face inscrutable and calm, with dark, reproachful eyes,
That gaze on me from limpid depths, or gusty autumn skies.

And there may be a reason why I shun the blatant street,
To seek a distant mountain glen where three bright waters meet.
But why I shun the doors of men, their rooms a-light and warm,
To camp in forest depths alone, or face a winter storm,
Or why the heart that gnaws itself will find relief in rhyme,
I cannot tell: I but abide the footing up of Time.

We rose at six and packed in near-darkness, postponing breakfast to get away before the wind kicked up. So intent were we on zippers and stuff sacks that at first we didn't notice the light show unfolding over the marsh to our left. Raquette Lake had twice tried to drown us, but on this morning it showed us its loveliest self. Mist rising off the water was refracting the first rays of sun and creating billowing blooms of purple and pink and orange over the rushes. Even Winslow Homer, master of light and water, could not have rendered such a scene. This was no inferential sunrise; this was a Statement.

The mist reduced visibility to about half a mile, but the water was mercifully glassy. We circumnavigated Osprey Island, where W. H. H. Murray camped for several summers and where, in the early 1870s, H. Perry Smith found him. "The particular spot . . . where Mr. Murray and his party were encamped," Smith wrote, "he has 'dubbed' Terrace Lodge, it being an abrupt bluff on the water side, surmounted by a green plateau on which was pitched his tents. These numbered, that season, six or eight, and as they stood basking in the sun, backed by the thick foliage of the woodland, and surrounded by the gay party, their appearance was picturesque in the extreme. Add to this a crooked path down to the lake, a dozen boats of as many colors, guides in and about them dressed in colored shirts, and it made up a scene from fairy land."

Ten years later Murray had lost everything. By then, one of W. W. Durant's cousins had built Camp Fairview on the western end of the island. Sears paddled past and observed that the main building looked rather like a Swiss villa. The day before, he told his *Forest and Stream* audience, Fairview's owner had "organized a hunt of feudal proportions" that had involved nineteen guides, thirty-six hunters, and about thirty hounds. With some satisfaction Sears reported that the effort had netted exactly one buck and one small yearling, for a cost, it was rumored, of a thousand dollars. Fairview burned in 1920.

From Osprey's south shore it was only a few hundred feet to Saint Hubert's Isle, where Durant built the Episcopal Church of the Good Shepherd to serve the spiritual needs of the Brahmins he hoped to lure to the area. (Nearby, on the mainland, he built a Catholic church for the local populace.) Parishioners were called to worship by a small cannon, and although this ecclesiastical artillery now graces the Adirondack Museum, the church operates to this day.

The light was strengthening as we made our way back into the bay we'd paddled down yesterday as we entered Raquette. This time we poked along the south shore, looking for the site of Ed Bennett's hotel, Under the Hemlocks, where Sears liked to stay. When he stopped by with the *Sairy,* "nearly all the [guests] turned out to have a look at the little canoe. To lift her and exclaim on her lightness. To ask questions of the rough-looking little old duffer who had cruised her from side to side of the wilderness, and pretty well back again by a different route." It was all Sears could do to dissuade the 170-pound Bennett from getting in and trying her himself.*

There are still hemlocks on Long Point, but no sign of the hotel, which—quick, class, what happened?—burned in 1899. By the time we regained the axis of the lake, the mist had dissipated and Raquette was glittering in the sunshine. We passed two of Durant's Great Camps, Echo and Pine Knot, and then, just as Sears did, struck out directly across South Bay for the lower shore of the lake. We were making good time through a light swell and admiring the hills all around, Blue Mountain visible far off to the east, when we heard a sound we'd been waiting for all month, the lovely two-tone honking of Canada geese. We rested our paddles and drifted, scanning the sky. There they came, directly above, thirty-two birds in a loose **V**. Moments later we spotted another flock off to our right and still another, the biggest skein of all, disappearing over a low ridge dead ahead.

We were passing a marina on the south shore when we

* Unsuitable admirers had been a problem from the beginning. In late November 1882 the spanking-new *Sairy* had just been given her final coat of shellac when a well-heeled visitor stopped by J. Henry Rushton's shop. "W. W. Durant . . . was here the other day," the boatbuilder wrote Sears. "He saw the 'Sairy.' He is near six ft. and 170# (guess). I had hard work to keep him from ordering a duplicate."

caught a glimpse of a restaurant across the highway. Did I imagine it, or did a whiff of bacon grease waft past my nostrils? I looked at John, who was looking speculatively at me. Long cohabitation having honed our communication skills, we turned as one for the boat ramp. Our powdered milk and stale cereal could wait another day.

We stowed our boats behind a gas station and were soon sipping coffee in the cheery warmth of a local hangout. We'd been colder and hungrier than we'd realized, and when our eggs arrived we hoovered them up in a state approaching ecstasy. A white-haired man drove up in a Cadillac, his boat trailered behind, wife in the front seat. He was off to Florida for the winter and had come in to say good-bye. Our waitress made a nice fuss over him and gave him a warm hug.

"You stay out of trouble now," she told him.

"Oh, I guess I will," he said. "Hard not to at my age."

In the bathroom a canister with a hand-lettered sign suggested that nonpaying customers could contribute to the local ambulance company. If I'd had any cash on me I'd have emptied my pockets.

A collection of housekeeping cottages occupies Rush Point, where "Honest Joe" Whitney (no relation to the Whitney Park family) had his camp and where Sears lingered an extra day on his way north. On his return trip, he ran into Whitney and a young guide named Billy Cornell at Under the Hemlocks. Joe had business elsewhere but delegated Cornell to look after the old woodsman, so the two paddled side by side to Rush Point. Sears must have taken to the boy, because he let him take the *Sairy* out for a paddle. (A likable fellow who built boats when he wasn't guiding, Cornell stayed on when Whitney sold out in 1917, and some time thereafter drowned near Echo Camp.) We could see why Sears dawdled here. The view up the lake, with Big Island in the foreground, is magnificent.

The sky was graying off as we continued around South Bay but our luck held, and the winds remained light. It took some poking around in the rushes to locate the entrance to Brown's Tract Inlet, but soon we were working our way up the channel. This time I had no trouble negotiating the beaver dam under the bridge, where a layer of branches, leaves still green, had just been added to the top. I suppose I shouldn't have, but along the way I picked a white water lily and threaded its stem through my zipper pull so I could inhale its scent as I paddled. A heron and a kingfisher leapfrogged ahead of us, and on a dying pine I spotted a yellow-shafted flicker. Dead and dying trees, primarily spruce and tamarack, dot these marshes, because although seeds can germinate and reach respectable heights here, there is almost no soil to anchor them. Their shallow root systems can't sustain these trees, which are eventually toppled by blustering winds.

At one of the inlet's innumerable tight bends, three mergansers came steaming toward us, eyes submerged as they peered for fish. The trio looked up unalarmed, squeezed politely into single file, and as soon as they were past us resumed their hunt. Not five minutes later a flock of mallards accosted us at a shallow backwater. Like our visitor of the previous evening they seemed flabbergasted that we had nothing for them and followed some distance before giving up.

At the floating dock where we'd watched over her, I thought of Chelsea and wondered how she'd weathered her ninety-mile odyssey. Much had changed in the weeks since we'd been here: stampeding Canoe Classic racers had churned the muck at the end of the dock to a wallow, and the carry trail was ankle deep in beech and maple leaves. With a good deal of foliage down, you could see deeper into the woods. Now I was aware that the mile-long path traverses another major divide, this one between the Raquette and Moose River watersheds.

The wind was up by the time we emerged at Eighth Lake, where in the 1880s the recluse Alvah Dunning had a shanty.

Here Sears had stopped for breakfast after leaving Rush Point and getting caught in a shower. He intended to dry out indoors, but the key wasn't where Dunning had said it would be, so he camped in the lee of the shack, brewed a pot of tea, and passed a couple of hours lounging and smoking his pipe.

His absent host was a legendary character who had little use for people and none at all for the game laws they tried to impose on him. He lived by hunting and trapping, but he took only what he needed and like Sears he despised those who killed for trophies. His education had been rudimentary: to the end of his days he believed that the world was flat and stationary, and anyone who thought otherwise was crazy. Tall and spare, Dunning had what Alfred Donaldson termed a "vulturesquely beaked nose." He had been young when he fled to the woods after beating his unfaithful wife so savagely that his neighbors went looking for him. Seclusion agreed with him, and thereafter he lived alone in remote corners of the central Adirondacks, occasionally consenting to guide people he liked. He was honorable in his own way and as skilled in woodcraft, it was said, as Mitchell Sabattis. He loved dogs, and when Ned Buntline shot one of his hounds no one could believe Dunning had not dropped him on the spot.

The Adirondacks in the last quarter of the nineteenth century proved a poor choice for a man who relished solitude. Encroaching civilization drove Dunning from Blue Mountain Lake to the shores of Raquette Lake and then to a hut on Osprey Island that he shared with W. H. H. Murray. When the Durant family made it known that they had plans for the island, Dunning claimed that Murray had given Osprey to him and threatened to shoot anyone who set foot on it. Where masculine posturing failed, feminine persuasion succeeded. In 1880 W. W. Durant's mother invited Dunning to Camp Pine Knot, listened to him sympathetically, and plied him with tea. This courtesy, sweetened by a modest cash settlement, did the trick.

"Alvah can be coaxed," Dunning later explained, "but he can't be druv."

Whereupon he went to the lone island on Eighth Lake. When someone built a shanty nearby he returned to Raquette but was again driven away, this time by the arrival of the railroad. In 1899 a disgusted Alvah headed for the Rockies, but within a year he was back at Raquette Lake. By then he was declining, and spent the winters in nearby cities. The modern world he detested finally did him in: in March 1902 he went to bed in a Utica hotel and never woke up. The gas jet in his room leaked.

We ate lunch at the island's lean-to and decided to call it a day. Clouds had rolled in, and we knew the wind would be raking Seventh Lake. I lounged on the deacon's seat, tried to decipher the 1930s-era graffiti on the walls, and watched a chipmunk forage around the fireplace. Both of us were a little melancholy at the realization that this was our last night out-of-doors, the rest of the journey a matter of day-trips.

A light rain began at 5:30 and continued through the evening. We heard more geese, but they were hidden by the overcast. Dark came so fast we barely had time to finish our supper and brush our teeth. In the lean-to we lay in our sleeping bags and watched headlights streaming along the far shore. As usual, we slept as if we'd been poleaxed.

EIGHTH LAKE TO MINNEHAHA

Sears was still lounging at Alvah Dunning's shanty when a guide named Fred Loveland paddled past. Loveland was also bound for the Forge House, so Sears proposed that they travel together. Neither was in a hurry; Loveland was saddled with a boat that weighed more than a hundred pounds and was happy to have help getting under it for the carries. The two paddled off into a headwind and what Sears termed "a short snappy sea."

Similar conditions prevailed when we awoke, a light but persistent south wind creasing Eighth Lake, the morning light muted by scudding low clouds. After a perfunctory breakfast we pushed off for the south end of the lake, where we found the campground that had been jammed in August all but deserted. Again we opted for the shortcut, but now the half-mile trail seemed no more than a leg-stretcher.

Seventh Lake was calm at its sheltered eastern end but choppy wherever the wind could get at it. It was worse when

Sears and Loveland got here. Dismayed by the sight of whitecaps, Sears allowed that while he was able to keep pace with Loveland, it seemed "rather an unsocial way of traveling, that one should go ahead with a long, sharp boat, and his companion come puffing along in the rear with a canoe little larger than a bread tray. Wherefore I fell in readily with the suggestion that the larger boat would 'trim' better with two than one. Also, I may have had some doubts as to whether I could make the opposite shore at all." He gratefully took a seat in the stern of the guideboat and, grasping the *Sairy*'s painter, towed her along. In this way he went all the way to the foot of Fourth Lake.

At Arnolds Rock, where we camped on our first night out, we stopped to use the privy and have a sentimental look around. Then it was on to Sixth, where one plane took off and another landed while we were paddling the short distance from inlet to outlet. The noise in the little basin was ferocious, but we enjoyed riding the broad wakes the pontoons left behind. So adept had we become at rigging our gear that in minutes we were striding along the highway, past a low white building with a sign offering Showers $1. Wind buffeted our boats and tugged at our paddles until we turned off to descend the hill to Fifth Lake, where at the muddy landing a fresh deer track restored a sense of wildness. Soon we were well down the channel to Fourth, passing below the row of stores and houses that front the highway. The backsides of these buildings reminded me of the bad old days, not so long ago, when the channel was less than pristine.

There was a time when people here thought nothing of dumping raw sewage into the water, a problem that prevailed throughout the region, exacerbated by leaking leach fields and the universal practice of tossing garbage into the lakes. You could find everything from used diapers to cigarette butts bobbing in the waves, but most people ignored the detritus floating by the shores. By the mid-1960s the Fulton Chain was one large cesspool registering astronomical coliform counts. Concerned citizens, many of them summer residents, banded together and forced local and state authorities to act. The result has been dramatic improvement in water quality throughout the region.

As anyone who has worked at the local level knows, an educated citizenry can be a potent force for change. In another victory for ecologically minded residents, the Town of Webb (the large township that includes Old Forge) has at last stopped its program of aerial spraying to control blackflies and mosquitoes. The sprays its subcontractor applied—Malathion, Dibrom-14, and Scourge—were less harmful than the DDT once used but still potentially toxic to fish, bees, birds, aquatic invertebrates, and wildlife. While informational campaigns by agencies such as the nonprofit Adirondack Council brought an end to spraying in most other communities, the Town of Webb clung to its program, fearful that more insects meant fewer tourists. The anti-spray arguments gathered force when enough residents were inadvertently doused: it didn't take too many ruined barbeques and drenched boaters to convince people that a substance that stung their skin and eyes might not be good for them or for wildlife. Now the town is paying workers to hand-treat streams with BTi, a highly specific bacterium that attacks blackflies and mosquitoes in the larval stage without adverse side effects.

The final section of channel leading to Fourth Lake is a straight shot between man-made wooden retaining walls. On windy days the swell bulging in from the lake ricochets off these palisades and intensifies. Nowhere else had we encountered such waves: steep, triangular, arhythmic, and definitely unpleasant. Pitching and bobbing, we timed our strokes to hit the crests and fought our way out. As we passed the town beach, the same man who had shooed us away in August was securing his perimeter, alert to any hint of incipient merriment.

A short pull through broadsiding rollers took us to the state boat ramp. Fourth Lake, an unrunnable mass of whitecaps, would have to wait another day; already my face was radiant with windburn. Offshore the replica steamboat *Clearwater* chugged by, its few passengers huddled on the enclosed lower deck.

The autumnal equinox dawned bright and crisp, with fall colors blazing and fog hiding the lakes. At eight o'clock Fourth Lake was still blanketed, visibility only a few feet through a dense curtain of gray. I was paddling straight out from shore when John called me back. In three strokes I had disappeared completely, and he was convinced I was heading in the wrong direction. We should stay within sight of land, he said, even if hugging the shore added a mile or two. I soon saw his point: we were disoriented by every small bay and would have been hopelessly lost without the shoreline to guide us. It was also safer in the shallows. We could hear the odd powerboat pulsing slowly through the soup and could imagine being rammed in open water.

The surface was glassy as we *plip-plopp*ed past a couple of baronial estates and then a string of cottages jostling for waterfront. Slowly the mist thinned and patches of blue began appearing overhead. First the south shore revealed itself, then the sweep of the lake, the far end softened by the lifting haze. This time we could see what clouds had obscured on the first day of our trip: we were in a deep basin ringed by middling hills, their slopes now brilliant with fall color.

For Sears the Stormy Fourth again lived up to its name. Whitecaps and a "stiff topsail breeze" made him glad to be in Fred Loveland's boat; the waves, he judged, "were piling up in a way that would have made it impossible for the *Sairy* to advance a rod in an hour. . . . Every wave would have lifted half her length out of water, the wind would have caught under her full bearings, also on the broad blades, and any progress would have been out of the question." As it was, Loveland had his hands full. The guideboat "was sometimes brought to a standstill as we rounded an exposed point. Then there would come a lull and we would go ahead again." Halfway down the lake they spotted a lean-to and pulled in for lunch, Loveland contributing sandwiches, cheese, and bread; Sears adding tea, sugar, butter, and bacon. "It was," Sears wrote, "one of the impromptu, wholesome woodland dinners that are remembered through life, while the memory of more pretentious feasts have 'Gone, like the tenants that left without warning,/Down the back entry of Time.'"

At the northern tip of Alger Island we stopped to unkink tired muscles and have a look around. We were glad we hadn't stayed there on our way north. The lean-tos were too close together for any sense of privacy, but of course we'd been thoroughly spoiled. The wind was rising as we entered Third, where this time we could see the cottages strung out along the northeast and south shores. The last three lakes are small and, as Sears would say, soon passed over. Of them, Second is the nicest because it's least developed.

We entered First Lake on the opposite side of the strait we'd groped our way through on day one, passing the tall boathouse once owned by President Benjamin Harrison. His camp was so modest that in 1899 Martin Van Buren Ives wondered "why such a man can content himself with camping there when there are so many grander sites further on." Local legend holds that Harrison was so shy he hid behind trees when tourists rowed by.

Directly ahead lay a shallow bay with here and there a dead tree standing starkly in the slack water. There were more of them when Sears first saw the place in 1880, a mile or so of dead "hop poles," and the sight filled him with anguish. The desolation, he wrote, was "evidence of the effects of civilization and progress," in this case the dam at Old Forge Pond.

"Motionless in the fiercest storm, they stand with their dead feet and legs in the dull, sedgy marsh. Almost imperishable, they have stood there for more than a generation, and a generation yet unborn will see the same ghastly sight."

More ghastly, to my eyes, is the crowded north shore of First Lake, dominated by the former Hollywood Hills Hotel. The largest log hotel in the East, it opened during the Depression and was to be the centerpiece of a twenty-one-hundred-lot housing development. Streets and electricity were already in place when the entrepreneur behind it died and the project languished. The hotel, divided into condominiums, sports a lurid green roof.

At the entrance to the channel to Old Forge Pond, a man lounging on his dock gave us a cheery wave.

"Saving gas, huh?" he said.

"Yup," I told him. "Burning calories."

Lots of calories. When I got home I discovered that in just under a month I'd shed seven pounds. (If we'd stuck with freeze-dried food, it could have been twenty.) Seven pounds isn't that much, until you factor in the muscle I'd added, which is heavier than fat. One day toward the end of the trip, as I picked up John's pack and slung it into the back of the car, I remembered what a struggle that task had represented not long before. In fact all of our gear felt lighter and more compact, and carries that had challenged me on the way north seemed shorter by half.

Down the gamut of cottages and boathouses we went, and at 12:45 we scraped onto the children's beach we'd left twenty-six days before. Although we still had one more leg to paddle, I was elated. We'd all but done it, and tomorrow's cruise, down the Middle Branch of the Moose, would be a breeze. *Yeeee-hah!*

But for Sears, the paddle from Fourth Lake to the Forge House held no elation. He had parted company with Fred Loveland at Third Lake in order to visit with friends. From there, he wanted to travel alone. "I had a fancy," he wrote, "for taking in the lower three lakes by moonlight once more; for I had a presentiment that I was likely to go over them no more." He was right. He never saw them again.

"And when the moon rose, orange-red and large and full," he told *Forest and Stream*'s readers, "I paddled, very quietly and a little sadly, over the Third, by the Eagle's Nest, across the Second, by the Stickney camp and over the First, and so down by the Indian Rock and down the channel until I made the lights of the Forge House. I landed at the boathouse, tied in, and at 8:30 o'clock the *Sairy* was resting by the maple tree where my canoes have so often found a safe resting place."

If I seemed to be dragging my feet toward the end of our cruise, at least I could claim precedent. Sears too had trouble tearing himself away. When he paddled up to the Forge House he had been in the Adirondacks a month and a half. His time was up, yet he stole another week. He wanted to do some deer hunting, and I imagine he made the rounds of friends' camps to say good-bye.

While he postponed his departure, the American Canoe Association was holding its fourth annual meet in Ontario. The young organization was experiencing phenomenal growth, and not only among men:

> The Canadian canoeists have succeeded in interesting their wives, daughters, and sweethearts in the sport, and seventy lady canoeists are reported to be in camp at the Peterboro meet. . . . We have a few lady canoeists on this side of the line, but American girls will surely not suffer themselves to be outdone by the fair Canadians in adopting a sport that is far better adapted for feminine muscles than is rowing.

New-York Times
August 22, 1883

Rain pummeled our cabin roof during the night but morning arrived dry, albeit chilly and gray. Below the dam in Old Forge the Middle Branch of the Moose is rocky, so we asked permission to put in at a local outfitter called Tickner's, a little farther down. We were welcome to use his dock, a pleasant young man told us, and we could leave our car in his lot. He traced the river's sinuous course on a topo map, twelve miles of water where the road takes six, and waved away my offer to pay.

"The Middle Branch is a nice day-trip," he said. "I don't know why more people don't paddle it."

The river was narrow at the put-in but broadened almost immediately, when the North Branch came in on our right. A slanting rain began and my glasses, fogged to begin with, were of no further use. I paddled through a soft-focus world, past indistinct houses and docks until the shores turned marshy.

When Sears paddled the *Sairy* down this stretch, the river had fallen out of use and was choked with downed trees. Only three years before, it had been a pleasant excursion, and he had stopped at Herreshoff Manor. Known in Sears's day as Arnold's, the Manor was "quite a tragical place," he noted. After Charles Herreshoff's suicide and Nat Foster's murder of the Indian Drid, a final chapter darkened the house's history. In 1837 Otis Arnold and his wife moved in and proceeded to raise ten girls and two boys there. They planted crops and kept cows, and in time they put an addition on the back to accommodate travelers on the Brown's Tract Road. One of the boys, Ed, became a respected guide; the daughters, Amazons all, were proficient in every aspect of farm work and were also renowned equestrians. The Honorable Amelia Murray, Joel Headley, H. Perry Smith, and many other passersby marveled at their skills. "Not only did they ride their horses bareback over the flat land of the clearings at reckless speed," wrote Joseph Grady, "but they broke the untamed colts to saddle and harness and trained them to come at their call. . . . The girls rode saddle-less and bridle-less with the mere touch of the hand for guidance, swam their mounts through the swollen waters of the Moose River and walked them across the ice."

The family prospered until the fall of 1868, when the normally level-headed father had a misunderstanding with a guide over ownership of a dog collar. The argument took an ugly turn, whereupon Arnold seized his rifle and shot his opponent, who died in considerable pain five hours later. Stunned by what he'd done, Arnold walked to nearby Nick's Lake, filled his pockets with rocks, rowed away from shore, and rolled out of his boat. His body was not recovered until the following spring; in the interim his wife died. When the Arnold offspring sorted through their parents' effects, their father's trunk yielded ten thousand dollars in gold. The children moved away, and the house was left to disintegrate.

Sears spent a couple of hours at the Manor, inspecting broken furniture, moldy barrels, discarded cookware. "The ruins of a dozen castles on the Rhine would have less interest for me," he said. "There was a rusty scythe hanging in what was once the drawing room, and in an upper room was a bunk, well filled with soft dry grass. An old tin pail, half full of ashes, had recently been used for making a smudge, and the bunk had been used within two or three days by some sleeper who had come to the clearing to watch for the deer which feed at early morning or late evening in the lonely fields." Eventually the building was razed and the hillside it occupied was eaten away by a sand pit. The flats where the Arnold girls raced their horses, now part of a community called Thendara, are shared by railroad tracks and a highway.

Not far below Thendara there used to be a cascade known as the Little Rapids. It could be run in a canoe in both directions if conditions were right, but on the day Sears took the *Sairy* down the Moose, the gate at the Old Forge dam had been raised and the river was high and turbulent. "While I was hanging on at the head of the rapids, back-paddling and making up my mind whether to 'shoot' them or carry around," he wrote, "fate decided the question. One of those colorless boulders caught the prow of the canoe, whirled her broadside on, and the next instant I *was* shooting the rapids, stern foremost. I think it was not five seconds until I was safely by the rocks and on the level, foamy current below. One bump and a jump on a rock that nearly threw me out, and I was calmly floating on deep, clear water." He was, he admitted, a little shaken by the incident.

There are no longer rapids where Sears had his adventure. They were drowned in 1888, when an eight-foot dam was built, with a lock for the side-wheeler *Fawn*. We carried around and saw from downstream that the dam was crumbling and the lock had all but vanished. The river bottom below the falls was littered with sunken timbers and logs strewn every which way, giant jackstraws passing just beneath our hulls.

Beyond the dam the river changed abruptly, the languid, marshy Moose giving way to a narrower, quicker river that wound through deciduous forest interspersed with corridors of conifers. The woods crowded in on us, their silence broken only by the *dee-dee-dee* of chickadees. At one bend we surprised two otters playing on the bank. They slipped into the water and swam ahead of us for a time, little round heads bobbing at the surface. On a long straightaway I pulled over and got out to snap off the tip of a balsam bough so I could inhale its tangy scent. (I kept it on my desk for weeks, its odor growing sweeter as it dried, the memory of the river at my fingertips.)

While the rain came and went, the cold intensified. Occasionally we could see the embankment of the New York Central tracks, and finally Flatrock Mountain, microwave tower on its summit, materialized out of the scrim. No sooner had it done so than we were caught in a downpour, fat drops hobnailing the surface and hammering the hoods of our slickers. It was a marvelous tumult, like a hailstorm in a tin-roofed shed.

Near a grassy flat, a giant boulder in the stream marked what Sears called "the foot of navigation." This is where the Peg Leg railroad ended, where the *Fawn* docked, and where, before either of them came into being, Jones's Camp had stood. Sears had stayed at Jones's on both of his previous trips and was much attached to the place. It was, he declared, "emphatically a place of rest. The low, constant murmur of the rapids, a hundred yards below, is audible at all hours of the day and night. To me it is somnolent music. Often . . . I dropped asleep over pen and paper, lulled by the low, unvarying monotone of rushing waters, and at night it was better than an opiate."

But in 1883 something had gone amiss between Eri Jones and Sears. Perhaps Jones saw him as a freeloader (which he could be; he was a poor man), or Sears may have unwittingly offended the owner on his previous visit. At any rate, in a rare breach of woodland etiquette, Jones had refused, when the two met elsewhere, to disclose the location of the camp key. Sears was furious, the near-disaster at Little Rapids still on his mind. "I stood about one chance in fifty of needing [the key]," he wrote. "But if I did need it, I should need it badly." And so he sat outside and with great satisfaction watched a red squirrel race in and out of the barn: "I hope he will eat up ten bushels of chop-stuff and oats and call in his sisters, his cousins and his aunts."

After half an hour, Sears shouldered the *Sairy* for the nine-mile trek to Moose River Settlement, and early in the afternoon he emerged on the north shore of the river. "I . . . ferried myself over, landed in the Tannery ooze, drew the *Sairy* up into the fresh, green grass, wiped her frail siding clean and 'tied in' neatly and carefully. Then, amid the questions and congratulations of a dozen good-natured friends, I mounted her on my head for a last short carry to the hotel and walked wearily up to the hospitable door of the Moose River House. I laid her down carefully on the shady porch, as a mother would a tired infant, and the cruise of the *Sairy Gamp* was ended." It was the twenty-fourth of August. The following week, the *Boonville Herald* noted:

> The little boat of G. W. Sears, of Wellsboro, Tioga county, Pa., has returned to us all right after a trip of 261 miles through the woods. Having gained three quarters of a pound in the trip it now weighs eleven and one fourth pounds. The little man did well not to smash the little boat in the rough country he had to travel in.

Since there is no public access to the Moose below Thendara, canoeists turn around when they see Flatrock Mountain and head back to town. We planned on going a bit farther. A friend with a camp just downstream had showed me an overgrown footpath we could use to get to the road. Between us and that path lay the only whitewater on our trip, a series of short rapids that I had scouted one February day. Now, of course, they looked quite different. The first was a straightforward chute that I negotiated easily, the Kevlar bulging under my fanny as I slid over a couple of boulders. The *Sairy Damp* felt wonderfully stable, and I was impressed with how easy it was to maneuver her with the double blade. Correction was instantaneous, a matter of dipping whichever tip was needed. John also got a lumpy but safe ride.

An island split the river ahead, with rapids on both sides. Exposed rocks all down the channel showed the water level was too low for passage, so we had to get out and walk. It was a miserable haul. The banks were overgrown, which meant we had to stay in the river, stumbling over slick rocks, through water that was waist-deep in spots, our feet plunging into ankle-grabbing holes. Thoroughly soaked, we both began shivering. It was all we could do to keep the painters from slipping through our whitened fingers.

Beyond the island we reembarked, but only for a minute or

two, when another stretch of fastwater appeared. We pulled into an eddy to reconnoiter and saw a runnable short chute with a broad right turn at the bottom. This time John went first, maneuvering into midstream and then shooting through the black **V** between rocks. In seconds he was bobbing in the foam below and I followed, pulse quickening as the current sucked my bow toward the wedge. Down I sailed, keeping one boulder on my left, stroking to miss another on the right, then trailing my paddle to carve a turn through the bend.

My heart sank. Before us lay another impassable stretch, a boulder garden a hundred yards long. This wasn't supposed to be there; were we on the wrong river? Backpaddling, we stared stupidly downstream, unable to take in what we were seeing, unable to figure out what to do next. Duuuuh. In fact we were sliding into hypothermia, blood retreating to vital organs, brains abandoned in the scramble. We might still be sitting there, eyes dull, mouths agape, had something not clicked in my oxygen-starved brain, some synapse getting just enough juice to fire. Then I knew where we were, in the scattering of summer camps known as Minnehaha. In the woods to our right we would find a trail, a house, and beyond it the road and our car.

With enormous relief we swung into a cove, but when we stumbled up the bank there was no sign of the path. We had landed about fifteen feet too early, and the bushwhacking required to get to the trail was more than we could contemplate. There was a straighter shot and we took it, lurching through tangles of blackberry to emerge in someone's backyard, my water-filled boots making cartoon squishes. Fifty yards down the road sat our car, a profoundly welcome sight. Before we'd reached it our friend Herm Albright, who styles himself the mayor of Minnehaha, appeared out of the drizzle to offer congratulations.

The forty miles back to our cottage passed in a peculiar blur.

When we'd retrieved the other car I tucked in behind John, but along the way he managed to pass a lumbering RV and disappeared. I hadn't the energy to follow. I drove in a daze, heater blasting, wipers slapping, the towel under me now as wet as my pants. Although I knew the road intimately, I kept jerking out of my reverie to find myself on another highway, until a familiar sign or view snapped the landscape into place. Past Seventh Lake I drove, then Eighth, where the dark maw of our last lean-to flashed through the trees. I surfaced briefly at Raquette Lake, and at Utowana. A final downshift, a turn onto a winding gravel road, and I cut the engine in front of the cabin. Only then did I believe our trip was over.

John ran a steaming bath while I got out the Mumm's. We peeled off our sodden clothes and squeezed into the tub together, moaning as the heat flooded into our bones. The cork hit the ceiling and champagne foamed in our battered plastic mugs.

"Cheers," John said.

"Cheers," said I. "To George."

EPILOGUE

When George Sears so gently deposited the *Sairy Gamp* on the verandah of the Moose River House, he could not have imagined that her odyssey was only beginning. He arranged to have her taken to Boonville and then shipped the 250 miles to his home in Wellsboro. There, he reported, "she sits lightly on a shelf, where I can rest my eyes on her."

She did not sit there long. As early as November 1882, when her varnish was still tacky, J. Henry Rushton was thinking about her publicity value. "Regarding her final disposition," he wrote to Sears, "can't we get her an honored position somewhere? In Washington or New York. If she takes you through the woods safely I think she will be as deserving of honor as the 'Rob Roy' or the Paper Canoe . . . " As it turned out, Sears's dispatches in *Forest and Stream* generated considerable interest in her, and after a month the little canoe was returned to her maker. "To-day I send you back the *Sairy Gamp*," Sears wrote Rushton.

She is of no further use to me. There is not a lake in Tioga County, and I am not going to rattle her over the stones of Pine Creek. She has astonished me; she will be more of a surprise to you. Remember the advice you gave me about bracing, etc. Remember you said you "would not warrant her for an hour; she may go to pieces like an

> *eggshell." That's what you said; she don't go to pieces worth a cent. I have snagged her, rocked her, got her onto spruce knots, and been rattled down rapids stern foremost; and I send her back, as tight and staunch as the day I took her at Boonville. There are more than a hundred cuts, scratches, and abrasions on her thin siding, there are red and green blotches on her strips, from contact with amateur boats, and longer streaks of blue from collisions, with the regulation guide boat, but she does not leak a drop. I once said in* Forest and Stream *I was trying to find out how light a canoe it took to drown a man. I never shall know. The* Sairy Gamp *has only ducked me once in a six weeks' cruise, and that by my own carelessness.*

A few months later, Rushton wrote Sears about a canoeing meet at which Sears and his boat had been the talk of the day: "They hardly knew which to admire most, the little craft or the reckless (!) woodsman who would risk his life in such an eggshell. However, all had only the kindliest words for 'Nessmuk' and his light canoe. The canoe is in Forest and Stream office [in New York] right where everyone who goes in must see her and can examine. . . . She is a 'Card' alike for her paddler and her builder." After all her travels, he reported, she was still "staunch and tight." "Yes, the *Sairy Gamp* is tight," the editor of *Forest and Stream* added. "We filled her half full of water the other night and launched a yacht model by gaslight."

In the fall of 1884, Rushton arranged with the U.S. Department of Agriculture to have the *Sairy Gamp* featured at the Cotton Centennial, in New Orleans, and nine years later she turned up in the *Forest and Stream* exhibit at the World's Columbian Exposition in Chicago. Later she was acquired by the Smithsonian Institution, whose collection she adorned for roughly seventy years.

In 1918 she left Washington briefly when the Smithsonian loaned her to a former speedboat builder named W. Starling

Burgess. Burgess, who manufactured biplanes and was experimenting with seaplane design at his factory in Marblehead, Massachusetts, used the *Sairy* as a model for a lifeboat light enough to be carried on naval aircraft. How useful she proved isn't clear, but Burgess was obviously a Sears fan. "Last Saturday," he reported, "she was cradled aboard my car and run to the New Hampshire border for a taste once more of woods and running water. My son and I dropped down the river that afternoon; and picking her out of the water at the edge of the forest carried her back to camp. It was high adventure in our little camp that night—thrilling indeed, the reading of 'Woodcraft' with Nessmuk's very boat amongst us."

At last, in 1965, she returned to the scene of her triumph, when she was sent on permanent loan to the Adirondack Museum. By the time she arrived in Blue Mountain Lake her thwarts were missing but she was otherwise intact.

From the moment I first laid eyes on her, I'd longed to touch this boat, and my chance came in the spring of 1992, when I arranged to have her photographed beside the *Sairy Damp*. One morning in May curator Hallie Bond and I lifted her from her cradle and maneuvered her over the exhibit barrier. She felt surprisingly light, more like nine pounds than her original ten and a half. Could she have dried out over the years? Hallie thought not. At any rate, she seemed terribly frail, "her sides no thicker than the shell/Of Ole Bull's Cremona fiddle," as Sears put it in "Our Camping Ground." I could feel her strakes working as we carried her outdoors. In the sunlight her oil-and-varnish finish was a deep chestnut, and when we rolled her over we discovered bright splotches where she had been patched. She was shorter and even shallower than I'd realized, her lines infinitely more graceful. With her oval shape and closely spaced ribbing she looked like an ancient, burnished beech leaf.

After he had sent the *Sairy Gamp* off to her maker, Sears spent the winter writing *Woodcraft*, his *omnium gatherum* of camping lore. The following summer he stuck close to home, making brief forays down Pine Creek and other favorite waters. The persistent cough that doubled him over made work difficult, and a note of self-pity crept into his articles, though leavened with a characteristic dash of humor. "And now I am lounge-ridden," he told his *Forest and Stream* fans, "and my canoes hang idly in their slings, while my guns are rusting, and Jeff, my hound, is eating himself into the shape of a seed cucumber, out in the country."

Unable to face another Wellsboro winter, "the trying time for northern invalids," he accepted an invitation to join *Forest and Stream* contributor Samuel D. Kendall at Tarpon Springs, on Florida's Gulf coast.* He sailed from New York in January 1885 and after several adventures managed to connect with his friend. A week of paddling his latest Rushton canoe, the ten-and-a-half-foot *Bucktail*, proved more than he could take. His arms, he reported, "were so lame and swollen that I was absolutely disabled . . . and forced to call a halt." He built himself a shanty and befriended a flock of quail, which he then could not bear to shoot. A high point was the arrival of the eight-and-a-half-foot *Rushton*, which he delighted in paddling around sheltered lakes and streams. Once, he boasted, he cruised her twenty miles down the coast and back "without shipping a drop." After almost sixteen months he returned home, but the improvement in his health didn't last. The Florida climate had brought on a recurrence of malaria, and he was wracked by chills and fever.

* Kendall, whose byline was "Tarpon," had in 1882 performed the not-inconsiderable feat of sailing a homemade canoe, the *Solid Comfort*, some thirty-eight hundred miles, from Lake George, on the eastern edge of the Adirondacks, to Tarpon Springs.

In October 1886 he finished the introduction to *Forest Runes,* the poetry collection he had begun assembling almost six years before. (The manuscript, bound in deerskin, had been kicking around the *Forest and Stream* offices for some time before the editor decided to take a chance on it.) The book, available by subscription for one dollar, appeared in March 1887.

Sears had been home only a few months when he was offered another chance to get away. It was clear that travel improved his spirits, if not his health, and he accepted this new invitation with alacrity. On Christmas morning 1886 he left New York City for what would be his last jaunt, a leisurely tour to Florida's east coast on the steam yacht *Stella.* The ship put in at Charleston and at one of the Georgia Sea Islands; in Saint Augustine Sears saw what was left of Geronimo's Chiricahua Apaches: 448 ragged men, women, and children reduced to begging for food. "Accustomed as they have always been to the freest life and the pure mountain air of their native fastnesses," he observed with callous detachment, "it is likely the low, malarious lands of southern Florida may soon solve the Indian question as far as they are concerned, and it is as well so. Humanity has no use for them."

Tired of his stateroom, he went ashore near New Smyrna and spent a week camping alone. "And the old, old story was taken up once more," he wrote, "the story that is acted over and over again but never tires. Loafing silently through the woods, sitting on a log, getting an occasional shot at a squirrel or rabbit, lounging about camp, cutting night-wood and 'fixing up.' A real woodsman is always 'fixing up' the camp when there is nothing else to do, and the camp is always growing more easy and comfortable the longer it is occupied." As a camper, Sears was definitely an otter. Returning north in April 1887, the *Stella* lost her rudder and came close to foundering in the worst storm Sears had ever experienced at sea.

The late 1880s were grim years for Sears as his health deteriorated and his income dwindled. His application for a military pension was rejected,* and his diary entries became despondent. At one point he considered suicide; eventually the journal was abandoned altogether. When Captain L. A. Beardslee, the *Forest and Stream* contributor he'd met at the Forge House, invited him to sojourn aboard the battleship *Vermont,* he sadly declined. "Time and 'physical disability' will . . . beat every mother's son of us and I do not complain," Sears wrote his old friend. "Few men have had as much of life in the woods as I have, and memory at least can not be taken away from me while my senses hold good. . . . No. I have not written much for the press in the last year or so. I can not get over the inane listlessness and laziness induced by a long, tedious siege of malaria, and it seems as though the old-time energy and vim would never return. I have lost all ambition."

Another *Forest and Stream* writer received one of Nessmuk's last communications, a postcard written March 10, 1890: "Friend Stratton. Your letter is before me, and should have been answered sooner; but I must write when and as I can. It is not every day I can write even my name. A constant cough, heart failure and great weakness are telling on me, and I shall probably never get a mile from home. I have not been beyond the front yard since last October. I should like to see the birds and apple blooms once more, if it may be, but am quite resigned to what fate may have in store for me."

The man who for more than fifty years had roamed at will was ultimately housebound. Release came in the early hours of May 1, when at age sixty-eight, Sears embarked on what he called "the Dark Carry." The following week a notice appeared on page one of *Forest and Stream:*

* The Civil War was a week old and Sears was a thirty-nine-year-old father of two when he shaved four years off his age and enlisted in the "Bucktails," a Pennsylvania regiment composed largely of loggers and sharpshooters. Less than two months later, after twice being hospitalized for asthma, he was discharged.

> The sad intelligence, which came to us last Saturday, announcing the death of "Nessmuk," was not altogether unexpected. For several months past it had been known to his friends that Mr. Sears was in a very feeble condition. . . . Last summer, too weak to make a camping excursion to the woods, yet powerless to withstand the longing for a taste of the old life, he pitched his tent beneath the hemlocks of his home yard and there with his grandson, "played" at an outing. After the long and weary confinement of the winter just past, he craved outdoor life: and on the last day of April, supported by loving arms, he went out for a little while under the same trees. The next morning at 2 o'clock, May 1, he passed away. Last Saturday, in the spot he had selected beneath those same hemlocks, they laid him at rest.

"He was gifted with a superior intellect," the editors wrote, "and it did not stagnate in the woods. Uneducated in the schools, he was yet self-taught, and well taught. He knew the best authors. That was no idle boast of his, on being asked what books he took into the woods, that he found it necessary to take none, seeing that he carried Shakespeare and other poets under his hat. He possessed a rich store of mother wit, a vast fund of practical common sense, a philosophy of his own. He commanded the respect of intellectual men with whom he came in contact. A distinguished clergyman once wrote us after spending a fortnight in camp with 'Nessmuk,' 'Of all the men I have ever met, Sears is the best worth knowing.'"

There were many tributes, among them a forgettable poem by James Whitcomb Riley entitled "Nessmuk" in which Riley invoked the spirits of Chaucer, Robin Hood, and "Ike" Walton: "These three, O Nessmuk, gathered hunter-wise,/Are camped on hither slopes of Paradise,/To hail thee first and greet thee, as they should."

Sears had always entertained a healthy skepticism about the hereafter. On April 26, 1875, he had dropped in to see his friend Hugh Young, a Wellsboro banker and state legislator who, like many of Sears's friends, called him Bacchus. Young's diary relates: "Geo. W. Sears, 'Bacchus,' called in today and we read and laughed over some of the obituary verses in the Philadelphia *Ledger*. He wrote on the margin of a newspaper the following verse and requested me to have it 'sculped' into his tomb stone if I survived him:

> Life is the dullest of jokes—
> He's a fool who supposes it serious.
> Death puts a *nub* to the hoax
> And the rest is immensely mysterious."

Sears left behind a curious document, a medical will drawn up in April 1884. In it he described various of his symptoms and directed his physicians, a father and son, to perform an autopsy—"It may be of benefit to the living." A further clause enjoined these doctors to "articulate my bones and preserve the same where the blessed sunlight can sometimes reach them. And I charge both doctors to set their faces firmly against the modern prejudice that would first make a funeral of me and then relegate my body to a wet, dismal hole in darkness and dirt. If a man has one indefensible right on this earth, it is the right to himself: to his personality, the ownership of his own body . . ." His wishes were ignored. No autopsy was performed because, as the younger physician recalled many years later, "I knew the community, particularly the widow, would look on the proceedings with horror." Besides, he added, there was no mystery about what killed Sears; it was an ordinary case of pulmonary tuberculosis.

And so a man who abhorred convention was given a conventional funeral and buried among the hemlocks he had planted in his yard. His travels, however, were not quite over. Improvident in all matters, he had lost title to his homestead through foreclosure; the sister-in-law who redeemed the mortgage had given George and Mariette a life lease on the place, but when she objected to a grave on the property, Sears was reinterred in the Wellsboro cemetery. *Forest and Stream* took up a collection for a memorial, and fans from around the country sent contributions. In 1893 a granite headstone with a bronze bas-relief was erected. The portrait, by George T. Brewster, is a reverse view of the *Forest Runes* frontispiece. Oak and laurel leaves, a perched owl, and Sears's signature decorate the bronze; the supporting boulder bears an image of his trademark hatchet. Mariette and their children, left to shift for themselves as usual, are buried elsewhere. The solo traveler sleeps alone.

A prosperous community of lovingly tended shade trees and nineteenth-century buildings, Wellsboro remembers Sears with a plaque on its common and a dusty display of his belongings at the county historical society. The high school yearbook is called *The Nessmuk.* A summit overlooking nearby Marsh Creek is named Mount Nessmuk, and another plaque greets visitors to the east rim of his beloved Pine Creek Gorge, the thousand-foot chasm now known as the Grand Canyon of Pennsylvania. Sears's house on the banks of Morris Brook was eventually moved and remodeled beyond recognition, and the brook was dammed—ironically, considering his views on dams—a half mile above his property to create Lake Nessmuk. A few years ago, December 2, his birthdate, was proclaimed George Washington Sears Day in the state.

Despite the memorials, I did not find Sears's spirit in Wellsboro, a town he escaped every chance he got. For me he lives on in the great watersheds of the Adirondacks: the Moose, the Raquette, the Saranac, the Saint Regis, all the way from Old Forge to Paul Smiths. Before he had ever seen the Northern Wilderness, he understood what was at stake there. The same scenario had been played out at Yosemite, Yellowstone, and Niagara Falls. "I have traveled in foreign lands," he wrote, "have been twice to the Amazon Valley; and I rise to remark that there is but one Adirondack Wilderness on the face of the earth. And, if the great State of New York fails to see and preserve its glorious gifts, future generations will have cause to curse and despise the petty, narrow greed that converts into saw-logs and mill-dams the best gifts of wood and water, forest and stream, mountains and crystal springs in deep wooded valleys that the sun shines on at this day."

He did not live long enough to see it, but two years after he died, New York State did preserve those glorious gifts by creating the Adirondack Park. And as Nessmuk predicted, the tanners and lumbermen moved on and the forest began to recover. In two hundred years, one ecologist has estimated, all signs of their presence will be gone, at least in the publicly owned Forest Preserve. The drowned lands that so distressed him no longer exist, except as shadowy stumps passing beneath your hull. The mammoth hotels burned, and the steamers that bustled up to their landings were long ago broken up for scrap.

Yet for those who cherish, as Sears did, the best gifts of wood and water, the fight to preserve the Adirondacks for future generations continues. Perhaps the greatest challenge of the next century will be striking a balance between the needs of the park's 130,000 permanent residents and those of the nine million people who visit it each year. In a region plagued by unemployment, development often looks like salvation: many Adirondackers believe that zoning restrictions should be eased. Those who oppose them note that housing construction has increased fifty percent in the last twenty years and want zoning tightened, particularly on lakeshores and in the backcountry.

Often, as we paddled along, I was reminded of a line in a Gerard Manley Hopkins poem: "After-comers cannot guess the beauty been." In some ways this is true: acid rain has killed more than two hundred Adirondack lakes, and nowhere can you safely drink the water. Alpine flora are at risk from too many feet, and it's harder to find true solitude. But some things are better now than they were in Sears's day. We no longer shoot everything that moves, and we're restoring some of the species our forefathers hunted to oblivion. Pesticides are out, recycling is in. Most campers pack out what they pack in, and leave a little firewood besides. A canoe trip through the park is still a wonderful experience. At dawn and at dusk, when the waters still and the wildlife goes about its business, it is indeed possible to guess the beauty been. Some things endure: the way a heron stalks a marsh, the shapes of mountains and bays, the sound of water lapping granite.

We couldn't always follow Sears's trail, yet in the end the distances we covered were almost the same. Although Sears wrote that he had paddled and carried the *Sairy Gamp* 266 miles, roughly 82 of those miles were made with assistance. Guides were always relieving him of his knapsack or his canoe. On the longer carries he hired wagons to tote his gear, and thirty-odd miles were accomplished on the decks of steamers. Under his own power he covered about 183 miles; we covered 180. He spent one night under canvas; we spent twelve. But the numbers don't really matter. What matters is the work itself, the sheer energy required to push a small canoe from Old Forge to Paul Smiths and back again. We were younger and by far healthier than Sears was, and we were better nourished and better equipped. In spite of this we found ourselves exhausted every night—happily so, but still exhausted. By the time we staggered out of the woods at Minnehaha, we felt enormous respect for his accomplishment.

George Sears gave me three enduring gifts. First were the friends I made all along his route, people whose kindness and encouragement I will always remember. Another was the gift of Adirondack history. In the beginning I saw the cruise of the *Sairy Gamp* merely as geography, as a necklace of lakes strung on rivers. But the more I learned about the past, the more I saw that my route was really a necklace of stories. There were so many stories; so many lives were shaped by that geography, so many consumed by it. The farther I paddled, the richer the experience.

Sears's final legacy was the joy of canoeing, and this gift has changed both our lives. Now, from ice-out to freeze-up, whenever we can get away, we imitate Nessmuk and head for the woods. The canoe, that most elegant mode of travel, takes us to places where silence calms the spirit and where perspective returns. "Wherefore," as Sears wrote at the end of *Woodcraft,* "let us be thankful that there are still thousands of cool, green nooks beside crystal springs, where the weary soul may hide for a time, away from debts, duns and deviltries, and a while commune with nature in her undress."

As usual, George had it right.

AFTERWORD

Eight years have glided by since I pulled the *Sairy Damp* out of the chilly waters of the Moose that September afternoon in 1990. A lot has happened in the Adirondacks since then. Properties have changed hands, structures have been replaced, and several people have passed over what George Sears called the Dark Carry. The intervening years have also given me a deeper understanding of Sears as a person. A year ago I was granted access to a private archive belonging to a great-grandson of Nessmuk, the late Dr. James F. Madison. This collection includes seven of Sears's diaries and assorted manuscripts, correspondence, travel and military documents, financial records, and personal artifacts (one, a business-size envelope, contains two coppery locks of his hair). The information gleaned from the Madison archive has fleshed out my original portrait, providing deeper shading here and smudging earlier convictions there.

Sometimes I feel as if the shade of George Sears won't leave me alone. I've lately been immersing myself in the yellowed pages of *Porter's Spirit of the Times* and *Forest and Stream*, the periodicals in which most of his prose appeared from 1860 to 1890, for a projected volume called *The Nessmuk Reader*. These long-forgotten travel pieces include vivid accounts of camping excursions on his home ground in Pennsylvania, and chronicles of more ambitious expeditions: to Michigan when it was a frontier, to a largely undiscovered Florida, and, a year after Louis Agassiz ventured there, into the jungles of the Amazon. Neglected for more than a century, these evocations of a vanished era also bring Sears's life into sharper focus.

Finally, in the years since *An Adirondack Passage* appeared, many readers have written me, to take exception to my opinions, to correct me in matters large and small, or simply to share their own canoeing experiences in this wonderful region. For all these reasons, I'm delighted to have this chance to update and amend my original text.

SEARS'S TRIP

To begin at the beginning, Sears did not, as it turns out, start his cruise in the first week of July 1883. His diary for that year reveals that it was not until Wednesday, July 11, that he left Wellsboro, and from the outset things went badly. He missed his rail connection at Lyons, New York, and had to spend the night there ("had a cussed time"). The next morning he "reached Utica in a tornado." Thus it was not until the afternoon of July 12 that he swung down from the train in Boonville to claim the *Sairy Gamp*.

He spent four days at Moose River Settlement, fishing and trying out his featherweight canoe, and on the last day "had an audience like a side show at a circus." Quite likely the *Boonville Herald* reporter who noted his preparations was one of the spectators. There followed a week of fooling around the first four lakes of the Fulton Chain as he visited friends and tried to get his arms into shape for the upcoming voyage. It seems that Sears counted this social mileage in his overall trip tally of 266 miles (a figure that always confused me, since the objective distance was roughly 180 miles). Some 80 of those miles, then, consisted of short paddles to welcoming Fulton Chain camps on both the northbound and southbound legs of his cruise.

Perfunctory as it is, his 1883 diary shows that his account for *Forest and Stream* glosses over some of his more expedient travel arrangements. Thus I learned that after his first sojourn at Joe Whitney's camp, when he told his readers "I left the Raquette for Forked Lake," he did not, as he implies, do so under his own power. What he really did was paddle three miles up to Kenwell's hotel on Tioga Point, take lunch there, and shoot the breeze with tourists and guides all afternoon. It was, after all, a lovely day, one "to mark with a white pebble." He stayed on for supper, and then he and his diminutive canoe caught the steamer *Killoquah* to Forked. There, his dyspeptic view of his stay at Fletcher's may have owed as much to the "wretched bed in the garret" he fumed about in his diary as to the rainy weather cited in his official dispatch.

At Paul Smith's hotel, at the northern end of his route, he was treated better. Here the proprietor, a canny operator renowned for his skill in separating guests from their cash, "[would] not take a cent for my bill," Sears told his journal. Also unmentioned in his published itinerary was a day and a half layover on Upper Saranac Lake as he headed south. Having missed the last wagon on the Sweeney Carry, and thus his connection with the Raquette River steamer, he ended up spending two nights at the carry hotel, socializing with passersby and on August 9 visiting a camp belonging to the Woodruff family.

By August 18 he was back at the Forge House, in no hurry to conclude his cruise. "Laid off doctoring for lameness and resting," he scribbled in his diary. "The days go by dreamily and all too fast. I paddle and visit." His journal entry for August 24 doesn't mention his hair-raising plunge down the rapids, only that he reached the Moose River House, "tired as a dog. . . . Had my room, no. 7 as usual." Then he summed up: "Cruised 113 miles out, 143 back, 46 miles of it carries." *Forest and Stream*'s total was 118 miles out and 148 back, a

10-mile discrepancy that may have arisen from Sears's shakily scrawled figures. Whether the total was 256 or 266 miles, however, his cruise was a signal accomplishment.

SEARS HIMSELF

His diaries and correspondence highlight recurring patterns in George Sears's life. As early as 1847, when he was twenty-five years old and living in Brockport, New York, he complained of poor health, a "bad pain in side" and other ailments that left him "indisposed to work." Yet he seldom felt ill when he was hunting or visiting friends. He wagered on cockfights, hired out at haying time, and occasionally rewarded himself with a small luxury. On September 30, 1847, he confided to his diary, "Got me some drawers." The next day he "Commenced wearing drawers. Feel pretty nice." By his mid-twenties he was already a confirmed wanderer, abandoning the family home to walk from town to town, working as a cobbler for a few days and then obeying his "notion to tramp" again.

A series of seventeen letters written between 1853 and 1857 to Mariette ("Mett") Butler of Wellsboro casts a different light on his marriage. George Sears was not, as I'd assumed, a reluctant groom. Rather, these letters reveal a man smitten with a young schoolteacher. In letter after letter he declares his yearning, in the superheated language of his day, to crush her to his breast and press his lips to hers. He chides his beloved for her laconic replies and urges her to reveal her feelings. This George Sears was a surprise to me, as was the father who doted on his daughters, especially Jenny.

To supplement his income from shoemaking, Sears submitted poems and articles to numerous periodicals. The earliest of these I have found were two series in *Porter's Spirit of the Times*, in spring and summer 1860. In my original text I misstated Sears's relationship with this sporting journal. He did not disappear from its pages after *Porter's* changed hands; *Porter's* was a spin-off of another, much older publication known as *The Spirit of the Times*, whose editor, William T. Porter, had left his post to launch his own journal. *Porter's* existed only from 1856 to 1861, when social and logistical dislocations caused by the Civil War shut it down. By that time Sears was serving in a regiment of Pennsylvania sharpshooters he himself had helped raise. Another correction is in order here: none of his military documents cite asthma as the reason for his discharge; apparently he fractured a foot while drilling his company and was unable to march. Nor was he denied a pension. In August 1889 he was notified that his claim had been approved, but the news did him little good: nine months later he was dead.

His diaries don't alter our understanding of the shape of Sears's life, but the nuggets they contain add depth to every era. The journal for 1870, for example, documents his second trip to Brazil. Traveling by schooner, he was chagrined by his persistent seasickness, an affliction he considered shameful in a former whaling man. In Pará (now Belém), while he waited for government officials to appropriate funds to buy his rubber-making system, he collected butterflies (and the skin of at least one vampire bat). Three and a half months passed as he waited for audiences with assembly members and watched his modest stake, furnished by Wellsboro investors, dribble away. His view of Brazilians changed as his initial elation darkened into disillusionment. He couldn't wait to leave, but once afloat, his seasickness returned. "What I want is to get out of this on any terms," he wrote as squalls battered the *Ocean Pearl.* "Hell must be a middling comfortable place."

Also intriguing is his journal for 1881, in which he describes his second Adirondack cruise. As in 1883, the trip started off inauspiciously: his July 6 entry reads, "Left home for the wilderness. Sick. Poisoned with Paris green." Rain and a brisk north wind bedeviled him, and by the time he reached the

Fulton Chain he'd caught a nasty cold. He never really recovered, and physical weakness forced him to curtail his trip. What I hadn't known was that all along the route, for reasons he did not divulge, he was prospecting for ginseng. Perhaps this was another get-rich-quick scheme, or perhaps ginseng was an ingredient in one of the remedies he habitually collected. Whatever his motivation, he never found any *Panax quinquefolius*, although it did grow in the region and can still be found today, despite serious overharvesting.

A less than heroic episode that never found its way into print occurred on this trip, as he made his way out of the woods on August 9. "Started from Forge House," he told his diary, ". . . for a walk to Moose River. Was attacked by unruly cattle at the Arnold clearing, thrown down, hooked, tossed & trampled, until nearly exhausted. Got away by a piece of good luck and managed to reach Moose River." The next day he felt "Sick, sore & beaten. Nothing to say for myself. Only wish I was at home. Can hardly walk or feed myself. . . . Had a night of delirium chills and fever."

From 1884 on, two matters preoccupied him: his deteriorating health, and his alcoholic son Charles. Charlie had proved unable to hold a job, and when he wasn't in jail or off looking for employment he lived at home, straining his parents' already meager resources. Sears used the endpapers of his 1888–89 diary to note his son's comings and goings, and the months' worth of unpaid board. At the bottom of the tally he raged, "Am done keeping a free 1 horse inebriate asylum." But year after year, Charlie kept turning up. He'd appear, drunk, in the middle of the night, sleep off his bender, eat his fill, steal valuables, and depart a few days later. He borrowed money and seldom repaid it, and he seems to have been a sullen drunk. "Stood him off with the revolver," Sears wrote one July day. "Like to shoot him." When Charlie went after Jeff, Sears's hound, Sears gave his last hunting companion away. Interestingly, Sears himself occasionally got tight; almost always he recorded his shame at having done so.

Another unsuspected side of Sears was his attitude toward his wife, to whom he often referred as "Mrs. Bacchus." She almost never appeared in his dispatches, and when he traveled he seems to have written primarily to his brother Charles, not to her. But he clearly cared for her. In these later years Mett often worked outside their home to help make ends meet, and it's touching how often Sears mentions missing her and looking forward to her return. More than once he says he treasures the days when only the two of them are at home.

"Am failing and fading," Sears noted in late July 1884, and this theme would be sounded repeatedly in his last years. "Tired of life," he ended this journal. Still, he could occasionally muster some gallows humor. On April 18, 1888, he noted, "Roscoe Conkling died this a.m., Emperor Frederick on his last legs, and I not feeling well myself!" That year saw a stream of relatives and boarders passing through his house. Despite constant disruption and the weakened condition of his lungs (his "breathing works"), Sears continued to write for *Forest and Stream* and *Outing*, although now the material he produced came from his memory, not from fresh experience. His trips to Florida, in 1885 and 1886, had been his last ventures beyond Wellsboro. Now he puttered around his yard, raising chickens, grafting plum and apple trees, putting up honey, repairing equipment, tending hop vines and the garden. The spring of 1888 marked the last time he was able to plow his small plot himself. Easily exhausted, he more and more let others make the short trip downtown for the mail. There was no shoemaking work to be had; desperate for income, he sold off all royalty interest in *Forest Runes*, applied for back pay and other Civil War service claims, and sold two lots in Florida that he'd purchased while camping there in 1885. Eventually his writing tailed off and depression settled over him. On December 2, 1888, he told his journal, "My birthday. Am 67 years old. Don't feel much like celebrating it. My life has been a troubled dream. It has not been worth living, and I would not go through it again for a million dollars. Once is quite enough."

Sears's last entry was for April 2, 1890, a month before he died. After commenting on the weather and family matters, he scrawled, "I am weakening & failing day by day. I cannot sleep nights for coughing, and cannot last very long so. I have a high fever daily too." And that was all he wrote.

In addition to the unorthodox medical "will" he left behind, Sears drew up a conventional instrument that bequeathed his estate to Mett and summed up his situation in typically direct fashion. "I owe much," he stated, "I own little and must die in debt to my friends. I leave them my heartfelt gratitude."

THE ROUTE OF THE *SAIRY DAMP*

As Heraclitus observed, "One cannot step twice into the same river." Landforms for the most part endure, but we humans and our puny works are forever vanishing—"Gone," as Sears would put it, "like the tenants that left without warning, / Down the back entry of Time." Today you will not see the same bridge I saw straddling Brown's Tract Inlet and beneath which I nearly capsized as I negotiated a beaver dam. The bridge has been rebuilt, and the dam has disappeared. Nor will you find the bridge I passed under in 1990 between Simon Pond and Tupper Lake. A year or so ago that steel-girder structure was replaced by a lower, concrete span that arcs gracefully over the water.

On the day eight years ago when we paddled under that bridge, we dodged past a man who was tacking industriously across the channel in a homemade sailing rig. "I thought you might be interested in learning," Tupper Lake historian Louis J. Simmons later wrote me, "that the 'old man' you encountered . . . was my brother, Lawrence Simmons. He died on Oct. 5,

1993, at 82. He was an electrical engineer . . . and had a number of patents under his name on railroad gear. . . . He enjoyed sailing on area waters and added his own personal touches to the sport—a keelless row boat, plastic sheets for sails, a jerry-rigged rudder, and devout trust in his guardian angel, who never let him down, despite frequent dunkings. . . . He was the last of my seven brothers and sisters. I miss him." Bridge and man have vanished, and so too has the writer of this letter.

Also departed, in February 1998, is Robert L. Lyon, who never completed his biography of George Sears but who kindly shared with me the fruits of his research. After *Adirondack Passage* was published, Bob wrote me to defend Charlie Sears:

> Charlie was my good friend, generous, intelligent (he read a basketful of books from the library every week), witty, helpful, went out of his way to befriend a young boy. Wise (I remember more of his statements and advice than any other person's). . . . Few knew him; he was a very private soul, and the one who knew him best (I) was hardly a contemporary. He was 60 when I was 14. "Ending his days as an indigent in the county home" [you wrote]. Loggers, even if they didn't drink, could not save money enough for retirement. And when I visited him in the poorhouse (then in my 20s), he was surrounded by old men who idolized him. He couldn't smoke the cigar I gave him. After a few puffs he said he would keep it till later. He didn't mention that he was dying of cancer. Praised the treatment inmates received, and was courteous, gentlemanly, and brave. . . . He wasn't perfect. But he was one of the finest persons I have ever known. I loved him.

Some major land transfers have occurred since my book was published. In the first, state acquisition of a choice piece of real estate was made possible when, after years of indifference, monies were set aside for open-space protection. In July 1993 the legislature approved establishment of a landmark Environmental

Protection Fund. Three years later voters approved a $1.75-billion Clean Water/Clean Air Bond Act, some of whose funds could be used for preservation. Thus it was that the core of what may some day be a Bob Marshall Great Wilderness was transferred to New York State. It happened this way: In December 1992 Cornelius Vanderbilt ("Sonny") Whitney died, and his 51,000-acre park passed to his wife, Marylou. In 1996, Mrs. Whitney applied for permission to subdivide her lands on Little Tupper Lake, and the threat of development forced the state's hand. On December 22, 1997, Governor George Pataki announced the purchase of 15,000 acres surrounding the lake for $17.1 million. As it has so often, the Adirondack Nature Conservancy played a key role in this happy denouement. In the summer of 1998 canoeists were at last able to paddle one of George Sears's favorite places. The William C. Whitney Recreation Area does not encompass Stony Pond or the two Slim Ponds Sears traversed to reach Long Lake, but officials hope that in time the remaining 36,000 acres of the estate can be acquired.

In the private sector, Marjorie Merriweather Post's estate on Upper Saint Regis Lake, which had passed from the state to hot-dog maven Roger Jakubowski and then, in spring 1993, to a New Jersey bank, was bought by a Texan named Harlan Crow. Son of Trammell Crow, who built a real-estate empire in the Lone Star State only to see it wither in the recession of the late 1980s, Harlan took over his family's business, turned it around, and diversified its holdings. Now in his late forties, he's well on his way to billionaire status. At present he and his wife, Kathy, are spending millions to renovate Topridge.

In December 1993 it still seemed likely that 14,600-acre Follensby Park, site of the 1858 Philosophers' Camp, would be purchased by the state. The McCormick family, which owns the preserve, had signaled its intention to keep the land out of developers' hands and several times in the prefund era had extended an option deadline when the state could not marshal sufficient funding. "It belongs to the park," John McCormick was quoted as saying. "We'd hate to see it dismembered." What happened isn't clear. Some say the family decided the state would not be a good custodian; others think too many people were telling the McCormicks what to do. Whatever the reason, negotiations ceased. Although Follensby Park remains on the state's wish list, hopes for its acquisition have faded.

On a smaller scale, a few other changes have taken place along the *Sairy Damp*'s route. An excursion train now trundles down the old New York Central tracks from Thendara to Minnehaha, where John and I took out for the last time. The view from its cars will remain pristine, thanks to the Adirondack Nature Conservancy and the Adirondack Land Trust, which purchased a 950-acre tract in Minnehaha. The parcel includes five miles of riverfront on the Moose and preserves a wildlife corridor linking the Ha-De-Ron-Dah and Black River wilderness areas.

And finally, I'm pleased to report that the Indian Carry trail marker dedicated to Paul Jamieson has not, as he expected, been defaced. Better yet, the navigation rights issue he set in motion has successfully made its way through the courts. A final appeal will be heard by the state's highest court in late October 1998. In a recent letter Paul told me, "It seems unlikely that, even conservative as it is, [the Court of Appeals] will overturn the lower courts' rulings that recreational users have right of passage on all navigable streams. It might rule, against evidence plain to paddlers, that the South Branch of the Moose is unnavigable, but that would not affect the other principal rivers of the park, which have a long history of both commercial and recreational use."

TWIST TIES, AFFAIRS OF THE HEART, AND OTHER IMPORTANT STUFF

While I'm discussing changes, one technological innovation ought to be mentioned. In 1990 Adirondack campsites were littered with twist ties, but time has marched on. Today most campers use zippered plastic bags, and the twist tie is fading into the pine duff of history. Sic transit effluvia.

In the I-stand-corrected department, Hallie Bond, curator at the Adirondack Museum, has pointed out that the small steamers that plied the lakes were not clangorous, as I claimed; only their whistles were loud. And Jim Meehan, curatorial assistant at the museum, has observed that BTi applied to fast-moving streams kills only black fly larvae, not those of mosquitoes. Mosquitoes breed in still water.

Also, loons are not the oldest birds in North America. "I don't know where that came from," says *Gavia* expert Judith McIntyre, who teaches at Utica College of Syracuse University. "Loons are no older than cranes and ducks and herons."

It is no longer true that I have not heard a single word in defense of Ned Buntline, aka Edward Zane Carroll Judson. Robert Pepper of Palo Alto sped to his defense: "He was indeed a rascal and a rogue male . . . but he was generous and, believe it or not, had many longtime friends. . . . " Pepper explained that much of Ned's misbehavior was attributable to Demon Rum, and that Ned quit drinking in 1867. Pepper also eloquently defended Buntline's military record and his relationship with Bill Cody. Another positive view of Buntline can be found in the obituary *Forest and Stream* ran in 1886.

"Amaroogian," the term of disapprobation that Buntline applied to Alvah Dunning, was a new one on me. Robert Pepper explained it as "a northwestern lumberman's term meaning a foreigner or generally unpleasant person." *The Dictionary of American Regional English* defines "amarugian" as "A crude, unruly person; a member of a rough party of funmakers—orig. applied to residents of Fulton Co., Illinois."

A gentleman from Katonah, New York, chided me for my "selfish" views. "You seem to believe," he wrote, "that only backpackers or canoeists should be permitted to use the park and the fewer people the better. The taxpayers of the state of

NY paid for the park and [its] use by all should be encouraged. . . . Motor boats should be allowed wherever they can navigate, motor vehicles should be allowed and roads should be built to encourage them. This would encourage the handicapped, the old, families, and others to enjoy the park. When we go to [our favorite pond] we fish, water ski, swim, shoot guns, set off fireworks, hike, have campfires, and have a great time without disturbing others." Hmmmm. It seems to me that some activities are more appropriate to wilderness areas than others. (And however nice they are, I don't want to camp within three miles of these folks.)

In August 1995 I received a letter with a photograph of a nice-looking woman at a lean-to. "During August of 1988," a reader named Dan explained, "I took my girlfriend on a canoe trip to the St. Regis Canoe Area. We spent a marvelous four days at the lean-to on St. Regis Pond. . . . In case you haven't guessed, the enclosed picture is of Kristen, who said yes! and made me happy! She is shown sitting on the deacon's seat of the St. Regis lean-to, enjoying our engagement dinner. Kristen having said yes, we were married just over a year later, and she still makes me happy. The proposal came as somewhat of a surprise to her, and it wasn't until the next morning I received my response. It was then as I lay in my sleeping bag I carved what you read (well, somewhat later, I suppose)."

I loved this story and told all my friends about Dan's charming letter. A month ago I called him to see if I could use his words here, and when I asked how things were going he said, "Well, Kristen isn't making me happy anymore." After nine years of marriage they'd just split up. (The log on which he carved his declaration is gone too; not long after John and I stayed there, the lean-to was given a wood floor, and in order to install it the DEC crew had to remove the bottom logs of the walls.) "But you know what?" Dan said. "Go ahead and use the story anyway. It's a really nice story." It is.

In 1992, at age forty-nine, Peter Hornbeck, who built the *Sairy Damp* and who has hiked and paddled all over the park, had a heart attack. It changed his life, forcing him to modify his diet and the way he dealt with frustration. His wake-up call also gave Pete a chance to think about what he really wanted to do with his time. Deciding to quit teaching and devote himself full time to building Lost Pond boats, he hired an assistant and now sells about two hundred canoes a year. He's made a conscious decision to keep his business low-key enough to be manageable, and he usually takes the month of October off so he can go canoeing or kayaking himself. Despite his scare he retains his impish sense of humor.

My love of canoeing has only grown since *Adirondack Passage* was published, and the friendships Nessmuk brought me continue to flourish. For help with this afterword I thank Betsy Folwell, editor of *Adirondack Life*, who was always ready with facts and phone numbers; Janet Decker, who routinely fields queries historical and botanical; Andrea Masters, publications director for the Adirondack Mountain Club, who told me of her interest in an ADK edition as soon as she'd read the book; Chuck Brumley, who very kindly furnished the hitherto unpublished photograph of Sears in middle age; and all of you who wrote to tell me what you thought.

I owe a special debt to Dr. Joan Madison and her children, Jim, Jennifer, and John, for granting me access to the family's Sears archive. Joan provided food and board while I worked in her den, typed lists of documents from my loopy scrawl, and let me carry off diaries and correspondence to transcribe at my leisure. Her generosity has meant more than I can say.

October 1998

SELECTED BIBLIOGRAPHY

BOOKS

Abbott, Henry. *The Birch Bark Books of Henry Abbott*. Harrison, N.Y.: Harbor Hill Books, 1980.

Allen, Richard S., et al. *Rails in the North Woods*. Lakemont, N.Y.: North Country Books, 1973.

Armour, Marylee. *HeartWood: The Adirondack Homestead Life of W. Donald Burnap*. Baldwinsville, N.Y.: The Brown Newspapers, 1988.

Barnett, Lincoln. *The Ancient Adirondacks*. New York: Time-Life Books, 1974.

Beetle, David H. *Up Old Forge Way*. Utica, N.Y.: North Country Books, 1984.

Birmingham, Stephen. *"The Rest of Us": The Rise ofAmerica's Eastern European Jews*. Boston: Little, Brown and Company, 1984.

———. *The Right People: A Portrait of the American Social Establishment*. Boston: Little, Brown and Company, 1968.

———. *"Our Crowd": The Great Jewish Families of New York*. New York: Harper & Row, 1967.

Brandon, Craig. *Murder in the Adirondacks: An American Tragedy Revisited*. Utica, N.Y.: North Country Books, 1986.

Brenan, Dan., comp. *The Adirondack Letters of George Washington Sears, Whose Pen Name Was "Nessmuk."* Blue Mountain Lake, N.Y.: Adirondack Museum/Syracuse University Press, 1962; revised edition retitled *Canoeing the Adirondacks with Nessmuk*, 1993.

Brown, Henry A. L., and Richard A. Walton. *John Brown's Tract:*

Lost Adirondack Empire. Providence: Rhode Island Historical Society, 1988.

Bryan, Charles W., Jr. *The Raquette, River of the Forest.* Blue Mountain Lake, N.Y.: Adirondack Museum, 1964.

Burdick, Neal S., ed. *A Century Wild: Essays Commemorating the Centennial of the Adirondack Forest Preserve.* Saranac Lake, N.Y.: Chauncy Press, 1985.

Burroughs, John. *Wake-Robin.* Boston: Houghton Mifflin and Company, 1900.

———. *Locusts and Wild Honey.* Boston: Houghton Mifflin and Company, 1900.

Colvin, Verplanck. *Report on a Topographical Survey of the Adirondack Wilderness of New York.* Albany, N.Y.: Argus Company, 1873.

Coolidge, Louis A. *An Old-Fashioned Senator: Orville H. Platt of Connecticut.* New York: G. P. Putnam's Sons, 1910.

Crowley, William. *Seneca Ray Stoddard: Adirondack Illustrator.* Blue Mountain Lake, N.Y.: Adirondack Museum, 1982.

Cutright, Paul Russell. *Theodore Roosevelt: The Making of a Conservationist.* Urbana and Chicago: University of Illinois Press, 1985.

———. *Theodore Roosevelt the Naturalist.* New York: Harper & Brothers, 1956.

DeSormo, Maitland C. *Summers on the Saranacs.* Saranac Lake, N.Y.: Adirondack Yesteryears, 1980.

———. *The Heydays of the Adirondacks.* Saranac Lake, N.Y.: Adirondack Yesteryears, 1974.

———. *Noah John Rondeau, Adirondack Hermit.* Utica, N.Y.: North Country Books, 1969.

Dickens, Charles. *The Life and Adventures of Martin Chuzzlewit.* Philadelphia: John Wanamaker, 1886.

DiNunzio, Michael G. *Adirondack Wildguide: A Natural History of the Adirondack Park.* Elizabethtown, N.Y.: Adirondack Conservancy Committee/Adirondack Council, 1984.

Donaldson, Alfred L. *A History of the Adirondacks,* 2 vols. Mamaroneck, N.Y.: Harbor Hill Books, 1989; reprint of 1921 edition.

Gilborn, Craig. *Durant: The Fortunes and Woodland Camps of a Family in the Adirondacks.* Blue Mountain Lake, N.Y.: Adirondack Museum, 1981.

Grady, Joseph F. *The Adirondacks: The Story of a Wilderness.* Old Forge, N.Y.: North Country Books, 1933; third edition, 1972.

Graham, Frank, Jr. *The Adirondack Park: A Political History.* Syracuse: Syracuse University Press, 1984.

Hammond, S. H. *Wild Northern Scenes.* New York: Derby & Jackson, 1857.

———. *Hills, Lakes, and Forest Streams: Or, A Tramp in the Chateaugay Woods.* New York: J. C. Derby, 1854.

Headley, Joel T. *The Adirondack: Or, Life in the Woods.* Harrison, N.Y.: Harbor Hill Books, 1982; reprint of 1875 edition.

Heinrich, Bernd. *Ravens in Winter.* New York: Summit Books, 1989.

Hooker, Mildred Phelps Stokes. *Camp Chronicles.* Blue Mountain Lake, N.Y.: Adirondack Museum, 1964.

Hochschild, Adam. *Half the Way Home: A Memoir of Father and Son.* New York: Viking, 1986.

Hochschild, Harold K. *Township 34: A History, with Digressions, of an Adirondack Township in Hamilton County in the State of New York.* Privately printed, 1952.

Hoyt, Edwin P. *The Whitneys: An Informal Portrait, 1635-1975.* New York: Weybright and Talley, 1976.

Ives, Martin Van Buren. *Through the Adirondacks in Eighteen Days.* New York: Wynkoop Hallenbeck Crawford, 1899.

Jamieson, Paul. *Uneven Ground.* Canton, N.Y.: St. Lawrence University/Friends of the Owen D. Young Library, 1992.

———. *Adirondack Pilgrimage.* Lake George, N.Y.: Adirondack Mountain Club, 1986.

———. *The Adirondack Reader.* Lake George, N.Y.: Adirondack Mountain Club, 1982.

———. and Donald Morris. *Adirondack Canoe Waters: North Flow.* Lake George, N.Y.: Adirondack Mountain Club, 1987.

Kaiser, Harvey H. *Great Camps of the Adirondacks.* Boston: David R. Godine, 1982.

Longstreth, T. Morris. *The Adirondacks.* New York: Century Company, 1917.

Manley, Atwood. *Rushton and His Times in American Canoeing.* Syracuse, N.Y.: Adirondack Museum/Syracuse University Press, 1968.

McCullough, David. *Mornings on Horseback.* New York: Simon and Schuster, 1981.

McIntyre, Judith W. *The Common Loon: Spirit of Northern Lakes.* Minneapolis: University of Minnesota Press, 1988.

McKibben, Bill. *The End of Nature.* New York: Random House, 1989.

McMartin, Barbara. *Hides, Hemlocks and Adirondack History: How the Tanning Industry Influenced the Region's Growth.* Utica, N.Y.: North Country Books, 1992.

Morris, Edmund. *The Rise of Theodore Roosevelt.* New York: Coward, McCann & Geoghegan, 1979.

Murray, William H. H. *Adventures in the Wilderness: Or, Camp-Life in the Adirondacks.* Syracuse: Syracuse University Press/Adirondack Museum, 1989; reprint of 1869 edition.

Nash, Roderick. *Wilderness and the American Mind.* New Haven: Yale University Press, 1982.

Northrup, A. Judd. *Camps and Tramps in the Adirondacks.* Syracuse, N.Y.: Davis, Bardeen & Company, 1880.

Prime, W. C. *I Go A-Fishing.* New York: Harper & Brothers, 1873.

Proskine, Alec C. *Adirondack Canoe Waters: South and West Flow.* Lake George, N.Y.: Adirondack Mountain Club, 1986.

Robins, Natalie, and Steven M. L. Aronson. *Savage Grace.* New York: William Morrow, 1985.

Roosevelt, Theodore. *Theodore Roosevelt's Diaries of Boyhood and Youth.* New York: Charles Scribner's Sons, 1928.

Russell, Don. *The Lives and Legends of Buffalo Bill.* Norman: University of Oklahoma Press, 1960.

Sears, George Washington, pseud. "Nessmuk." *Woodcraft.* New York: Dover Publications, 1963; reprint of 1920 edition.

———. *Forest Runes.* New York: Forest and Stream Publishing, 1887.

Seaver, Frederick J. *History of Franklin County.* Albany, N.Y.: J. B. Lyon, 1918.

Shepard, Richard F., and Vicki Gold Levi. *Live & Be Well: A Celebration of Yiddish Culture in America from the First Immigrants to the Second World War.* New York: Ballantine Books/Hilltown Press, 1982.

Simmons, Louis J. *Mostly Spruce and Hemlock.* Tupper Lake, N.Y.: N.p., 1976.

Smith, H. Perry. *The Modern Babes in the Wood, or Summerings in the Wilderness.* Hartford: Columbian Book, 1872.

Stillman, William J. *The Autobiography of a Journalist,* 2 vols. Boston: Houghton Mifflin and Company, 1901.

Stoddard, S. R. *The Adirondacks: Illustrated.* Glens Falls, N.Y.: Glens Falls–Queensbury Historical Association, 1983; reprint of 1874 edition.

Terrie, Philip G. *Forever Wild: Environmental Aesthetics and the Adirondack Forest Preserve.* Philadelphia: Temple University Press, 1985.

Timm, Ruth. *Raquette Lake: A Time to Remember.* Utica, N.Y.: North Country Books, 1989.

Todd, John. *Long Lake.* Mamaroneck, N.Y.: Harbor Hill Books, 1989; reprint of 1845 edition.

Trowbridge, Catherine C., ed. *Durand Camp.* Privately printed, 1975.

Tyler, Helen Escha. *The Story of Paul Smith: Born Smart.* Utica, N.Y.: North Country Books, 1988.

Wallace, E. R. *Descriptive Guide to the Adirondacks.* Syracuse, N.Y.: Watson Gill, 1872.

White, William Chapman. *Adirondack Country.* New York: Alfred A. Knopf, 1987.

Wright, William. *Heiress: The Rich Life of Marjorie Merriweather Post.* Washington, D.C.: New Republic Books, 1978.

PERIODICALS

In addition to the pamphlets and articles listed below, I have plundered back issues of the *Adirondack Daily Enterprise, Adirondack Life,* the Adirondack Museum's "Guide-Line," *Forest and Stream,* and the *New York Times.*

Decker, Janet P. "Early Settlers on the Indian Carry." *Franklin Historical Review,* vol. 28, 1991.

Jamieson, Paul. "Rights of Passage." *Adirondack Life,* May/June 1988.

Ketchledge, Edwin H. "Born-Again Forest." *Natural History,* May 1992.

Kunstler, James Howard. "For Sale." *New York Times Magazine,* 18 June 1989.

Lyon, Robert L. "The Odyssey of Nessmuk." *Conservationist,* March-April, 1992.

———. "Nessmuk." *Pennsylvania Game News,* July 1990.

———. "Nessmuk." *Adirondack Life,* Winter 1972.

———. "Who Was Nessmuk?" Wellsboro, Pa.: Wellsboro Chamber of Commerce, 1971.

Manley, Atwood, and Paul Jamieson. "Nessmuk and Rushton." *Adirondack Life,* July/August 1982.

McKibben, Bill. "Adirondack Reprise." *Outside,* November 1991.

Mitchell, John G. "A Wild Island of Hope." *Wilderness,* Fall 1989.

———. "Spirits of the Mountains." *Adirondack Life,* March/April 1992.

Porter, William F. "High-Fidelity Deer." *Natural History,* May 1992.

Schneider, Paul. "The Adirondacks: The Remaking of a Wilderness." *Audubon,* May/June 1992.

Seaman, Frances, and Jessie Stone. "Long Lake: A Brief History." Long Lake, N.Y.: Town of Long Lake, n.d.

Shoumatoff, Alex. "Forever Wild." *Condé Nast Traveler,* September 1989.

Simmons, Louis J. "Town of Altamont, 1890–1990." Tupper Lake, N.Y.: Town of Altamont, 1990.

———. "Raquette Falls Lodge." *Franklin Historical Review,* vol. 8, 1971.

Van Valkenburgh, Norman. "The Death of 'Adirondack Harry.'" *Adirondac,* January/February 1992.

Verner, William. "Nessmuk and the Cruise of the Sairy Gamp." *Conservationist,* May/June 1976.

Walsh, James J. "A Young Catholic Explorer." *Forest Leaves,* Autumn 1915.

INDEX

The Adirondack Mountain Club, Inc.
814 Goggins Road, Lake George, NY 12845-4117
(518) 668-4447/Orders only: 800-395-8080 (M–F, 8:30–5:00)

BOOKS

85 Acres: A Field Guide to the Adirondack Alpine Summits
Adirondack Canoe Waters: North Flow
Adirondack Canoe Waters: South & West Flow
The Adirondack Mt. Club Canoe Guide
to Western & Central New York State
Adirondack Park Mountain Bike Preliminary Trail and Route Listing
An Adirondack Passage: The Cruise of the Canoe *Sairy Gamp*
The Adirondack Reader
An Adirondack Sampler I: Day Hikes for All Seasons
An Adirondack Sampler II: Backpacking Trips
Adirondack Wildguide (distributed by ADK)
Classic Adirondack Ski Tours
Climbing in the Adirondacks: A Guide to Rock & Ice Routes
Forests & Trees of the Adirondack High Peaks Region
Guide to Adirondack Trails: High Peaks Region
Guide to Adirondack Trails: Northern Region
Guide to Adirondack Trails: Central Region
Guide to Adirondack Trails: Northville–Placid Trail
Guide to Adirondack Trails: West-Central Region
Guide to Adirondack Trails: Eastern Region
Guide to Adirondack Trails: Southern Region
Guide to Catskill Trails
Kids on the Trail! Hiking with Children in the Adirondacks
Our Wilderness: How the People of New York Found,
Changed, and Preserved the Adirondacks
Trailside Notes: A Naturalist's Companion to Adirondack Plants
Winterwise: A Backpacker's Guide
With Wilderness at Heart:
A Short History of the Adirondack Mountain Club

MAPS

Trails of the Adirondack High Peaks Region
Trails of the Northern Region
Trails of the Central Region
Northville–Placid Trail
Trails of the West-Central Region
Trails of the Eastern Region
Trails of the Southern Region

Price list available on request.